Enlargement & Integr...
European Union

D0084564

The enlargement of the European Union in the 1990s, to encompass countries of Central and Eastern Europe has become critical for the future of European integration. The possibility that the EU might expand to thirty members in the first quarter of the next millennium poses fundamental questions concerning both the objectives and processes of the EU.

Enlargement & Integration in the European Union addresses the key issues that surround the EU's 'mission' to expand. Christopher Preston begins by setting the context for evaluating the enlargement process. Analysing the traditional 'Community method' of expansion he finds many shortcomings with its ability to handle future enlargement. The chapters explore: the past experience of enlargement, assessing what lessons can be drawn; the impact that enlargement has had on EU policies, institutions and on the new members themselves; and the likely future developments in the enlargement process.

This study of the crucial decisions facing the EU focuses on the Mediterranean, Central and Eastern Europe. With the theme of enlargement becoming ever more fundamental to the future of the EU, this book will be essential reading for students, specialists and practitioners of European Politics.

Christopher Preston is an adviser and author on European Integration. He is the British Know How Fund's EU Integration Programme Director for Poland. He has lectured widely at universities in the UK and Scandinavia on European Integration, and has acted as an adviser on European affairs to a number of government and parliamentary bodies and international companies.

The Routledge/University Association for Contemporary European Studies series

Series editor: Clive Church, University of Kent

Integration and co-operation in Europe
Brigid Laffan

The European Union and the South
Relations with Developing Countries
Marjorie Lister

Enlargement & Integration in the European Union

Christopher Preston

London and New York

First published 1997
by Routledge
11 New Fetter Lane, London EC4P 4EE

Simultaneously published in the USA and Canada
by Routledge
29 West 35th Street, New York, NY 10001

Typeset in Times by Routledge
Printed and bound in Great Britain by Mackays of Chatham PLC,
Chatham, Kent

British Library Cataloguing in Publication Data
A catalogue record for this book is available from the British Library

Library of Congress Cataloguing in Publication Data
Enlargement & integration in the European Union / Christopher
Preston
p. cm.
1. European Union countries. 2. Europe–Economic integration.
3. Europe, Eastern–Economic integration. 4. Europe, Central–Economic
integration.
I. Title.
HC241.2.P6639 1997
337.1'42–dc21: 96–47506

ISBN 0–415–12001–2 (pbk)
ISBN 0–415–12002–0 (hbk)

Contents

Acknowledgements

Many people have supported the writing of this book. In particular I would like to thank Professor Clive Church at the University of Kent who encouraged me and commented helpfully on the drafts; Professor Helen Wallace at the University of Sussex, with whom I have debated many of the arguments surrounding EU enlargement; the librarians at the Royal Institute of International Affairs at Chatham House in London who provided excellent research facilities and backup whilst writing; and to Sheila Ogden who so patiently word processed the drafts.

The book is dedicated to my wife, Susan, without whose support the book would never have been written.

Christopher Preston
Warsaw, Poland, March 1997

Abbreviations

ACA	Agriculture Compensation Amount
ACP	Africa, Caribbean and Pacific
CAP	Common Agricultural Policy
CDP	Common Defence Policy
CEEC	Central and East European Countries
CET	Common External Tariff
CFP	Common Fisheries Policy
CFSP	Common Foreign and Security Policy
COREPER	Committee of Permanent Representatives
CSF	Community Support Framework
CSCE	Conference on Security and Co-operation in Europe
DG	Directorate General
EBRD	European Bank for Reconstruction and Development
ECSC	European Coal and Steel Community
EC	European Community
ECJ	European Court of Justice
EDC	European Defence Community
EEA	European Economic Area
EFTA	European Free Trade Area
EMU	Economic and Monetary Union
EP	European Parliament
EPC	European Political Co-operation
ERDF	European Regional Development Fund
ERM	Exchange Rate Mechanism
ESF	European Social Fund
EU	European Union
FDI	Foreign Direct Investment
FEOGA	Agricultural Guidance Fund
GATT	General Agreement on Tariffs and Trade
GDP	Gross Domestic Product

GNP	Gross National Product
GSEE	General Confederation of Greek Workers
GSP	Generalised System of Preferences
IGC	Intergovernmental Conference
IMF	International Monetary Fund
IMP	Integrated Mediterranean Programme
MEUA	Million European Units of Account
MFA	MultiFibre Agreement
NATO	North Atlantic Treaty Organisation
ND	New Democracy
OECD	Organisation of Economic Co-operation and Development
OEEC	Organisation of European Economic Co-operation
PASOK	Pan Hellenic Socialist Movement
PCE	Spanish Communist Party
PCP	Portuguese Communist Party
PSD	Social Democratic Party
PSOE	Spanish Socialist Party
QMV	Qualified Majority Voting
SEA	Single European Act
SEV	Confederation of Greek Industries
TEU	Treaty of European Union
UCD	Democratic Union Coalition
WEU	Western European Union

Part I

Enlargements of the EC/EU

1 Introduction

EUROPEAN INTEGRATION: THE NEW CHALLENGES

By the mid-1990s the further enlargement of the European Union, to encompass the countries of Central and Eastern Europe has become critical for the future of European integration. Whilst other projects, in particular European and Monetary Union, may command more public attention, the possibility that the EU might expand to thirty members in the first quarter of the next millennium poses fundamental questions, concerning both the objectives and processes of the EU. So fundamental are these questions that they shape the debate on all aspects of the EU, from the CAP to institutional and decision making reform. The key question is: 'How much diversity can the EU accommodate before it ceases to be a durable community?'

Enlargement has always been part of the EC/EU's 'historic mission'. In more than doubling its membership from six to fifteen over its forty-year history, such questions have been asked many times before. Though the answers have often been carefully qualified, they have reaffirmed the basic dynamics of enlargement. Despite the strains imposed on both the Union and its new members, the queue of applicants, stretching from the Southern Mediterranean, through Central and Eastern Europe, into the former Soviet Union is proof of its attractiveness. Despite its arcane rule book, opaque procedures and high membership fee, the EU is still considered to be the 'best club in Europe', worth making sacrifices to join.

Yet the issues raised for the Union by the possibility of nearly doubling its membership again in a shorter time-scale, are qualitatively different from those faced before. In the past, the enlargement debate was more fragmented, and focused on the problems of particular states and policy areas. Though the EC has, from time to time, engaged in a more wide-ranging debate about the effects of diversity, for instance in the late 1970s and early 1980s, as the likelihood of enlargement into the Mediterranean increased, pragmatic compromises were usually found, and the more fundamental implications of recasting the whole system were left unexplored.

The collapse of the USSR, leading to the creation of new sovereign states, to the political, economic and strategic reorientation of Central and Eastern Europe, and to changes in the Mediterranean region, has transformed the environment in which further EU enlargement will take place. The assumptions of integration, based on the shared objectives and historical experience of a core group of West European states, though continually modified, are now challenged more openly.

How the EU deals with this issue depends on whether the dynamics and methods by which enlargement has been handled in the past are still valid. Hence this book seeks to explore:

- The past experience of enlargement, to assess what lessons can be drawn from it
- The impact which enlargement has had on candidates, policies and institutions and what light this throws on the problems of deepening
- The likely future development of the enlargement process in the light of the above. It also seeks to evaluate the difficulties of extending further the way the EU has handled the process.

THE MAIN THEMES OF THE BOOK

The introductory chapter sets the context for the evaluation of the enlargement process. It examines the present goals of the EU, and how these are affected by the possibility of enlargement, the dynamics of the integration process and the tensions between widening and deepening, the strengths and weaknesses of the Community's 'classical method' of enlargement, an account of the formal accession procedures, and a review of the principles underlying enlargement which have shaped the process so far.

The first part of the book then traces the sequence of enlargements to date. Chapter 2 examines the EC's first round of enlargement, from the 1961 application from the UK, Denmark, Ireland and Norway through to accession (for the first three) in 1973. It examines the policy debates that surrounded enlargement, the wider pressures confronting the EC, the attitudes of existing member states, the domestic debate in the applicant countries, and an analysis of the accession negotiations. Chapters 3, 4 and 5 follow a similar format for the second (Greece), third (Spain and Portugal) and fourth (Sweden, Austria and Finland) enlargement rounds.

The second part of the book goes on to assess the effects of enlargement. So, to begin with, Chapter 6 examines the impact that accession has had on the EC's new members. It explores the political and economic adjustments necessitated by full membership, and the role played by the EC in facilitating these adjustments. It argues that the success of a new member's integration into the EC/EU is determined more by its own willingness to make fundamental changes than by the specific terms negotiated during accession. Chapter 7 examines the impact that enlargement has had on the EC's principal internal policies, in particular on agriculture, the structural funds, the budget, the internal market and monetary union. It argues that, whilst enlargement has encouraged the extension of the EC's policy domain into areas previously considered to be in the exclusively national domain, EC policy priorities are still determined by member states. Chapter 8 examines the impact of enlargement on the EC's major external policies, in particular trade, and the initiatives to develop a Common Foreign and Security Policy. It comes to similar conclusions to those of Chapter 7. Chapter 9 examines the impact of enlargement on the EC/EU's institutional structure and decision-making processes. It argues that, whilst enlargement has led to some increase in the power of Community institutions to underpin the expansion of its policy domain, it has consolidated the power of member states in the Council of Ministers, and therefore the intergovernmental nature of the EC/EU. The final part of this book seeks to apply this to future enlargement.

Chapter 10 examines the pressures for further enlargement in the Mediterranean. It argues that despite its strategic importance to the EU, Turkey is not presently a credible candidate for membership, whilst Malta and Cyprus pose institutional questions for the EU which have to be dealt with by the IGC. Chapter 11 examines the prospects for further enlargement in Eastern Europe. It examines the measures taken so far to create economic and political links through 'Europe Agreements'. It argues that the EC needs to undertake further policy reform, particularly of agriculture and 'cohesion' policies before enlargement is realistic. Chapter 12 draws together the main themes of the book, reviews the development of the classical method and examines the options for reform as the EU faces a dramatically increased membership.

THE PRESENT MISSION OF THE EU

The completion of the Internal Market and the commitment to achieving EMU before the year 2000, raise the accession threshold for a group of states undertaking the transition process from a different economic base than in the past. Both these internal and external developments have also led to changes in the Franco–German axis which has, to date, been the motor of integration. The Federal Republic footed the bill for the adjustment costs of integration, whilst France set the agenda and policy priorities of the EC/EU. This implicit bargain allowed both parties to claim that there was a net gain to the whole EC to have West Germany anchored into the Western European political and economic system, and to have France shape the grand design of European integration. The unification of Germany and the geopolitical changes in Eastern Europe have modified many of these assumptions. The increased need for Germany to pursue a new form of 'Ostpolitik' within an EU framework is straining the Franco–German alliance at a time when moves towards EMU are themselves creating difficulties. The new challenge is to accommodate a wider range of new interests into the EU system during a period of uncertainty amongst the EU's key actors about what are, and in the future should be, the EU core competencies and commitments.

WIDENING AND DEEPENING

Despite the new context of the enlargement debate, there has been a striking degree of continuity about the way in which the enlargement process has been managed to date. Many of the dynamics of the process have deep roots in the origins of the EC and the basic objectives of the integration process. Since the Rome Treaty was signed, the Community has been driven by the need to balance the demands of widening and deepening. At different points in the EC's development, the emphasis has been either on widening or deepening. The initial configuration of the EC was shaped by the six founder members who were willing to transfer sovereignty to supranational institutions and invest in common policies within a customs union. Whilst the choice of core policies, in particular, agriculture, reflected the political preferences of the key actors, France and Germany, rather than a rational economic calculation of optimal trade creation, the goal of economic integration, leading to political integration was clearly established. Hence Article 2 of the Treaty states that:

The Community shall have as its task, by establishing a common market and progressively approximating the economic policies of Member States, to promote throughout the Community a harmonious development of economic activities, a continuous and balanced expansion, an increase in stability, an accelerated raising of the standard of living and closer relations between the States belonging to it.[1]

Progress towards integration has also always depended on favourable economic circumstances. During the boom years of the late 1950s and 1960s, the Community focused on deepening, concentrating on completion of the customs union, the creation of the Common Agricultural Policy and the establishment of its own budgetary resources. During the 1970s and early 1980s, the EC's commitment to further integration faltered. The post-1973 oil crisis recession led to a long period of stagnation and 'eurosclerosis', which did not lift until the economic growth of the mid-1980s smoothed the way to the completion of the Internal Market in 1992. In the mid- and late 1990s, the plans to achieve EMU before the year 2000 have been affected by the prolonged recession of the early 1990s.

Although the will to deepen has always been fundamental to the dynamics of integration, the expectation of widening has always existed. The EC was founded at a time of wide-ranging debate about the value of different economic and political frameworks to the peace and prosperity of Europe. The Six who signed the Rome Treaty opted for the intensive model of integration. Yet it was always recognised that this integration process should not be isolated from the wider European context and, if successful, was likely to generate pressures for enlargement. Hence Article 237 of the original Rome Treaty opened with the statement that 'any European State may apply to become a Member of the Community'.[2] Whilst the criteria for acceptance into the EC have often proved complex and contentious, this basic commitment to widening has opened the door to a continuous process of expansion. Within four years of signing the Rome Treaty, the Six were faced with applications from the UK, Ireland, Denmark and Norway. Although the de Gaulle veto postponed enlargement, it was never far from the integration debate. Following de Gaulle's death, the first enlargement was pushed vigorously, though it was made conditional on the applicants accepting the commitment, made at the 1969 Hague Summit, to monetary union.

Within several years the enlarged Community of nine was again called upon to substantiate its Article 237 commitment, following the collapse of dictatorships and the restoration of democracy in Greece, Spain and Portugal. The possibility of a twelve-member, more economically and geographically diverse Community led to an active debate about the impact of widening on deepening. However, following the decision to pursue Greek accession urgently, and the prolonged difficulties in finding an internal consensus on the conditions of Iberian, in particular Spanish, accession, the debate proved inconclusive. The Community therefore faced the late 1980s with the same mindset when new pressures for enlargement were generated by both the commitment to complete the internal market, and the more fluid political environment in Central Europe and Scandinavia.

The search for balance between widening and deepening is therefore a fundamental dynamic of the EC. Although widening has been recognised as unavoidable at particular critical moments, the key EU actors, France and Germany, have always favoured deepening as vital to maintaining the momentum of the original integration project. Enlargement has, therefore, only proceeded when the risks of dilution have been minimised, by linking enlargement to new, deepening, projects, and by demanding further reassurances from prospective members.

THE COMMUNITY METHOD OF INTEGRATION

The difficulties in resolving the tension between deepening and widening are integral to the 'Community method' of integration. This 'method', developed by the early pioneers of integration, in particular Jean Monnet in his plans for the European Coal and Steel Community, founded in 1952, sought to identify sectoral policy areas where member states' interdependence gave them strong incentives to co-operate. The expectation that successful co-operation would lead to further incremental pressures for joint decision making in related policy areas would, over time, create a regime with durable institutions and an expanding policy domain. During the 1960s, this process generated the theory of 'spillover'[3]. As member states 'pool' their sovereignty, so the structures and processes of the EC acquire greater legitimacy, thereby generating demands for further integration. Though it has created complex and opaque procedures which have led to wide-ranging concerns about effectiveness and accountability, the Community method has endured. Once 'locked in' to the system, it is extremely difficult for a member state to 'opt out' of policy developments that may not have been its preferred choice, but which it can accept with some modification. Though the Community method may produce 'lowest common denominator' policies, these are still seen by enough member states as preferable to the alternatives.

THE CLASSICAL METHOD OF ENLARGEMENT

The Community's 'classical' method of enlargement is an integral component of this underlying Community integration method. Over the four enlargement rounds to date, there has been a consistent pattern both to the formal accession procedures adopted, and to the implicit assumptions and principles which have shaped the expectations of the participants and the progress of negotiations.

Despite being severely tested at each enlargement round, the classical method has endured. Its major strength has been to establish at the outset of negotiations what the key outcomes should be: the integration of new members into a club with an ever-expanding rule book. 'The subject matter is not so much a future pact between the parties as the way in which one party will apply the rules of the other party's club.'[4] This alters the balance of the dynamics of negotiation. By pushing the major onus of responsibility for adjustment on to the new members, it gives them a strong incentive to conclude negotiations quickly. Any outstanding disagreements are therefore left until the new member is inside the club and has full decision-making and voting rights. The classical method also insulates accession negotiations from wider integration debates which might slow down the enlargement process even further.

However, the classical method also has serious weaknesses. The expectation that the bulk of the adjustment costs should be borne by new members, can create lingering resentments which can disrupt the whole integration process once internalised by the EC. The failure to address the predictable budgetary problems arising from the UK's trade structure led to a renegotiation of entry terms in 1975, and an acrimonious budget dispute that was not settled until 1984. Similarly, the terms pressed on Spain, particularly for agriculture and fisheries, have led the Spanish to take a hard line on subsequent CFP and CAP negotiations, and to increase their demands for side payments. The narrow focus of enlargement negotiations also reinforces the perception that the EC is an exclusive organisation more concerned with maximising the benefits to its present members than meeting its wider responsibilities.

ACCESSION NEGOTIATION PROCEDURES

The framework for negotiating accession was set out in Article 237 of the Rome Treaty. Now modified to include the assent of the European Parliament, in Article O of the Treaty on European Union, it states that:

> Any European State may apply to become a Member of the Union. It shall address its application to the Council, which shall act unanimously after consulting the Commission and after receiving the assent of the European Parliament, which shall act by an absolute majority of its component members. The conditions of admission and the adjustments to the Treaties on which the Union is founded, which such admission entails, shall be the subject of an agreement between the Member States and the applicant State. This agreement shall be submitted for ratification by all the contracting States, in accordance with their respective constitutional requirements.[5]

Accession negotiations follow an intergovernmental procedure and are therefore unlike most other EC negotiations with third parties, which are usually led by the Commission acting on a negotiating mandate granted by the Council. This is primarily because, as one participant has observed, negotiations are not between 'us' and 'them', but about relations between the 'future us'.[6] The sensitivity of the mutual adjustments necessary is therefore greater than in conventional EC negotiations or, for instance, multilateral fora such as the GATT.

THE DECISION TO APPLY

The decision of whether, and then when, to apply formally for membership is determined primarily by the domestic politics of the applicant state. Whilst individual member states may informally encourage a state to apply, and act as an unofficial 'sponsor', the EC itself has never solicited applications. This is largely because the EC/EU's agenda has always been busy enough without adding new issues. Table 1 shows the calendar for the EC's four enlargements to date.

Whatever the nature of the applicant's previous relations with the EC, the decision to apply is a major 'historical choice', involving the construction of a domestic political consensus to support a credible application. Whilst the EC does not take a formal position on these domestic political considerations, it clearly influences the shape of negotiations and any concessions made in particularly sensitive areas.

Table 1: Calendar of Enlargement

	Application	Opinion of Commission	Opening of Negotiations	End of Negotiations	Accession
UK	09.09.61		08.11.61	29.01.63	
	10.05.67	29.09.67	30.06.70	22.01.72	01.01.73
Denmark	10.08.61				
	11.05.67	29.09.67	30.06.70	22.01.72	01.01.73
Ireland	31.07.61				
	11.05.67	29.09.67	30.06.70	22.01.72	01.01.73
Norway	30.04.62				
	21.07.67	29.09.67	30.06.70	22.01.72	——
Greece	12.06.75	29.01.76	27.07.76	28.05.79	01.01.81
Portugal	28.03.77	19.05.78	17.10.78	12.06.85	01.01.86
Spain	28.07.77	29.11.78	05.02.79	12.06.85	01.01.86
Turkey	14.04.87	14.12.89			
Austria	17.07.89	01.08.91	01.02.93	12.04.94	01.01.95
Sweden	01.07.91	31.07.92	01.02.93	12.04.94	01.01.95
Finland	18.03.92	04.11.92	01.02.93	12.04.94	01.01.95
Norway	25.11.92	24.03.93	05.04.93	12.04.94	——
Switzerland	26.05.92				
Malta	16.07.90	30.06.93			
Cyprus	04.07.90	30.06.93			
Hungary	31.03.94				
Poland	05.04.94				
Romania	22.06.95				
Slovakia	22.06.95				
Estonia	24.11.95				
Latvia	13.10.95				
Lithuania	08.12.95				
Bulgaria	14.12.95				
Czech Republic	17.01.96				
Slovenia	10.06.96				

Note: Following de Gaulle's rejection of the UK's first application in 1963, the applications of Denmark, Ireland and Norway were dropped. They were reactivated when the UK reapplied in 1967. In 1972 and 1994, referenda in Norway rejected the terms of accession. The application from Switzerland was suspended, though not withdrawn, following the rejection of the EEA Treaty by referendum in December 1992. Malta's application was suspended following the election of a Labour government in October 1996.
Source: Avery, G.[7]

The timing of an application is also strongly determined by its linkage to other applications. Although the negotiating procedures accord a notional equality to applicants, in reality there are 'leaders' and 'followers'. However, it is not the case that the followers are necessarily less enthusiastic about membership than the leaders. Thus the timing of the Danish, Irish (and initially Norwegian) applications was effectively determined by the complex politics of the British application. Though Greece managed to de-couple itself from the other Mediterranean applicants, Portugal's application was shaped by Spain's. In the recent EFTA enlargement, the early application by Austria, even before the EEA negotiations had started, affected the timing of the Scandinavian applications.

COUNCIL DEFINITIONS OF PROCEDURES

The formal negotiating procedure is usually defined internally by the Council before the start of accession negotiations. The framework adopted in December 1992, prior to the EFTA enlargement negotiations, which is a standard procedural model, contained eight elements:[8]

1 The accession negotiations should be conducted according to uniform procedures by the EU.
2 The Council has responsibility for determining the common position of the EU, though this should not prevent COREPER from defining common positions if it is able to.
3 To ensure agreement with these common positions, the Commission is invited to make proposals on all problems posed by the negotiations on matters relating to the Treaties. Since the Maastricht Treaty, the Presidency, in liaison with Member States and the Commission, can make proposals on 'second pillar' (Common Foreign and Security Policy) and 'third pillar' (Justice and Home Affairs) matters.
4 In keeping with Article 151 of the EC Treaty, COREPER has responsibility for preparing the work of the Council concerning common positions.
5 Negotiating meetings between the EU and the applicants are chaired on the EU side by the acting Presidency of the Council.
6 Common EU positions are set out and upheld by the Presidency, or by a decision of the Council and the Commission, if existing EC policies are concerned.
7 The rules of 5 and 6 also apply when negotiations are conducted at COREPER level.
8 Particularly in cases where existing common policies are concerned, the Council gives the Commission the task of seeking out solutions to problems with candidate countries and reporting these to the Council for further guidance.

Apart from the provisions dealing with the second and third pillar issues, this framework is very similar to those adopted for previous enlargements. Formally, it accords the leading role to the Council, unlike in most other external negotiations in which this responsibility is given to the Commission. Although this 'role reversal' is important in reminding applicants and member states of the sensitivity of the mutual adjustments they may have to make, in fact the Commission still plays a pivotal role in the whole process. As the formal 'guardian of the Treaties' and positioned equidistantly from all the member states, it plays the role of 'honest broker' in the process.

REQUEST FOR COMMISSION'S OPINION

A formal application to the Council for membership does not automatically lead to the opening of negotiations. The Council then requests the Commission to prepare its Opinion ('avis'). The Opinion is a comprehensive analysis of the fitness of the applicant for membership, reviewing the capability of the applicant to take on the acquis, and to identify likely areas for negotiation should the EC proceed. Although the Commission's Opinion is not a legal prerequisite of opening negotiations, it has always been critical in shaping the accession debate, and consolidates the role of the Commission as pivotal to the whole process. The preparation is undertaken by the Commission's Services in collaboration with the relevant Ministries in the applicant countries. The quality and preparedness of the applicant's public service is therefore an important factor in the process.

PREPARATION OF OPINION

The time taken to prepare an Opinion has, in the past, varied from four months (for Norway in 1993) to three years for Turkey, Malta and Cyprus (see Table 2). This is determined both by the sensitivity and complexity of the application. In the Norwegian case, a decision had already been taken to open negotiations with Austria, Sweden and Finland, and with Norway, as soon as the Opinion was available. Given the detailed level of knowledge of the Norwegian situation gained through the negotiation of the EEA and, from the EU's perspective, the lack of any major obstacles to negotiations, the preparation of the Opinion was straightforward. By contrast, Turkey's 1987 application was an embarrassment to the EC. The three years taken to prepare the Opinion reflected the reluctance of the EC to take a public position on Turkey's eligibility.

Table 2: Periods of different stages of enlargement

	Preparation of Opinion (months)	Decision to open negotiations (months)	Duration of negotiations (months)	Total period (years, months)
UK	05	33	19	5 years, 7 months
Denmark	05	33	19	5 years, 7 months
Ireland	05	33	19	5 years, 7 months
Norway	02	33	19	——
Greece	07	06	34	5 years, 6 months
Portugal	14	05	80	8 years, 9 months
Spain	16	02	76	8 years, 5 months
Turkey	32			
Austria	24	18	13	5 years, 5 months
Sweden	13	06	13	3 years, 6 months
Finland	08	03	13	2 years, 9 months
Norway	04	01	12	2 years, 1 month
Malta	35			
Cyprus	36			

ADOPTION OF THE OPINION

The Opinion is formally the decision of the College of Commissioners acting by majority vote. In controversial applications, their endorsement may itself be the subject of lengthy debate. In most cases the Opinion recommends that the EC should open accession negotiations, though it may recommend the opening of delay whilst the EC deals with internal issues, for instance postponing Malta's and Cyprus' accession negotiations until after the 1996 IGC. The Opinion on Turkey, in concluding that its economy and political system was far from ready for EC membership, amounted to a rejection, though its position was carefully reserved.

Following its adoption by the Commission, the Opinion is sent to the Council of Ministers for the decision on whether to proceed and on the shape of the negotiating mandate. This is the critical decision point since accession negotiations require a major commitment of human and diplomatic resources, and imply a willingness to conclude negotiations. The time taken from the issuing of the Opinion to the opening of negotiations has also varied considerably. For the first enlargement round, the relatively uncontroversial 1967 Opinions on the UK, Ireland, Denmark and Norway were followed by a long period of internal debate about the effect of the UK, in particular, on the EC's ambitions for deepening. The possibility of negotiations only became realistic when Pompidou became President of France in 1969.

PROBLEM CANDIDATES

The delay caused by 'problem' candidates is frustrating for applicants linked to them, though there is usually little that they can do to 'de-couple' themselves. Only Greece was able to pre-empt the likely problems arising from the impending Spanish application, and move quickly to full negotiations. This decision is therefore taken at head of government level in the light of previous commitments made in European Council meetings. Although the Commission's Opinion is critical, it can be overridden for political reasons. The Opinion on Greece recommended that a long pre-accession period was necessary before Greece would be ready to take on the acquis. Yet, following intensive lobbying by the Greek Government, that delay might endanger the fragile Greek democracy, the Council set aside the Opinion and moved immediately to open full accession negotiations.

THE ACCESSION CONFERENCE

Following a decision to open negotiations, the Council convenes an 'Accession Conference' with each of the applicants, which meets at Ministerial or Ambassadorial level. Procedurally, the Conferences are separate despite the linkage between applications and the frequent need to find common solutions. The Council, Commission and applicant all set up special groups of high-ranking officials drawn from different relevant ministries, who are dedicated to the enlargement negotiations. In the applicant state, the group is usually located in the Foreign Ministry though, in some cases, it may report directly to the Prime Minister. The Commission establishes an enlargement task force located in DG1 (External Relations) which co-ordinates the work of other DGs in preparing common positions for the Council.

EXPLORATORY PHASE

The first task of the Accession Conference is to define the areas for negotiation, with the different aspects of the EC's activities being divided into chapters. Enlargement negotiations divide into exploratory and substantive phases. The first phase, largely undertaken by the Commission in consultation with the applicant's delegation involves exhaustive study of the acquis in order to classify which secondary legislation would be immediately applicable on accession, and where technical adaptations, either of Community acts or national legislation, would be necessary. Some part of this work is undertaken in the preparation of the Commission's Opinion, though the quality of information available varies from applicant to applicant. In the Greek case, the Commission noted in its Opinion that there were major areas requiring further study. These were not approached until full accession negotiations were opened. Conversely, in the EFTA case, most of this exploratory work had been undertaken as part of the EEA negotiations.

SUBSTANTIVE PHASE

During this phase both sides are gearing up for the more substantial negotiations to come. For the Community this process is necessary for the Commission to prepare a 'vue d'ensemble' of the applicant's case before proposing common positions to the Council. However, from the applicant's perspective, this period involves watching and waiting for the internal politics of the EC to be resolved. The most difficult parts of accession negotiations are those that take place in COREPER and the Council. The fact that unanimity is required for common positions prolongs the search for compromise. The most arduous aspects of enlargement negotiations are therefore those where adjustments to existing Community policies fall disproportionately on one, or a minority of member states. The length of the negotiations with Spain and Portugal was largely determined by the need to find a solution to the issue of extending the agricultural acquis that would be acceptable to France and Italy (and to a lesser extent Greece). Here, the role of the Commission as an honest broker, exploring the limits for compromise on all sides, is critical. Ultimately, however, only political will at head of government level can break a serious deadlock.

COMPLETING NEGOTIATIONS

Once negotiations have reached this substantive phase, the Community normally sets a target date for their completion. This schedule also incorporates a period for ratification procedures to be completed in time for new members to accede on 1 January, thereby simplifying budget deals. This concentrates the search for solutions and exposes the issues that determine the success or failure of the whole process. In each enlargement round there are usually several dossiers which are critical to the acceptability of the accession terms in the applicant states; in the EFTA enlargement, for instance, the issue of environmental standards was critical to domestic public opinion. Finding acceptable compromises that meet applicants' needs without breaching the acquis communautaire involves intensive detailed work by the Commission, matched by a political determination by key Community actors to find solutions. In the final stages of the process, the linkage between the applications can become critical. Despite the relative ease with which they could have concluded negotiations, the Portuguese could not close until the EC and Spain had found an acceptable compromise on agricultural support and transition periods. Where one applicant has particular difficulties with one policy area, the fear of failing to close negotiations when others in the group have succeeded can overcome the final hurdle. Thus the closure of negotiations with Austria, Sweden and Finland in early March 1994 pushed Norway to accept a deal on fisheries three weeks later.

ENDORSEMENT AND RATIFICATION

The conclusion of a political agreement leads to the deal being endorsed by the next European Summit before ratification procedures are commenced. In the recent EFTA enlargement, the European Parliament also gave its assent under the co-decision procedure. Ratification in the applicant states utilises parliamentary or referendum procedures, or a combination of both. Despite the accession negotiations and the ingenuity of the compromises in the final deal, this can still be a major hurdle to cross. In the EFTA enlargement all four governments mobilised a major political campaign, given the finely balanced state of public opinion. Despite the ingenuity of the fisheries deal, the Norwegian electorate rejected the accession terms by a narrow margin, similar to their rejection of the 1972 accession terms. The ratification procedure in member states' parliaments is more of a formality. Immediately a new member accedes, even though it may be subject to derogations and transitional periods, it assumes the full rights and obligations of membership. However tortuous and acrimonious the negotiations have been, it thereafter proceeds to pursue its interests according to the formal rules and informal norms, in the same way as the other member states.

KEY PRINCIPLES OF THE CLASSICAL ENLARGEMENT METHOD

Underpinning these formal procedures are a set of implicit principles which determine the negotiating process, define the limits of compromise and shape mutual expectations. These principles are derived from the Community's method of integration, with its stress on incrementalism. Despite the diversity of the issues arising in the four enlargement rounds, the principles have endured.

Principle 1   Applicants must accept the acquis communautaire in full. No permanent opt-outs are available.

The concept of the acquis is one which has become more explicit over the years, as the scope and complexity of EC activity has expanded. The statement made to the EFTA applicants at the start of negotiation in March 1993, affirmed this principle clearly:

> Accession implies full acceptance by your countries of the actual and potential rights and obligations attaching to the Community system, and its institutional framework, known as the acquis communautaire. This includes the content, principles and political objectives of the Treaties, including those of the Maastricht Treaty.

- legislation adopted pursuant to the Treaties and the case laws of the Court of Justice;
- statements and resolutions adopted within the Community framework;
- international agreements concluded among themselves by the member states relating to Community activities.[9]

This principle has been a core component of the Community method since its earliest days.

De Gaulle's rejection of the UK's application in 1963 was, in effect, a judgement that the UK was incapable or unwilling to adapt to the acquis. The progress of negotiations between 1961 and 1963 excited de Gaulle's fears that the UK's desire to retain residual Commonwealth trade preferences and an open external trade regime with its former EFTA partners was incompatible with the fundamental commitments of EC membership.

Since then the extension of the acquis into new, more politically sensitive areas, such as the Common Foreign and Security Policy, has raised the membership threshold. Applicants have to engage in a searching domestic debate prior to application. This also increases the weight of the baggage that the EU has to carry forward into the next enlargement round. Yet the principle acts as a discipline on potential members and reduces the risk that accession negotiations will undermine some of the complex package deals between existing member states.

Principle 2   Accession negotiations focus exclusively on the practicalities of the applicants taking on the acquis.

Given the complexity of these package deals, the Community method avoids radical policy innovation in already sensitive negotiations. The adjustment process therefore focuses on negotiating time-limited transitional periods, setting target dates for the reciprocal reduction and removal of tariffs and quotas, and for legal harmonisation and policy alignment. Again, the EFTA applicants were advised that:

> The acceptance of these rights and obligations by a new member may give rise to temporary (not permanent) derogations and transitional arrangements to be defined during the accession negotiations, but can in no way involve amendments to Community rules.[10]

Some of these adjustments can be quite far-reaching and significant enough to classify as amendments to Community rules. During the EFTA enlargement negotiations, the EC allowed the new members to retain their higher environmental standards for a period of four years, during which time the enlarged EU would search for common (by implication, higher) standards. The designation of new Structural Fund 'Objective 6' regions in Scandinavia, based on population density rather than per capita GDP eligibility criteria, is a further example of creative adaptation. The EU, however, always maintains that these adaptations are based on objective, universally applicable criteria, rather than on special-interest pleading, even when their implementation clearly benefits some member states more than others. The EC also carefully reserves its position on how these policies will be reviewed at a later date by the enlarged EC.

Principle 3   The problems arising from the increased diversity of an enlarged Community are addressed by creating new policy instruments to overlay existing ones, rather than by fundamental reform of the existing instruments' inadequacies.

Each enlargement raises problems of the fit between the applicant's economic structure, the priorities of Community policies, and existing problems of Community expenditures and receipts. These issues were raised most acutely in the UK and Spanish cases. Both the high level of food imports from cheaper external producers in the UK and the competitiveness of Spain's Mediterranean agricultural exports threatened the structure of the CAP. Strict application of the acquis in the Spanish case imposed adjustment costs on French and Italian Mediterranean farmers; in the UK case, it imposed high budgetary burdens on the UK treasury and consumers. In such situations, existing members prefer to stretch the technical adjustments and transitional periods as far as possible, load the bulk of the adjustment costs on to the applicant, and promise a revision of the acquis once the new member has joined. The EC also established new policies designed to buy off the most difficult interests in the applicant state and the member states most affected. The creation of the European Regional Development Fund (ERDF) in 1975 was mainly a response to the UK budget problem, rather than a serious attempt to address regional disparities in a Community framework. The creation of Integrated Mediterranean Programmes (IMPs) in 1984 to compensate French, Italian and Greek farmers for the Iberian enlargement was a similar exercise.

Given the new patterns of issue linkage that each enlargement might create, it would be unrealistic for the EC to return to first principles and rationalise the acquis each time a membership application is made. Yet none of these side payments have dealt with the underlying structural problems of the CAP, which undoubtedly caused many of the adjustment problems in the first place. The incremental policy overlay caused by four enlargement rounds has greatly increased the problem of policy reform.

Principle 4   New members are integrated into the EC's institutional structure on the basis of limited incremental adaptation, facilitated by the promise of a more fundamental review after enlargement.

The prospect of enlargement always opens a wider debate concerning decision-making procedures, institutional effectiveness and accountability. Although there have been temptations to explore institutional innovations in parallel with enlargement, explicit issue linkage has always been avoided. The participation of new members in the institutions has always been based on calculations of proportionality according to the criteria in use at the time. This was seen most clearly in the June 1992 Lisbon Summit decision to negotiate the EFTA enlargement on this basis, deferring institutional reform questions to the 1996 IGC. The UK, supported initially by Spain, challenged this principle close to the conclusion of the enlargement negotiations in March 1994, by arguing that such a proportionate increase in the number of votes needed to form a blocking minority in the Council would increase the bias towards small states. Although a compromise was found, the UK's core argument was rejected, and the principle retained.

Principle 5   The Community prefers to negotiate with groups of states that already have close relations with each other.

Three of the four enlargement rounds to date have been with states that had established trade and political links with one other. For the EU this creates some economies of scale in negotiations across the parallel accession conferences, particularly since these groups usually bring up similar issues for negotiation. It also allows the existing members to defray the adjustment costs of enlargement more widely. From the applicant's perspective, this linkage is usually unwelcome. Small states, such as Portugal and Denmark, which presented few problems to the EC, were inextricably linked to more problematic candidates. Only Greece managed to breach this principle, though this was subsequently regretted by many on the EC side.

Principle 6   Existing member states use the enlargement process to pursue their own interests and collectively to externalise internal problems.

Given that the decision to enlarge and that the closing of specific chapters of the accession negotiations requires unanimity, there are many opportunities for individual member states to extract side payments in return for consent. Greece, for instance, received money through the Integrated Mediterranean Programmes in return for removing its block on Iberian enlargement. The EC can also use the prospect of enlargement as a way of breaking a policy log jam. The agreement in 1970 on a Common Fisheries Policy was facilitated by the prospects of bringing in four new members with substantial fishing interests. The CFP thus became part of the acquis which applicants had to accept.

However, the CFP imposed too high a price on Norway, though it was reluctantly accepted by the UK, Ireland and Denmark. Similar considerations before Iberian enlargement led to the conclusion of a twenty-year CFP in 1983. Spain and Portugal subsequently demanded their early inclusion in the CFP as their price for agreement to EFTA enlargement in 1995, though again, the terms of the fisheries deal proved unacceptable to Norway.

THE INCREMENTALISM OF THE CLASSICAL METHOD

The durability of these principles is striking. Each time enlargement approaches the top of the EC's agenda, there is a debate about how far the EC can adopt a more 'strategic' approach, and recast its policies and institutions in a more rational framework, appropriate to the shared goals of its wider membership. Yet the pressures of incrementalism are formidable. Over nearly forty years it has proved impossible to recast fundamentally the shape of the EC as defined in the 1957 Treaty of Rome. Though enlargement has affected the EC, as subsequent chapters will show, the 'rules of the game' have become more entrenched. As Chapter 1 shows, the rules were already embedded by the time the UK applied in 1961. Much of the pain of the enlargement process results from the applicants' need to adapt their expectations of the EC, to reappraise their definition of national interest and to identify new points of influence within the EC framework.

2 The first enlargement
UK, Ireland and Denmark

INTRODUCTION

The core principles of the EC's classical method of enlargement were
established early in the development of the Community. By the time
the formal enlargement process commenced in 1961, with applications
from the UK, Denmark, Ireland and Norway, these principles were
clearly visible, most notably in the UK's case. Indeed, the protracted
enlargement process, which effectively lasted from 1961 until 1973, set
out the framework within which future applicants had to operate, both
in terms of the negotiations process and the extent of the domestic
adjustments needed to meet the requirements of membership.
Therefore, this chapter:

- Examines the debates and negotiations that took place during the
  1950s, up to the first accession applications in 1961, in order to
  explain the origins of the principles of widening and deepening;
- Analyses the enlargement negotiations from 1961 to 1973 in order
  to assess the way in which the Community's classical method
  became the model for future negotiations. This section focuses first
  on the UK negotiations, which determined the overall shape and
  schedule of the process, before examining in turn the negotiations
  of Denmark, Ireland and Norway.

THE ORIGINS OF WIDENING AND DEEPENING

Many of the principles underlying the classical enlargement method
and the reasons for the original configuration of the EC have their
origins in the 1940s and 1950s. The different perspectives of the UK,
France and Germany were particularly important in the light of future
enlargement debates.

In the early postwar period the need to reconstruct war-shattered economies and political institutions led to an open debate on the value of different models of development. The different experiences of the war, from the point of view of the major protagonists, were critical in shaping this debate. For France and Germany the overriding priority was to avoid war fought over disputed territory and the control of the raw materials, coal and steel in particular, necessary to make war. Britain, whose economic development had been based on the maintenance of maritime trade, gave priority to creating open trade arrangements.

Whilst all three nations supported the creation of the new postwar multilateral trade bodies, in particular the GATT, the IMF and the OEEC, there were differences of emphasis as to how these should be developed. The OEEC, established in 1947 in order to provide a framework for economic recovery in Europe, was seen by France and Germany as the foundation of a European customs union.[1] Whilst involving internal tariff liberalisation, the customs union model implied no necessary external tariff reduction, and therefore could be seen as potentially protectionist. Britain was not in favour of such developments, preferring to deal with tariff issues and sector-specific schemes within the GATT. Britain, therefore, supported by the Swiss and the Scandinavians, blocked the possibility of the OEEC developing as the economic base of a European Union. Although many of the debates were of a technical nature, they concealed more profound differences of perspective. Camps notes:

> To the British, Europeanism sometimes seemed to be a polite name for protectionism, while to the Continentals, the British attachment to the principles of the IMF and the GATT seemed to be a cover for a basic unwillingness to accept the concept of Europe as an economic unit. Motives were mixed on both sides of the Channel.[2]

THE EUROPEAN COAL AND STEEL COMMUNITY

British scepticism, however, did not prevent the Continental Europeans from pursuing their own vision of a more economically integrated Europe. In 1952, France, Germany, Italy and the Benelux countries signed the Paris Treaty and established the European Coal and Steel Community (ECSC). In creating a common market for coal and steel production under the management of a High Authority, chaired by Jean Monnet, the ECSC established both the institutions and processes of the Community method, which underpinned the later Rome Treaty.

THE MESSINA CONFERENCE, THE SPAAK COMMITTEE AND THE TREATY OF ROME

The Six moved quickly to build on the achievements of the ECSC and explored options for extending sectoral schemes and more ambitious integration models. This momentum led in 1955 to the convening of the Messina Conference in order to explore how extending economic integration might be given a new treaty basis. Britain was again sceptical and did not attend the Messina Conference. At this stage, the Six still wished Britain to participate in further plans and the Conference resolution recorded the agreement of the Six to invite Britain to participate in the Inter Governmental Committee set up to consider possible models for the economic development of Europe.

Britain signalled its attitude towards continental ambitions by sending a 'representative' rather than a 'delegate' to the Spaak Committee. This implied a desire to keep a watchful eye on developments, but with no particular Commitment to take decisions. British officials took a familiar line in the committee, arguing for a free trade area based on the OEEC rather than a customs union. In December 1955 the British withdrew from the Spaak Committee. Following the rejection by the French National Assembly of the ambitious plan to create a European Defence Community, the British believed that European developments were 'under control' and were unlikely to lead to further political integration.[3]

Although the ambitious federalism of the EDC proposal did not find favour, the more incremental approach of Monnet and Spaak was gaining ground, and was set out in the Spaak Committee Report of April 1956. The Common Market, proposed by Spaak saw the liberalisation of trade as a means to other, political ends, and the institutional framework proposed as a logical means to these ends. The Report stressed the importance of the overall internal consistency of the framework and, in effect, criticised the British free trade area proposals as lacking rigour and coherence.[4] This effectively established a core principle of the Community method which shaped future enlargements, that the acquis communautaire should be seen as a whole which is greater than the sum of its parts.

At this stage, the game was still open. Concerns were expressed amongst the Six, even in France, as to how far a customs union without Britain would be viable. The British were still willing to join a customs union so long as it excluded agriculture, given its likely effect on Commonwealth trade. Yet the British overplayed the attractiveness of their preferred free trade model and underestimated the determination of the Six to forge an 'ever closer Union'. Senior British officials were convinced that the Six would be unable to agree on an integration plan and that, even if they did, it would not endure. By early 1957 suspicions that Britain was prevaricating in order to undermine the Six's ambitions led them to move ahead, draft and sign the Treaty of Rome.

Some accommodation with Britain and the other non-signatories of the Rome Treaty still had to be found, however. Immediately following ratification, the OEEC, with the support of Britain, set up a committee to investigate the feasibility of establishing a European Free Trade Area encompassing the 'inner six' and the wider group who did not share their integrationist ambitions. In this sense, the search for a viable model of 'variable geometry' dates from the founding of the EC.

THE MAUDLING TALKS

Negotiations, known as the 'Maudling talks', led by the President of the Board of Trade in Britain, continued until 1959 and examined numerous proposals for developing a free trade area around the EC's customs union. Yet, by this point, the attitudes, particularly of the British and French, were beginning to harden. Despite careful consideration, no compromise could be found which reconciled the objective of tariff harmonisation, integral to the customs union model, with the preservation of tariff autonomy (combined in Britain's case with Commonwealth preference) implicit in the free trade area model.

ESTABLISHMENT OF EFTA

Following the breakdown of these talks, Britain opened discussions with the six non-EC states, Austria, Denmark, Norway, Portugal, Sweden and Switzerland on free trade arrangements. These led in 1960 to the signing of the Stockholm Convention, establishing the European Free Trade Association (EFTA). The looser model of co-operation, focusing only on industrial free trade, suited the disparate interests of the Convention's signatories. For Britain, it sought to demonstrate to other European states that it still had a leadership role to play. For the Scandinavians, and Portugal, it provided a flexible framework for managing their trade dependence on Britain. For Austria and Switzerland, it facilitated participation in West European trade liberalisation without affecting sovereignty or neutrality. Yet the long-term viability of EFTA was always debatable. As an organisation established in reaction to the EC, it was, from the outset, vulnerable to defections should circumstances change.[5] The trade dependence of Denmark, Ireland and Norway on the UK meant that they had little choice but to follow the UK should an application be lodged.

BRITISH REAPPRAISAL

By 1961 a fundamental reappraisal of Britain's foreign policy options was underway. The validity of Churchill's model of Britain as the pivotal point of three sets of relationships, with Europe, the Commonwealth and the US, had been progressively undermined. The Suez Crisis of 1956, the rapid decolonisation process which followed, and the cancellation of the Blue Streak rocket project in 1960 on cost grounds, dispelled illusions of Britain's role as a world power.[6] The strength of US support for the development of the EC also left Britain questioning the strength of the 'special relationship'. Fears about Britain's relative economic decline in a Europe committed to closer integration exacerbated the realisation of the scale of British miscalculations of the EC's durability.

This British reappraisal was also matched by a reconsideration by the EC Six of their longer-term political objectives. Whilst the Six remained committed to closer union, there was a recognition, particularly by the smaller member states, such as Holland, that Britain needed to be accommodated in some way. The Bonn Declaration of July 1961, whilst emphasising the development of European Union within an EC framework, also looked forward to the 'adherence to the European Communities of other European states'.[7]

1961 APPLICATION

On 31 July 1961, the British Prime Minister Harold Macmillan announced in the House of Commons, Britain's intention to seek membership of the EC.[8] In November the Government published a White Paper setting out its intentions.[9] The scale of the change in official British policy was confirmed by the Macmillan Government's commitment that, 'We accept without qualification the objective laid down in Articles 2 and 3 of the Treaty of Rome, including the elimination of internal tariffs, a common customs tariff, a common commercial policy, and a common agricultural policy.'[10] Britain's 'special problems' he argued, could be dealt with by means of special protocols, as had been the case with the original Treaty signatories.

Three areas of difficulties were identified. Commonwealth trade, in particular tropical produce, such as sugar, and temperate produce from New Zealand, gave the UK 'moral and contractual obligations'. The CAP, in utilising guaranteed prices for produce, rather than the deficiency payments system of income support for farmers used in Britain, posed policy alignment problems. Whilst accepting that preferential trade arrangements with EFTA would be incompatible with EC membership, the White Paper nevertheless looked forward to an association between an enlarged Community and the remaining members of EFTA.

At this stage, the extent of the EC's flexibility in accommodating Britain's special needs was untested. However, the Commission's (unpublished) opinion on the UK's application, whilst accepting that some adaptation would be necessary, stated that any protocols would only concern transitional arrangements. It noted that:

> Exceptions made must not be of such scope and duration as to call into question the rules themselves or impair the possibilities of applying these rules within the Community. The accession of new members must take place in such a way that they may subsequently share fully in the working out of common decisions in a Community spirit.[11]

This was the first, definitive statement of the classical method and has not changed substantially through all subsequent enlargement rounds. Whilst it left adequate scope for negotiations over transitional arrangements, it reminded the British Government that they would have to move more than half way to meet the EC's demands.

DE GAULLE'S VETO

Although de Gaulle's vigorous defence of the nation state had reassured the British Government that the EC was unlikely to become a full political union in the foreseeable future, Macmillan knew that de Gaulle was the major obstacle to British ambitions. Macmillan met de Gaulle in June 1962 in Paris to try and convince him of Britain's seriousness in making a commitment to the EC. They met again at Ramboullet in December, at which meeting de Gaulle reportedly expressed doubts about Britain's ability to make the necessary adaptations. However, the British and indeed, the other five EC member states were taken completely by surprise when de Gaulle expressed these doubts publicly at a press conference in Paris on 14 January 1963. Whilst not closing off the possibility of Britain ever becoming a

full EC member, de Gaulle's doubts were wide ranging and fundamental to British interests. He stated:

> England in effect is insular, she is maritime. She is linked through
> her exchanges, her markets, her supply lines to the most diverse
> and, often, the most distant countries. She pursues essentially
> industrial and commercial activities, and only slight agricultural
> ones. She has in all her doings very marked and very original
> habits and traditions. In short, the nature, the structure, the very
> situation that are England's differ profoundly from most of the
> continentals. [12]

Though humiliating for the British, de Gaulle's speech was a powerful
reminder to all applicants that full membership demands not only
technical and policy adjustment to the Treaties, but also a more
profound reorientation of political attitudes. Despite repeated British
claims that they accepted the acquis communautaire, de Gaulle
doubted that Britain accepted the EC's political goals, that is the
'finalite politique', however ambiguously defined. De Gaulle's political
criterion for membership therefore became an integral part of the
Community's enlargement method.

Despite the frustration of other member states at de Gaulle's 'veto',
the British (and the three other) applications effectively lapsed.
However, the long-run changes in Britain's foreign policy orientation
which had led to the 1961 application, though not profound enough
for de Gaulle, left Britain with no realistic alternative. At some point
the application would be reactivated. This point was recognised by the
incoming Labour Government of 1964. Despite strong anti EC opinions in parts of the Labour Party, the Prime Minister, Harold Wilson,
accepted the necessity of pursuing EC membership.

BRITAIN'S APPLICATION REACTIVATED

Following a series of meetings in 1966 led by George Brown, the
Foreign Secretary, to rebuild the goodwill lost three years earlier,
Wilson decided on a new diplomatic initiative to explore whether full
negotiations would be worthwhile. Wilson realised that developments
in the EC since 1963, particularly the financing of the CAP from tariff
revenues on third country imports, had already increased the accession
threshold for Britain. However, he emphasised that 'there is no future
for Britain in a little England philosophy'.[13]

Other EFTA Governments were supportive of the British desire for
full membership, since Britain's pivotal trading position was critical in

bringing about the wider, open European market to which both groups aspired. At an EFTA ministerial meeting in April 1967, they affirmed that an application 'would open up new prospects for a solution to the question of European economic integration'.[14]

Despite internal Labour Party disagreements concerning the costs of the CAP, the Cabinet decided in April 1967 to submit an application for EC membership. In his statement to the House of Commons on 2 May, Wilson stated the Government's intention 'to pursue our application for membership with all the vigour and determination at our command'.[15] He identified the, by now, familiar issues for negotiation as the effect of the CAP on British agriculture and the cost of living, and on Britain's balance of payments, arising out of its budgetary structure. Again the specific Commonwealth issues of New Zealand's temperate produce and the sugar producers were identified. There were, therefore, domestic political limits to the flexibility of the Wilson Government's negotiating position.

Given the experiences of 1961–63, de Gaulle's attitude remained critical to Britain's chances of success. At a press conference in May he welcomed the British application but reaffirmed the degree of change that would be necessary fully to integrate the UK into the EC. De Gaulle posed the dilemma of widening and deepening. This change, he argued, could either result from the dilution of the Community into a wider European and then Atlantic trading zone, some form of association between the UK, EFTA and the EC, or a 'profound economic and political transformation which would allow them (the British) to join the six continentals'.[16]

Given his previous statements, de Gaulle clearly favoured the last option, though, at this stage, he did not prejudge the outcome of negotiations. In October the European Commission published its preliminary Opinion on Britain's (and the other three) applications.[17] Whilst restating the, by now, familiar orthodoxy that successful enlargement required full acceptance of the acquis, the Opinion also identified the need to adjust sterling in order to fit into the EC's evolving monetary system, and the restoration of the British balance of payments equilibrium. Whilst retaining its definitive opinion on the applications, the Commission urged the opening of negotiations in order to explore these issues in more depth.

NEGOTIATIONS OPEN

Strong French concerns about the British application were put forward at ministerial meetings during the autumn of 1967. These familiar concerns were compounded by the growing balance of payments problems in the UK economy, which led to the devaluation crisis of November 1967. At a press conference in November, de Gaulle again restated his doubts concerning the ability of the UK to make the necessary adaptations, concluding that 'in order that the British Isles can really make fast to the Continent, there is still a very vast and deep mutation to be effected'.[18] Although the other five member states publicly stated their support for the British application, the December council meeting failed to agree on a way forward, noting that 'one member state considered that the re-establishment of the British economy must be completed before Great Britain's request can be reconsidered'.[19] Though less dramatically expressed than in 1963, this amounted to a second de Gaulle veto. However, this time de Gaulle was motivated by the fear that Britain's economic weakness would inhibit the development of the Community. In 1963 he had been concerned that Britain would dominate and 'Atlanticise' the EC.[20]

POMPIDOU SUCCEEDS DE GAULLE

No negotiating progress was made in 1968. France was also preoccupied with its own internal political problems which led to the resignation of de Gaulle. The election of Georges Pompidou as President in 1969 signalled a change in official French attitudes towards enlargement and a deeper reappraisal of French foreign policy. Until the late 1960s, French official policy had believed that West German inhibitions about asserting their own power gave France a pre-eminent political role in Europe. However, the launch in 1968/69 by Chancellor Brandt of a new 'Ostpolitik', combined with the Soviet invasion of Czechoslovakia and US pressure for possible troop withdrawals, left the French feeling more vulnerable.[21] Given this more unstable environment, Pompidou believed that enlargement could strengthen the EC. The Commission was requested to update its 1967 Opinion and, in its revised Opinion,[22] published in October 1969 recommended that negotiations with all four applicants should be opened immediately.

During the autumn of 1969, the Community was working towards a package deal that would make agreement on widening conditional on deepening. As noted earlier, the risk of dilution of the EC's achievements posed by enlargement required that new commitments to deepening should be made. These would then be added to the acquis presented to the applicants for membership. As well as widening and deepening, the French Government also spoke of 'completion'. Having completed the customs union ahead of schedule, questions were raised as to how far the other core goals of the Treaty could be turned into specific policies. The need to develop entirely new policy areas (e.g. regional policies) should enlargement take place, also entered the debate.[23] The Commission argued in its Opinion that 'only by returning to the letter of the institutional arrangements laid down in the Treaties, will the Commission be able to accept the risks involved in enlargement',[24] i.e. by using majority voting in the Council as the norm. It also argued for increased budgetary powers for the European Parliament, and for its members to be elected by universal suffrage.

1969 HAGUE SUMMIT

In the event, the Hague Summit of 1 to 2 December 1969 agreed that widening, deepening and completion were inseparable. It was agreed that accession negotiations would be opened immediately with the UK, that the Community would establish a system of 'own resources' (i.e. independent revenue), that the possibility of EMU should be examined by the Werner Committee, and moves towards a Common Foreign Policy would be looked at by the Davignon Committee. Negotiations would also be opened with Denmark, Ireland and Norway.

Though the commitment to deepening, in the long term, again raised the accession threshold for Britain, the domestic debate focused particularly on the budgetary costs of membership. The February 1970 White Paper estimated the direct budget costs at approximately £1 billion, though the paper argued that the potential gains from having access to the larger market were considerable.[25] The predicted costs of membership led to a decline in public support (measured by Gallup polls) in 1970, which fell consistently to just 20 per cent in mid-1971. This acted as a considerable constraint on the negotiating stand of British Governments. In the run-up to the June 1970 general election, it put stress on the bipartisan consensus on the necessity of membership.[26]

ACCESSION NEGOTIATIONS OPEN

Following the election of a Conservative Government led by Edward Heath, who had been the chief negotiator in 1961–63 in the Macmillan Government, accession negotiations opened on 30 June 1970. Britain requested that talks should focus on 'certain matters of agricultural policy, our contributions to the Community budget, Commonwealth sugar exports, New Zealand's special problems, and certain other Commonwealth questions'.[27]

In opening the negotiations, the President of the Council, the Belgian Foreign Minister, Pierre Harmel, restated the orthodox Community position on the acquis. He further reinforced this by stating that accession terms would involve only the minimum time necessary to adapt to Community rules, otherwise they would cease to be transitional arrangements and become derogations. They should further give benefits to all the parties involved and be identical for all four applicants. The EC also reserved the right to discuss EMU, as talks progressed.[28]

Early negotiations focused on the order in which the contentious issues should be tackled. Britain wished to tackle the budget issue first – for domestic political reasons and so that the concessions it would almost certainly have to make on sugar and New Zealand agriculture would not ratchet up its budget contributions. During the autumn of 1970, different transition periods were discussed for the introduction of industrial free trade, the CAP and Britain's budget contributions. Britain's request for an eight-year budgetary transition period was supported by some other member states, in particular Italy and Holland, with only Belgium supporting the French hard line. The role of the Commission was critical in brokering a compromise; it proposed a five-year phase which by January 1971 all the member states, apart from France and Belgium, had accepted.[29]

In early 1971 negotiations moved on to sugar and New Zealand agriculture with the French again taking a hard line on the run-down of imports within a strict five-year period. The other five member states supported the Commission's line that sugar imports should not be changed until 1974, pending a review of the Yaoundé agreement on trade with ACP countries, and that New Zealand imports should be only partially run down. Although by March 1971 agreement on these matters had still not been reached, the British requested that negotiations should be completed by May. Under pressure to reach agreement, the French suddenly insisted that the British should give specific assurances that they would reduce their sterling liabilities as part of the EC's preparations for EMU. Britain regarded these issues as being outside the scope of the acquis, as strictly defined, having already given general assurances concerning its adherence to the objective of EMU. The other five member states also expressed concern at the possible delay to negotiations at this late stage. Following several more inconclusive negotiating sessions, a summit meeting between Heath and Pompidou took place in Paris in May. The summit settled issues concerning the overall Anglo–French approach to future integration (and nuclear co-operation) and led to Britain's acceptance of a gradual run-down of sterling balances after accession, so as not to unbalance the EMU plans. The final negotiating session of 21 to 22 June settled the outstanding issues of New Zealand's dairy exports, which would be reduced to 71 per cent of existing amounts by the end of the transition period, and Britain's starting contribution to the budget at 8.64 per cent.

THE OUTCOME OF NEGOTIATIONS

In July 1971, the UK Government published a White Paper, setting out its interests in EC membership and the terms agreed.[30] The Paper accepted that Britain's role in the world had changed considerably, since the idea of a European Community had first been conceived, and that full membership of the EC was now vital to secure Britain's economic and political interests.

The objective of the transitional arrangements on industrial tariffs was 'to secure as quickly as possible the advantages for British industry of integration within a single European market while providing an adequate period of adjustment for our Commonwealth and other trading partners'.[31] This was achieved by a five-stage (20 per cent per annum) abolition of UK tariffs and a four-stage (starting a year later) adoption of the Community's CET.

For agriculture, the objective was to 'permit an orderly adjustment by our producers to the Community's system of support and marketing, avoid sharp increases in food prices, and prevent abrupt dislocation of the exports of our Commonwealth and other third country suppliers'.[32] The agreement involved adopting the EU's system of price support for most agricultural products immediately on accession but with initially lower intervention and threshold prices, moving to EC levels over a five year transition period. New Zealand exports would be reduced over the five year period, guaranteeing 80 per cent of butter, and 20 per cent of cheese exports. Lamb exports would face a 20 per cent CET pending the introduction of a sheepmeat regime. The budget settlement involved the phasing in of contributions over a five-year period, rising from 8.64 per cent to 18.92 per cent (broadly comparable with Britain's share of the enlarged Community's GDP). However, given the sensitivity and unpredictability of outline budget calculations, the EC accepted during the accession negotiations that if unacceptable situations should arise, the very survival of the Community would demand that the institutions find equitable solutions.[33]

The EC agreed that Britain could continue to buy sugar under the Commonwealth Sugar Agreement until the end of 1974, after which sugar producers would have access under new association agreements with the enlarged Community. Other Commonwealth exporters would continue their existing trade arrangements with Britain until the enlarged EC negotiated a successor to the Yaoundé Convention.

PARLIAMENTARY DEBATE

The House of Commons debate in October on the motion to approve the terms of accession cut across party lines. Harold Wilson, the Opposition leader, argued that the terms were too onerous, particularly in their impact on Britain's balance of payments. He pledged a future Labour Government to renegotiate terms, with no commitment to stay in the EC if better terms were not agreed. The motion, taken on a free vote, was passed by a majority of 112. However, of the 358 votes in favour, 284 were Conservative, 69 were Labour and 5 Liberal. Of the 246 against, 200 were Labour and 39 Conservative. Twenty Labour and two Conservative MPs abstained. The domestic debate in the UK and the Parliamentary vote demonstrated the difficulties that the classical enlargement method can create when there is only fragile domestic consensus in the applicant country for accession. From the EC's perspective, the accession terms preserved the integrity of the acquis and gave the UK transitional periods within which the necessary trade and policy adaptations could be made. However, the structural problems of the EC budget, highlighted by the accession negotiations, remained. The British 'problem' was internalised into the EC and continued to create difficulties, both in the EC and in British domestic politics.

THE COMMON FISHERIES POLICY

Despite agreement on the main negotiating package, the whole deal was put at risk by the newly agreed Common Fisheries Policy (CFP). The core principle of the CFP, which had been agreed just before enlargement negotiations commenced, was the right of access to all members' territorial waters. Given that the four applicants would bring with them 60 per cent of the enlarged EC's fish stocks,[34] they were convinced that the existing EC members had conceived the CFP as a way of externalising their own disagreements, particularly on excess fleet capacity. During the autumn of 1971, Britain refused to recognise the CFP as part of the acquis, given its last minute adoption.

As the January 1972 deadline approached, the ten existing and applicant member states eventually agreed to the ten-year transition period for the CFP, during which time the bulk of fish stocks would continue to be reserved for national fleets. The agreement opened the way for the signing of the accession treaty in Brussels in January 1972, giving 1972 for ratification procedures before accession on 1 January 1973.

RENEGOTIATION OF ENTRY TERMS 1974–75

Though the Conservative Government achieved a comfortable Parliamentary majority in favour of EC membership, the Labour Party remained unreconciled to the terms negotiated. When it formed a (minority) Government in March 1974, the Prime Minister, Harold Wilson, pledged to renegotiate entry terms. In April 1974, the Foreign Secretary, James Callaghan, set out the main areas of concern. The key issue was the constraints that membership had on the management of the British economy. He argued that the Paris Summit timetable for achieving EMU by 1980 was dangerously ambitious in forcing the pace of economic convergence and would undermine the Labour Government's full employment goal.[35]

Whilst concerns about Commonwealth trade also featured, the substance of Britain's case centred on Britain's budget contributions. Callaghan argued that in 1973, whilst only paying 8.5 per cent of the EC Budget, as part of the transitional arrangement, the UK was already the second largest net contributor. By the end of the transitional period, he estimated that the UK would be contributing 19 per cent of the EC budget against an estimated GDP share of 16.5 per cent at that point. Following the achievement of an overall Parliamentary majority in October 1974, the Wilson Government pressed to put renegotiated terms to the electorate within twelve months. Negotiations up to the Paris Summit of December 1974 focused on finding an appropriate 'correcting mechanism'. France, in particular, was resistant to revising the method of calculating budget contributions, since it would open up the possibility of member states expecting to receive in receipts what they gave in contributions (i.e. the principle of 'juste retour'). Though the Summit Communiqué acknowledged the commitment made to Britain to avoid 'unacceptable situations', it restated the orthodoxy that any correcting mechanism should be of general application, and based on 'objective criteria' during the period of convergence of member states' economies. In January 1975, the Commission published proposals defining the unacceptable situation as one in which, in addition to a member state being a net contributor, it also had a per capita GDP below 85 per cent of the EC average, a rate of growth of per capita GNP below 120 per cent of the EC average and a balance of payments deficit on current account.[36] In March, the proposals were discussed and accepted at the Dublin Summit, after which Prime Minister Wilson recommended a vote in favour of continued EC membership on the terms agreed. In the 5 June referendum there was a two-to-one majority in favour of continued EC membership.

The renegotiation of entry terms can be explained primarily in the context of British domestic politics and the need for Harold Wilson to retain internal Labour Party coherence.[37] The outcome of the renegotiations did little to solve the structural problem of the EC budget and Britain's trade patterns. The issue resurfaced again when the Thatcher Government came to power in 1979 and continued for a further five years. Despite their special pleading, the British had raised concerns also expressed privately by other member states about the structure of the EC budget which remained unaddressed for a further ten years. This demonstrated an inherent weakness of the classical method of enlargement. Faced with pressure from newcomers to rewrite the rules of the club, the preference of its existing members was to close ranks. Yet the failure to address budget reform head on, as a direct consequence of enlargement, slowed down the development of integration in other areas for many years.

IRELAND, DENMARK AND NORWAY

All three countries' policies towards European integration were strongly shaped by their relations with the UK. The calendar of their accession negotiations therefore matched that of the UK. For Ireland, Denmark and Norway, EC membership was a way of retaining trade links with the UK but within a larger, regional grouping that would reduce their historical dependence on the UK.

Yet these similarities conceal the extent of the differences between these three countries, which resulted in only two of them acceding to the EC in 1973.

IRELAND

In the years leading to accession, Irish policy towards European integration was dominated by two sets of factors. In the economic sphere, anxieties about the vulnerability of Irish industry as trade liberalisation quickened, and the predominance of agriculture in Ireland's economic structure, shaped perceptions of European initiatives. In the political sphere, the dominance of Ireland's bilateral relationship with the UK and adherence to neutrality were critical. The consequence of these factors was that Ireland's relations with the EC were inextricably bound up with Britain's EC relations. Ireland adopted a cautious approach to the trade liberalisation initiatives of the mid-1950s. In 1956, when the Six sought ways of reconciling the proposed Customs Union with the wider OEEC free trade area proposal, the official Irish position was that agriculture should be excluded.[38] Given the dependence of Irish agriculture on the British market, and the scepticism of Britain about integration of agriculture trade, this was inevitable.

Proposals for industrial free trade raised anxieties that Ireland would gain few new export advantages, but that dismantling its high tariffs and other protective measures would have serious consequences. The Irish Government, therefore, decided that no commitment to joining the proposed FTA should be made until adequate safeguards for the developing Irish economy had been secured. The Irish position, submitted to the OEEC in May 1957, was for a 25-year transition period to free trade, supported by safeguard measures and the preservation of tariff preference for British goods.[39]

Whilst the collapse of the OEEC talks was not itself significant to the Irish, it marked a shift in the emphasis of Irish economic policy. Whatever the specific framework for economic integration, the Irish economy needed to be adapted to cope with greater international competition. This was further reinforced by the plans to create EFTA which would erode Irish industries' preferences in the UK market. The failure of the Irish to improve their terms of trade with the UK as a result of the 1960 Anglo-Irish Trade Agreement, further reinforced the need to develop multilateral trade links. In 1960, Ireland explored the possibility of acceding to the GATT, underpinned by improved economic performance attributable to the 1959 Programme for Economic Expansion. However, the relative failure of agricultural production and exports to share in these growth rates was attributed to the lack of new assured export markets.

This greatly increased the attraction of the EEC where proposals for implementing the CAP were being developed. The possibility of some form of association with the EC, irrespective of British policy to the EC, was explored, though the outcome was inconclusive given the still overwhelming importance of trade with the UK. In the event, British moves towards the EC proved decisive for Ireland. Following rumours in April and May 1961 that a British application was imminent, the Irish Government submitted an aide memoire to the six EC member states, setting out its intention to seek EC membership. From that point the Irish Government sought maximum co-ordination with the British of its strategy towards EC accession. The main objective of this co-ordination was to avoid any new economic barriers being erected between Ireland and Britain as part of the transition process.

IRISH APPLICATION

The Irish application was lodged on 31 July 1961, as Macmillan announced to the House of Commons Britain's intention to apply. Meetings of the Council of Ministers in September and October indicated that the EC was taking a cautious line on the Irish application. Concerns about the adaptation of Irish industry to the customs union surfaced in preliminary exchanges of information.[40] In the wake of the Fouchet Committee's draft Treaty for a Union of States presented in October 1961, anxieties were raised, both in Brussels and Dublin, about the compatibility of Irish neutrality with the EC's political ambitions. Uncertainty continued through the spring and summer of 1962, exacerbated by the difficulties already encountered with the British application. Only following an intense round of diplomacy in EC capitals in October 1962, did the Taoiseach, Sean Lemass, persuade the Community to open negotiations.

In the event, these issues were never explored, since the enlargement negotiations broke down following de Gaulle's press conference of 14 January. Given the range of economic and political issues identified by de Gaulle as obstacles to enlargement, there was no realistic possibility for the Irish to pursue their application independently of the British. Irish policy, therefore, focused on negotiating an improved trade regime with the UK, which resulted in the more liberal Anglo-Irish Trade Agreement of 1965, in preparation for eventual EC membership, the continuation of internal structural economic reforms and the maintenance of contacts with Brussels and EC member states. The Second Programme for Economic Expansion, covering the period 1964–70, called for export-led growth accompanied by tariff reductions, and assumed that Ireland would be in the EC by 1970.

RE-PRESENTATION OF APPLICATION

The Wilson Government's interest in reactivating the British application led to renewed Anglo-Irish contacts in late 1966 and early 1967, and on 11 May 1967 the Irish application was re-presented. The Commission's Opinion on the four applications was published in September 1967 and did not identify any serious issues arising from the Irish application. However, as in 1963, the negotiations quickly deadlocked over French concerns about Britain, and Ireland was unable to pursue its application separately.

Following de Gaulle's resignation, Pompidou's succession as President of France and the Hague Summit of November 1969, events moved quickly towards full accession negotiations. In April 1970, the Government published a White Paper[41] on the implications of membership which identified the need to make constitutional amendments to accommodate EC law,[42] the substantial, if difficult to quantify, long-term economic benefit including a 30 to 40 per cent increase in agricultural output by the end of the decade. Given the uncertainty about the moves towards political union, its implications for Irish foreign policy autonomy were treated lightly by the White Paper. Initially Irish priorities during the negotiations focused on the transitional period, the status of the Anglo-Irish Free Trade Area during that transitional period, the implications of the agreement on establishing a common fisheries policy, and the maintenance of some specific animal and plant health regulations.

By the end of 1970, the negotiations had made considerable progress, with the Irish accepting a uniform transitional period of five years, the phasing out of Anglo-Irish trade preferences, so long as no new barriers were created in the meantime. The fisheries issue proved more contentious, and was not seriously tackled until later in 1971. The Irish wished to maintain their exclusive twelve-mile limit, until such point as the enlarged Community could come to a new common agreement. Eventually, the Community agreed (as with the other three applicants) to allow each member state to restrict fishing within a six-mile coastal zone until the end of 1982. Ireland was allowed to retain a twelve-mile zone on some parts of its north, east and west coasts.[43] The Werner Plan, presented in October 1970, to achieve European and Monetary Union (EMU) by 1980 also raised concerns in Ireland about regional and structural economic issues. Whilst, at this stage the EC had no active regional policy, the Irish were concerned that their special economic problems should be recognised. Eventually the Community agreed to the annexation of a protocol to the Accession Treaty, accepting Ireland's development needs, and committing the Community (unspecifically) to meeting these. This led the Community to take a more sympathetic view of the compatibility of Ireland's industrial incentives with the Treaty.[44]

The negotiations were concluded in January 1972 and led immediately to the publication of a White Paper setting out the terms of accession.[45] The debate on the accession terms lasted three days (21–23 March 1972). Whilst some concerns were expressed about the loss of sovereignty, and possible political dimensions of integration, the Government motion was easily carried by 89 votes to 16. This was followed, on 10 May, by a referendum on membership, resulting in approval of accession by 83.1 per cent.

The classical method posed few problems for Ireland. Irish negotiating priorities threatened neither the overall acquis nor any powerful domestic interest groups in the EC. At that stage in the development of the EC's foreign policy identity, Ireland's neutrality did not prove problematic either.

DENMARK

In line with the other Scandinavian countries, Denmark took a relatively sceptical position in the postwar attempts to forge a tighter political and economic union in Western Europe. It preferred closer Nordic co-operation with other states sympathetic to its social democratic model of domestic politics, combined with liberal, free trade policies. During the 1950s, Denmark participated actively in the development of the OEEC though, given the problems in the UK's policy at this time, there was an awareness that the wider, looser, OEEC framework might not emerge as the dominant model of European co-operation.

As one of Europe's largest food exporters, Denmark was vulnerable both to the possibility of a Common Market with agricultural preference, and the British plans for a free trade area in industrial goods whilst maintaining imperial preference for agriculture. Denmark was faced with the prospect of having to grant tariff-free access to approximately 90 per cent of its imports from Europe whilst about 70 per cent of its (agricultural) exports would be subject to protectionism. Given that Denmark's two main markets, the UK and Germany, would be likely to join different trade blocs, the key Danish objective during this period was to prevent any barriers being erected between the two groups.[46]

The breakdown of negotiations in the Maudling Committee to create a large free trade area, effectively forced Denmark to make a choice it had wished to avoid, and therefore, during 1959, it participated in the formation of EFTA. Denmark was adamant that EFTA should be seen as a vehicle for negotiating with the EC to resolve pan-European trade issues. Denmark succeeded in concluding bilateral agreements on agriculture with the UK and a long-term agreement with Germany guaranteeing access to its market until 1967.

Following the Bonn Declaration of July 1961, in which the governments of the Six expressed their desire to see the EC expand its role in developing European unity, the Danish Government announced its intention of applying for membership on the same day as the British application. Given the Danish Government's policy of seeking to have its main export markets in one bloc, it was taken as given that Denmark would join the EC with the UK. Thus Danish policy during this period was driven by rational economic calculations of national interest which overruled any misgivings concerning the possible political shape of the Communities.

The collapse of negotiations with the UK following the de Gaulle 'veto' of 1963 effectively terminated the Danish negotiations, despite the reported offer made by de Gaulle to the Danish Prime Minister, Jens Otto Krag, of either associate or full membership, since this would involve severing links with EFTA and the UK.[47] Despite its commitment to the development of EFTA, the issue of agricultural exports gave Denmark a particular interest in finding agreement with the EC. Although in 1960 Krag floated the possibility of the three Nordic members of EFTA joining the EC without the UK, this idea was not well received in Norway and Sweden.

The belief expressed by George Brown, the British Foreign Secretary, that circumstances were favourable for a renewed attempt at enlargement led to a formal renewal of the applications from the four EFTA members. In view of its experiences in the early 1960s and its scepticism as to whether de Gaulle had significantly changed his mind on the UK application, the Danish Government drew up contingency plans for more active Nordic economic integration, based on the EC model.

NORDECK NEGOTIATIONS

Following the effective breakdown of negotiations on enlargement, arising from the French view that the British economy was too weak to cope with integration, the Danes actively pursued the possibility of a Nordic customs unions (NORDECK) during 1968.[48] However, the situation changed following the resignation of de Gaulle, and the election of President Pompidou, known to be in favour of an early EC enlargement. The Hague Summit decision in December 1969 to open negotiations with applicant countries in the first six months of 1970 affected the NORDECK negotiations. Though many of the technical problems involved in creating a Nordic customs union were solved in 1970, it became clear that the political will no longer existed. However, the attempt and failure to create NORDECK was a key stage in the process of convincing Danish public opinion that there was no realistic alternative to full EC membership. Negotiations were opened in June 1970 and were relatively easy and unproblematic.[49] The Danes avoided identifying a long list of problems at the outset and accepted without reservation the 'acquis communautaire', but stressing the strong interest in participating in the development of these plans. The Danes requested that they should enter without any transitional periods for industrial or agricultural goods, and succeeded in getting the support of the French to their receiving home-market prices (very close to EC prices) immediately on entry. They also succeeded in obtaining a verbal statement that the right of veto contained in the Luxembourg Compromise of 1966 was still valid, since the Danes considered this to be an important factor in building public support for the referendum scheduled to take place shortly after the Norwegian referendum in October 1972.

The Danish referendum concentrated mainly on economic issues, and avoided speculation concerning the future development of the EC into a stronger form of union, instead stressing Denmark's participation in decision making and its ultimate right of veto. In the referendum two-thirds of the participating 90 per cent voted in favour of membership, with Denmark joining on 1 January 1973.

NORWAY

In common with Denmark, Norway's close trade links with the UK, and concerns about the political goals of the EC, led her to join EFTA. When the UK applied to join the EC in 1961, it was widely expected that Norway would immediately follow. However, domestic political concerns about sovereignty, combined with concerns about agriculture and fisheries, delayed the Norwegian application until April 1962.

Substantial negotiations never commenced before the de Gaulle veto in January 1963. Following the UK, the Norwegian application was reactivated in July 1967. However, after the breakdown of the UK negotiations in December 1967, Norway participated in the NORDECK talks.

Following the opening of full accession negotiations with all four applicants in 1970, the Norwegian Government set out its policy towards the EC in June. This involved seeking permanent exemptions for Norwegian agriculture, to ensure the maintenance of settlement in remote regions, as well as special arrangements for fisheries, given the overall importance of fishing to the Norwegian economy and its special significance for coastal communities.[50]

These demands directly challenged the EC's classical method, and led to difficult talks with EC negotiators. The strains also led to the collapse of the Norwegian coalition Government, and its replacement, in March 1971, by a Labour Government led by Trygve Bratteli. Negotiations were complicated by the EC's own internal discussions in the autumn of 1971 over the Common Fisheries Policy. The Norwegian Government pressed for a special protocol allowing it to maintain its twelve-mile exclusive limit indefinitely. In January 1972, the EC agreed to a twelve-mile limit for a ten-year transitional period, with vaguely worded assurances for the period after 1982. The EC also agreed to recognise the 'special problems' of agriculture, allowing Norway to maintain its own support policies for three years, after which they would have to be integrated into the Common Agricultural Policy.[51] The Norwegian Government accepted the terms and duly signed the Accession Treaty in January 1972.

Given only minority support in the Norwegian Parliament, the Bratteli Government had promised a referendum on the accession terms. Public opinion had always been finely balanced over EC membership, with northern, rural farming and fishing communities strongly opposed. The referendum took place on 24–25 September 1972, and resulted in rejection of the entry terms by 53.5 per cent to 46.5 per cent. The Bratteli Government duly resigned, to be replaced by a new coalition led by Lars Korvald, which negotiated a Free Trade Agreement with the EC, similar to those with other EFTA 'non-joiners'. The negotiations and the referendum had a traumatic effect on Norwegian politics. They confirmed that, no matter how ingenious an agreement concluded in Brussels, more fundamental concerns about political and economic identity cannot be overridden. They also tested the limits of the Community's classical method. Despite the EC's recognition of Norway's particular concerns over agriculture and fisheries, no permanent derogations were allowed. The principle held, to be tested again by Norway, twenty years later.

CONCLUSION

Taking the period 1961–73, the first enlargement negotiations have been the most protracted to date and, in the UK's case, the most problematic. De Gaulle's concerns, though humiliating for the British, and embarrassing for other EC member states, only highlighted the depth and breadth of adjustments demanded from all new EC members. The continuing difficulties that the UK has had with EC membership relate primarily to UK domestic political conflicts, rather than the terms of accession, though the EC budget and the CFP have, at critical moments, exacerbated these difficulties. The Norwegian negotiations demonstrated that accession is not inevitable and may depend on a very fragile domestic consensus.

Most significantly, the first enlargement negotiations set a framework for future enlargement rounds. Though the classical method continued to set tough challenges for applicants, the reality of the mutual expectations was much clearer.

3 The second enlargement
Greece

INTRODUCTION

Within three years of completing its first enlargement, the Community was faced with a new set of challenges in the Mediterranean region. As the military regimes in Greece, Spain and Portugal crumbled during 1974 and 1975, to be replaced by democratic governments committed to EC membership, so the EC was forced to confront once again the implications of a more diverse EC. However, Southern enlargement involved a much poorer group of states than the first enlargement (with the exception of Ireland), in a region fraught with political and military security tensions. Both the capacity of the applicants to implement the acquis, and the sensitivity of the EC's domestic interests affected by enlargement put the classical method under severe strain.

These pressures were first confronted in the case of Greece. This chapter therefore examines:

- the development of Greece's relations with the EC under the 1961 Association Agreement, until the 'freezing' of the Agreement during the military dictatorship
- the moves made by the democratic Greek Government in 1975 towards applying for full membership
- the attitudes in the EC towards Greek membership specifically and, more generally, towards southern enlargement
- the accession negotiations themselves, and how far the classical method of enlargement was adapted to take account of new realities.

FROM ASSOCIATION TO MEMBERSHIP APPLICATION

From the early 1960s, Greece's relations with the EC excited both hopes and fears as to what kind of economic and political impact

European integration might have on the Mediterranean regions. Greece applied to the Community for an Association Agreement, under Article 238 of the Rome Treaty, in June 1959. From Greece's perspective, the application was a choice in favour of the EC over the EFTA model of economic development, reflecting the hope of long-term full membership. The EC also covered agriculture, the critical sector in Greece's economic structure. The Community's motivation was essentially political. As a member of NATO, Greece was vital to the development of a Mediterranean security policy which also needed to encompass Turkey.

Following five years of negotiation, the Association Agreement was signed in Athens in July 1961 and set out the terms for the establishment of a customs union, some measure of policy harmonisation and financial assistance to Greece. At this early stage in the development of the Community's external relations, association could be seen either as an end in itself, to formalise relations with countries who had no chance of becoming members of the EC, or as a first stage of a process leading to full membership. The Athens Agreement, however, clearly saw membership as an eventual goal, with Article 72 stating the possibility, though with no specific timetable laid out.

TERMS OF THE ASSOCIATION AGREEMENT

The Agreement envisaged progressive trade liberalisation, though in view of the large economic gap between the two parties, the EC was to liberalise more quickly than Greece. It established a two-tier transitional period for industrial products, leading to an eventual customs union. Tariffs and quotas would be abolished over a 12-year period except for goods manufactured in Greece at the time, where restrictions would be removed over a 22-year period.[1] Similar provisions were agreed for agriculture. Greece also had to adopt the EC's Common Customs Tariff over the 12- or 22-year period, depending on the product categories.

Both parties were breaking new ground with the Agreement. No real economic analysis of the Agreement was made in Greece, though there was a widespread fear that the Agreement might undermine the fragile position of Greece's industry.[2] For the Community, the Agreement extended its political reach in the Eastern Mediterranean and led to the conclusion in 1964 of a similar Agreement with Turkey. The economic provisions of the Agreements were similar, though the Turkish Agreement envisaged a preparatory stage before the move to the transitional period. This move was not automatic, and reflected the caution with which the Community approached Turkey.

FREEZING THE ASSOCIATION AGREEMENT

Following the military coup in Greece in April 1967, the Community 'froze' the Agreement, limiting its implementation to tariff reductions, whilst suspending all the other provisions until democracy was restored. Tsoukalis argues that 'in the end the freezing of the association was not at a particularly low temperature'.[3] It suited both sides to maintain contacts, largely for reasons of economic self interest, though some opinions in the Community argued that it would give the EC some leverage with the regime.

Even before the 'freeze' there were differences of opinion as to what association would involve. The Greeks viewed the commitment to harmonisation of agricultural policy as giving them access to the institutional arrangements of the CAP, whilst the EC was adamant that no third country could be so involved in internal EC mechanisms. This was certainly an important factor in the eventual preference for full membership.

The economic effects of the Agreement are difficult to separate from other economic factors at the time. Growth rates throughout Europe were high in the 1960s and early 1970s. From 1962–77, Greece achieved average annual GDP per capita growth of 5.5 per cent in comparison with 29 per cent in the EC. Greece's trade patterns also moved markedly towards the EC, reaching 47.7 per cent of total trade in 1977.[4] Structural rigidities nevertheless remained. Despite the reduction in external protection, the tariff structure was still biased in favour of domestic producers who often retained oligopolistic market positions. The Agreement rather highlighted the extent to which far-reaching domestic structural reforms were necessary to develop the Greek economy.

THE COLLAPSE OF THE DICTATORSHIP AND THE APPLICATION FOR MEMBERSHIP

In July 1974, the military dictatorship in Greece collapsed, following the Turkish invasion of Cyprus and Greece's military withdrawal from NATO. This was a critical period in the re-evaluation of Greece's external political and economic relations. The US was widely perceived as having given the military regime at least tacit, if not active support. For Greece, the possibility of Community membership was seen as a way of strengthening its Western political orientation whilst distancing itself from the US. This reorientation was reinforced by the Cyprus crisis which led to a widespread political consensus that the greater threat to Greece's security came from Turkey rather than from the Communist regimes in the Balkans.[5]

In November 1974, the Greek Government submitted a memo to the EC announcing its intention of seeking full membership, and in June 1975 submitted a formal application. The Council of Ministers immediately requested the Commission to draw up its Opinion.

THE POLITICAL SITUATION IN GREECE

The political consensus on the sources of Greece's problems did not lead to consensus on solutions. The centre right New Democracy (ND) Government led by Karamanlis saw EC membership as marking the end of a long period of political isolation which would strengthen Greek independence and bargaining power in relation to third countries, while allowing Greece to actively participate in the political development of Europe. Karamanlis also saw a united Europe, independent of the superpowers as a pragmatic alternative to the, by now, discredited close engagement with the US, and adopted a 'Gaullist' perspective on foreign policy. The Socialist opposition Pan Hellenic Socialist Movement (PASOK) led by Andreas Papandreou drew very different conclusions. Claiming that the EC and NATO were synonymous, it pushed a more nationalist, populist line supporting non-alignment and direct co-operation with other Mediterranean socialist parties. This polarisation extended to the economic evaluation of EC membership. For ND, membership would act as a catalyst for structural reforms and would build on the developmental achievements of the Association Agreement period. Full participation in Community decision making would also overcome some of the limitations of associate status which involved acceptance of Community policies without direct influence on their shape.

PASOK's view was that the Mediterranean periphery would become increasingly dependent on the core economics of Western Europe. This dependence could only be broken by pursuing autonomous economic policies which were incompatible with the Treaty of Rome. EC membership would block the possibility of a socialist experiment.

The Confederation of Greek Industries (SEV) was actively in favour of membership. Its members were mainly larger companies who had most to gain from access to wider markets, whilst it was hoped that accession would provide an impetus to the reform of the Greek bureaucracy. The General Confederation of Greek Workers (GSEE) was also in favour, expecting improved labour legislation.

COMMUNITY ATTITUDES

Attitudes within the Community towards the possibility of Greek membership were ambiguous. Whilst the Association Agreement gave the Greeks the message that full membership was an eventual possibility, the difficulties in implementing some of its provisions led the Community to be cautious.

In his tour of European capitals which preceded the Greek application, Karamanlis stressed the importance of Greek membership in ensuring domestic political stability and maintaining Greece's Western orientation. Germany and the UK, concerned at the linkage with security issues, were worried that Greek membership might upset the delicate balance the Community had tried to strike between Greece and Turkey. Greece's application came at a time when the EC was trying to broker a deal in Cyprus. Neither the British nor the Germans favoured encouraging the Karamanlis Government to see the EC as an alternative to NATO. Only France, where President Valery Giscard D'Estaing had built close relations with Karamanlis, was actively in favour of Greek membership.

COMMISSION'S OPINION

The Commission's Opinion was adopted on 28 January 1976. It followed long discussions and disagreement between Commissioners and was eventually taken to a vote. Although the Commission recommended that 'a clear affirmative reply be given to the Greek request and that negotiations for Greek accession should accordingly be opened', the affirmation was half-hearted.[6] The core of the Commission's proposal was that a pre-accession stage should be established before any specific transitional periods came into effect. The Commission had three sets of concerns that led to this proposal. The first was the delicate state of Greco–Turkish relations. The Opinion noted:

> Until now the balance in the Community's relations with Greece and Turkey has found its expression in their identical status as Associates, both of them with the possibility of full membership as the final objective, albeit with different timetables.[7]

The EC was acutely aware that Greek membership would upset this delicate balance, since in June 1975 the Council had declared that examining the Greek application was without prejudice to Turkey's rights as an Associate.

The second set of concerns focused on the economic implications of accession. The overall macro-economic impact on the Community was deemed to be small, though the structural weaknesses of the Greek economy, in particular the size of its agricultural population and weak industrial base, meant that significant resource transfers would take place from the EU budget. Based on 1976 figures, the Commission estimated a net budget cost of about 300 MEUA though this did not take into account the effects of any transitional measures negotiated subsequently. The Opinion also pointed out the structural implications of adapting its pattern of agricultural imports to the Community's external trade policy.[8]

The third set of issues concerned the impact of Greek membership on the decision making and policy development of the EC. Here the Commission adopted its traditional role of arguing that widening should not be at the expense of deepening, and that steps towards European Union, such as direct elections to the European Parliament and EMU, called for an acceleration of the integration process.

All of these reservations led the Commission to propose a pre-membership period which would be more far-reaching than the completion of the Association Agreement timetable. This period would involve a substantial economic programme, utilising the Community's Structural Funds to bring about the necessary structural adjustments. Greece would be actively engaged in the process in order to familiarise herself with the EC's institutional and decision-making processes. The Commission also proposed that when full negotiations did start, priority should be given to the difficult issues first.

The proposals represented significant qualifications to the Community method of enlargement. The Commission was, in effect, telling Greece and the Council of Ministers that transitional arrangements and time limited derogations would not be enough to carry the burden of adjustment. A more open-ended period of political and economic convergence was necessary before the irrevocable step of opening full accession negotiations was undertaken. Yet, by arguing that Greece was not ready for full membership, the Commission was also seeking to protect the principles underpinning the classical enlargement method. The difficulties that the Commission had experienced in obtaining the appropriate level of information from the

Greek Government in preparing its Opinion, suggested that real difficulties lay ahead.

The Greek Government reacted strongly to the Commission's
Opinion. It argued that the Association Agreement had already served
as a pre-accession period and that the Opinion was a way of indefinitely postponing the Greek application. The linkage between the
Greek application, the wider implications of enlargement and relations
with Turkey, went beyond the proper terms of reference of the
Opinion.

COUNCIL REJECTION OF THE COMMISSION'S OPINION

The Commission's Opinion was almost immediately rejected by the
Council of Ministers. Karamanlis threatened to withdraw the Greek
application and lobbied member governments hard to override the
Commission's Opinion. The French Government rejected the idea of a
pre-accession period and, at a meeting on 2 February 1976, the Dutch
and German Foreign Ministers announced their support for moving to
full accession negotiations as soon as possible. At the Council meeting
on 9 February, the member states unanimously rejected the
Commission's Opinion, despite objections reportedly made by Britain,
Denmark and Belgium, and asked COREPER to prepare a negotiating mandate as soon as possible. The decision was facilitated by the
assurances given by Greece that, as a full member, she would not block
the EC's developing relations with Turkey.[9]

Despite the Council decision the Community was unenthusiastic
about Greek membership. The Commission's Opinion had identified
some of the wider implications of enlargement which were to become
more acute over the following five years. Although Spain and Portugal
had yet to apply for membership, their dictatorships had collapsed by
the time the EC agreed to negotiate with Greece and it was widely
appreciated that further Mediterranean enlargement was likely. This
raised wider questions about cohesion, regional disparities and, more
specifically, the development of market organisations for
Mediterranean agricultural produce. The Greek application could have
been postponed pending a wider review of these issues; that much was
implicit in the Commission's Opinion. The idea of taking all three
applications together, alongside a more fundamental review of the
implications of enlargement, was put forward by the French. This
showed some ambivalence on the part of the French Government who
were keen to open negotiations with Greece sooner rather than later.
This, however, did not necessarily indicate a willingness to conclude

negotiations; the possibility of an indefinite transition period was floated.[10] As was to be seen most clearly, during the Spanish and Portuguese negotiations, France sought to combine active promotion of Mediterranean enlargement with a vigorous defence of domestic sectional interests.

Ultimately, larger political and security issues tipped the balance in favour of immediate negotiations with Greece. Germany, in particular, was concerned that rejection of Greece's application might have further negative implications for its NATO membership. Full accession negotiations would help to reintegrate Greece into the Western security alliance at a time of tension in the Eastern Mediterranean. The Community was also keen to be seen taking an active role in consolidating democracy in the Mediterranean region which, at this stage, was still very fragile. Delaying the Greek application would also have sent the wrong signals to the Portuguese and the Spanish.

Having drawn up a negotiating mandate, the EC moved quickly to opening negotiations formally in Brussels in July 1976. The Commission, led by President Francois-Xavier Ortoli would provide analysis and play the role of honest broker. The Greek side was led by the Minister of Co-ordination, Panayotis Papaligouras.

Having agreed to open negotiations, the orthodox Community method of enlargement was restated. Greece had to accept in full the acquis communautaire. Transitional arrangements were acceptable only in so far as they did not hold back the process of further integration.

A supporting principle in the Greek case was that solutions agreed for one sector would not necessarily be applicable to others. Negotiation over the various dossiers was therefore fragmented with little attempt at policy integration.[11] This was largely a consequence of the decision to move to full accession negotiations at a time when there was such widespread uncertainty about the future direction of the acquis. Linking the policy dossiers together into a broader overview would have raised the wider issues about the future of the Community that the Council had sought to bypass by rejecting the Commission's Opinion.

THE NEGOTIATIONS

The classical Community method of handling accession negotiations involves two phases. The first, exploratory stage, as noted in Chapter 1, involves a detailed review of the acquis by the Commission and the applicant's delegation, to identify problem issues in implementing the acquis and where transitional arrangements might be needed. The second, substantive phase focuses on bargaining over specific issues in order to reach an overall agreement. In practice, the two phases cannot be so clearly delineated, with negotiating progress dependent on the sensitivity of individual sectoral dossiers, rather than on a coherent view of the whole process.

There was a basic imbalance in the negotiating strategy of the Community and Greece from the earliest phase of the negotiations. The Community side specified the overall principles relating to transitional arrangements, but was unwilling to put forward its own negotiating positions until it had acquired a comprehensive 'vue d'ensemble' of all the Greek positions. The Greeks were therefore put in a weak position from the outset. Given the complexity of interests on the Community side, this was not surprising. Despite the outward appearance of solidarity in the Community's insistence on the adherence to the acquis, there was considerable uncertainty as to how this might be moulded into specific negotiating positions. There were also differences in the negotiating positions of the Community. The Council would only enter into substantive negotiations, once the technical dossiers had been completed. For the Commission, progress on the technical dossiers was dependent on the substantive negotiations, that is, on a decision in principle being reached at the political level. Even two years into the negotiations, the Community still had not presented the Greek delegation with its detailed position on agriculture. This made for circularity in many of the arguments presented and was to be evident again in the negotiations with Spain and Portugal.

The first dossier to reach substantive negotiations was the customs union. Greece's overall negotiating strategy was to argue that the Association Agreement should form the basis of the accession negotiations, that the 'acquis d'association' should underpin the acquis communautaire. The Community took the very different view that association and full membership were qualitatively different, and that accession negotiations should be treated on their own merits. This was most clearly seen in the negotiations over the removal of Greece's residual import duties. Greece argued that these should be removed according to the association timetable, i.e. over the 22-year period originally negotiated. The Community argued that circumstances had changed in the mean time and that the timetable was no longer appropriate. The Greeks quickly abandoned their strategy in the face of Community determination and eventually settled on a five-year transition period, and that the different categories of products listed in the Association Agreement would be consolidated into a simple list. A similar agreement was eventually agreed for the Common Customs Tariff, with Greece's duties towards third countries being abolished in parallel with its duties on intra-Community trade over the same five-year period. Quantitative restrictions were also to be phased out during the transitional period.

Both sides were concerned about the impact of accession on Greek industry with its major structural weaknesses. The duty-free access of Community goods to the Greek market since 1974 said very little about the competitiveness of Greek industry, since these were mainly goods not produced in Greece.[12] The Greeks had also compensated for this tariff reduction by retaining or increasing non-tariff protection. Given that Community rules are clear in these areas, negotiations focused on how the transitional arrangements would be applied, with the immediate removal of measures 'having equivalent effect' with only some minor transitional exceptions being allowed.

EXTERNAL COMMERCIAL RELATIONS

Enlarging the Community necessarily leads to the renegotiation of trade relations with third countries with whom the EC had negotiated preferential trade agreements. In the Greek case, the extension of these trade agreements to other countries, particularly in the Mahgreb, had eroded the special benefits of Greece's Association Agreement. From the Greek perspective, the full acceptance of the Community's external commercial policy would expose the Greek economy to further import penetration and competition. The Commission's Opinion had identified the fact that the share of imports to Greece from these countries (6.6 per cent from EFTA and 10 per cent from the Mediterranean countries) was likely to increase and could cause some major sectoral problems.[13] Yet the Greek negotiations again had little room for manoeuvre since the core commitments of the external commercial policy were non-negotiable. The Greeks, for instance, dropped their request to retain their trade agreements with the state-trading (i.e. COMECON) countries, upon which some sensitive agricultural sectors depended. Overall, the detailed implementation of the common external commercial policy was integrated with the provisions of the transitional periods for the customs union.

AGRICULTURE

The central issue in the Greek accession negotiations was the agricultural dossier. Apart from the size and complexity of the agriculture chapters in the acquis, agriculture raised wider political issues both for Greece, and the Community. Wary of setting precedents for Spain and Portugal, the fragmented, labour intensive structure of Greek agriculture was predicted to create difficulties for both sides. The Commission's Opinion pointed out that on accession, land under cultivation would increase by 10 per cent, the farming population by 12 per cent, but the number of farm units by 19 per cent. Greek agricultural output per person was only 40 per cent of the EC average, which contributed 16 per cent of Greece's GDP, and employed 36 per cent of the population, compared with its contribution in the EC of 5 per cent of GDP, employing only 9 per cent of the population.[14] The predominance of Mediterranean products, in particular fruit, vegetables and olive oil in the Greek agricultural profile, inevitably affected the interests of French and Italian producers. Upward alignment to CAP prices would also stimulate overproduction in these sectors.

The Greek strategy was to play down the agricultural issue and argue that its overall budgetary implications were small. For the Community, wider interests were at stake. During 1977 the implications of enlargement to twelve member states came into sharper relief, following applications from Portugal in May and Spain in July. In June the French vetoed a Commission paper on agriculture addressed to the Greeks and argued for changes to market organisation in Mediterranean produce before Greek accession. This was soon reversed, with the French arguing for agricultural reforms in parallel.[15] In September 1977, Commissioner Natali, leading the enlargement negotiations, presented a paper to the Commission arguing for a global approach to the three applications involving a long transitional period, and a co-ordinated programme to reduce the economic gap between the applicants and the Community, focused on structural aid and diversification of production in order to avoid creating further surpluses in textiles, steel and shipbuilding as well as agriculture. The Commission rejected the paper; the economic costs to the existing member states were considered too high and were politically sensitive, particularly in France, where Parliamentary elections were scheduled for March 1978.

Linkage of the Spanish and Portuguese applications was a major problem for the Greeks. Whilst the opening of accession negotiations implied a willingness to conclude them, the risk of 'globalising' the Mediterranean enlargement was ever present. Beyond claiming that the overall impact of Greek accession was very small, there was little Greek negotiators could do to push the Community.

Progress in substantive negotiations in 1977 was very slow.

However, the result of the Greek general election in November helped to break the deadlock. Prime Minister Karamanlis called an early general election in order to seek a renewed mandate, particularly on the foreign affairs issues of EC and NATO membership. Although his New Democracy Party won, the election saw large electoral gains for the anti-EC PASOK Party. In January 1978 Karamanlis toured the member states' capitals in order to persuade EC governments that accession negotiations needed to be concluded speedily while a pro-EC party remained in power. Karamanlis' efforts helped to break the deadlock. He received assurances that the bulk of the negotiations would be concluded by the end of 1978 and that solutions would be found to the sensitive issues of agriculture, social policy and the length of the transition period.

FREE MOVEMENT OF WORKERS

The free movement of workers was a further sensitive issue during the negotiations. The Commission's Opinion on the Greek application had argued that outward migration would most likely fall after accession[16] and Greece expected complete free movement of its workers throughout the Community immediately after accession. The Community was concerned about the impact of outward migration from Greece, particularly at a time of high unemployment and recession. Germany, as the largest recipient of Greek workers, was the member state most concerned, though its fears were as much linked to Spanish and Portuguese workers.

The Greek Government continued to press hard for complete freedom from the moment of accession, which it considered vital for carrying public opinion. Although the Community was willing to grant Greek workers priority over third-country workers after accession, the final agreement specified a seven-year transition period. Germany had originally pushed for a 12-year period, though the final agreement also included a joint declaration 'reserving the right' of member states to bring to the Community's attention for solution any problems arising from the free movement of workers.

REGIONAL POLICY

Greece's key objective was that as much of the whole country as possible should be designed as a regional development area, so that Greece's own national industrial aids would be interpreted as regional aids, compatible with Article 92 of the Treaty. In this regard, the

Greeks were seeking parity with the agreement made with Ireland on her accession in 1973. Since this designation was a matter for the Commission to examine after accession, the Greeks sought and eventually achieved a protocol recognising the importance of industrial aids to Greece's economic progress.

CONCLUSION OF NEGOTIATIONS

The Community's negotiating strategy of seeking a 'vue d'ensemble' of all the key dossiers before an overall negotiating package could be concluded meant that the sensitive political issues were left until very late in the negotiations. Both sides had accepted that the overall 'basic' transition period should be set at five years, though the final haggling concerned the maximum period for the sensitive sectors. The Community side pushed for a maximum of eight years which was rejected by the Greeks at a ministerial negotiating session on 6 December 1978. Following intense lobbying by Karamanlis, a final compromise was reached on 20 December in which the maximum length of the transition period was settled at seven years, and would only apply to Greece's exports of peaches and tomatoes, and the free movement of labour. Whilst their overall impact on the Community was small, the member states were concerned about setting precedents for the more complex Spanish and Portuguese negotiations which had yet to start.

THE BUDGET

The settlement of the transitional periods opened the way for a conclusion of the budget issue. Greece calculated that the December 1978 agreement would leave her as a net payer during the transition period, in contrast to the estimates in the Commission's Opinion. However, the establishment of a transitional refund mechanism, with Greece receiving a digressive refund against its VAT contributions, ensured that Greece would be a net recipient of EC funds, a critical factor in ensuring domestic political support for the overall deal.

The final session of the Accession Conference took place on 23 May 1979, with the accession date being settled at 1 January 1981. The ratification procedure in the member states went smoothly, except in France, where the National Assembly ratified the Treaty with 264 votes in favour and 204 votes (mainly the socialists and communists) cast against. However, this was arguably more a protest vote against the prospect of Iberian enlargement. In the Greek Parliament, although the 93 PASOK and the 11 Communist Party deputies boycotted the debate and vote, the 193 votes in favour of the accession terms passed the three-fifths majority required for ratification.

CONCLUSION

The Greek accession negotiations took thirty-four months; longer than the first enlargement negotiations (although, in that instance, the decision to open negotiations took much longer) but considerably shorter than the Spanish (eighty months) and Portuguese (seventy-six months) negotiations were to take. For the Greeks, who sought to use the first enlargement as the basis of their strategy, particularly in relation to the basic five-year transition period, the negotiations took a frustratingly long time. Few substantive negotiations took place in the first year. Once the Spanish and Portuguese applications were made, there was a very real risk of issue linkage and indefinite delay. The Greek Government regarded this as the worst possible scenario, given the strengthening domestic opposition to EC membership during the negotiations, and used every diplomatic lever at its disposal to try and ensure a speedy conclusion. The personal credibility of Prime Minister Karamanlis, particularly with French President Giscard, was critical in this respect. The overall Greek negotiating strategy gave the highest priority to the speed of negotiation, even if this left some adjustment problems to be dealt with after accession. Tsalicoglou has written:

> Greece's emphasis on speed inevitably entailed a certain cost: it meant that, with the pressure of passing time, the assessment of the likely impact of accession entered only superficially in the formulation of her negotiation positions. The argumentation in the Greek position papers rarely rose beyond a mere identification of the sectors of the Greek economy that were considered 'sensitive', coupled with requests for temporary protection to avoid disturbances.[17]

Given the strength of the forces ranged against Greece, this was undoubtedly a rational strategy to follow. The initial stress on defending the 'acquis d'association' quickly gave way to a more 'flexible' approach. The key national interest was perceived as obtaining the rights of full membership as soon as possible, rather than in the defence of specific policy positions.

The Community side had a more complex set of positions to reconcile. No member state was really enthusiastic about Greek membership, though Germany considered that the geopolitical stabilisation issues in

the Eastern Mediterranean overrode the more prosaic economic arguments for and against Greek membership. As the Community's
paymaster, the German view was decisive.

The French view was more ambivalent. The long-held desire to be
seen as a 'bridge' between north and south Europe led the French to
sponsor Greek membership, though the potential effects on French
farming interests led the French to take a tough line during the agricultural chapter negotiations. However, following the French
parliamentary elections of March 1978, the French Government
became more flexible.

The British were agnostic on Greek membership, except in so far as
it might threaten the delicate Greco–Turkish balance over Cyprus. The
caveat in the Commission's Opinion that 'the application for membership must take account of certain wider issues of a political and
economic nature, including the problems related to the situation in the
Eastern Mediterranean' was reportedly inserted at the request of the
British.

From the Community's perspective, the Greek application was
significant because it presaged further Mediterranean enlargement.
The arguments surrounding the free movement of workers and
Mediterranean agricultural produce were rehearsals for the Iberian
negotiations. The Commission had a particularly difficult role to play
in acting as the defender of the Community acquis. Its Opinion on the
Greek application followed the orthodox line by arguing that Greece's
unpreparedness for membership might endanger the Community's
development; in effect that premature widening might endanger deepening. Yet the immediate rejection of the Opinion by the Council
suggests that the Commission badly misjudged the opinion of the
member states. The complexity of the issues raised by Mediterranean
enlargement clearly tested the Commission's role as an honest broker, a
role that came under more stress following the opening of the even
more difficult Iberian negotiations.

The Greek negotiations show that the classical Community method
of enlargement, with its exclusive stress on adaptation to the acquis
through transition arrangements, could be maintained, even during a
period of uncertainty about the future of European integration.
However, this explicit isolation of the accession negotiations from the
wider debates ranging through the EC was achieved at a cost. For the
Greeks, it meant constantly downgrading their negotiating positions,
fearful that taking a strong stand would risk entangling their negotiations with the Iberians'. For the Community, the stress on the classical
method risked internalising Greece's structural economic problems

before the Community had developed adequate policy instruments to deal with them. The capacity of the Greek economic and political system to wholeheartedly implement the acquis remained questionable. The demand for compensatory payments through the Integrated Mediterranean Programmes, which the Greeks demanded in 1984 as their price for agreeing to Iberian accession, shows how quickly the Greeks learnt to use their economic weakness to their advantage in Community bargaining. It marked the start of a shift of emphasis in the Community towards the South which was consolidated by the Iberian enlargement in the 1980s and was to continue until the fourth enlargement, the EFTA enlargement, in the 1990s.

4　The third enlargement
Spain and Portugal

INTRODUCTION

The wider implications of Mediterranean enlargement, raised by the accession negotiations with Greece, came into sharper focus once Spanish and Portuguese membership became a serious prospect. The need for policy adaptation within the EC, as well as extensive political and economic reform within the applicant states, became more pressing once the likely degree of diversity within the enlarged Community became clearer. The linkage between the second and third enlargements was, therefore, complex. Negotiations with Spain and Portugal opened before those with Greece had closed. The classical method consequently came under pressure both from the linkages between the two sets of negotiations, and from the wider policy debates which all three applications stimulated. This chapter therefore examines the third enlargement negotiations and the development of the classical method of enlargement. The first section examines Spain's and Portugal's relations with the EC up to the collapse of their dictatorships. The second examines the internal debates in Spain and Portugal leading to membership applications. The third examines the accession negotiations and the wider debates that surrounded them, concluding with a review of the effect of the negotiations on the classical Community method.

SPAIN'S AND PORTUGAL'S PRE-ACCESSION RELATIONS WITH THE EC

Spain's and Portugal's developing relationships with the EC were shaped by their experience of dictatorship. So long as both countries were ruled by autocrats and their economies organised on autarchic principles there was little possibility that relations could develop beyond the stage of limited trade agreements. Thus, the political changes that took place in both countries in the 1970s, in Portugal the 1974 revolution and in Spain the death of Franco in 1975, radically changed the context of European integration. By opening to the South, the Community faced an historic shift in its balance of power, away from the core founders of the EC and its close former EFTA northern associates, towards Europe's new democracies on its southern periphery. The third enlargement, therefore, became a critical test of the capability of the EC model to act as a stabilising influence in the region and to establish a framework for the development of pluralist political and economic structures and processes. It also became a test of the ability of the Community to adapt its acquis to accommodate a wider range of economic and sectoral diversity and to develop new policy instruments to deal with the issues of cohesion.

During the 1950s and 1960s, both Spain and Portugal were isolated from the mainstream of European political developments. The Franco regime in Spain, and the Salazar and Caetano regimes in Portugal pursued policies that would have rendered them both politically unacceptable to the Community and economically problematic. Yet, despite these disqualifications, Spanish and Portuguese policy during this period was, to a degree, shaped by the developments to their north, as the Community built its customs union and considered enlargement, initially, to the north.

SPAIN

Spain suffered from international isolation during the war years and the early postwar period which led her to pursue inward-looking, autarchic economic policies. It was not until the late 1950s and, in particular, the 1959 Stabilisation Plan that Spain embarked on a policy of limited economic liberalisation. The entry into the Government of the Opus Dei technocrats, interested in the experience of French indicative planning and with a growing awareness of the need to keep up with integration moves within the newly established EC, led to more outward-looking policies.[1]

The dependence of Spanish agricultural exports on the UK market led the Spanish Government to apply to the EC to negotiate an Association Agreement in 1962, following the UK application for membership in 1961. The request for Association looked to full membership at some point in the future. Despite internal disagreements within the Spanish Government, it marked a long-term statement of intent as to where its political and economic interests lay.

The application remained unanswered for nearly two years, with a decision in principle only being taken in 1964, negotiations starting in 1967 and concluding in 1970.

ASSOCIATION AGREEMENT

The agreement, initially provided for a first stage of six years, leading to a 70 per cent reduction in EC tariffs on Spanish industrial goods and a 40 per cent tariff reduction for citrus fruit. Spain agreed to reduce tariffs on EC exports in six stages up to 1977. The Agreement was an important stage in Spanish–EC relations by establishing the principle of reciprocal tariff and quota liberalisation. Despite the symbolic importance of the 1970 Agreement, its economic effects were limited. The Agreement was effectively opened for renegotiation in 1973–75 to take account of the accession of Denmark, Ireland and the UK, to whose market Spain's agricultural exports had previously enjoyed free access. The negotiations were, however, broken off in October 1975, following the execution of Basque prisoners by Franco.

PORTUGAL

The Salazar and Caetano regimes effectively isolated Portugal from the mainstream of European political and economic developments during the 1950s and 1960s. Economic growth in the 1950s was based on a policy of import substitution and preferential treatment for Portugal's African colonies. Largely because of its trade dependence on the UK, Portugal became a founder member of EFTA in 1960. In recognition of her economic circumstances, Portugal was given a longer timetable of tariff liberalisation, inside EFTA, together with the possibility of reintroducing new duties to protect infant industries. At the same time, the regime pursued the idea of a Portuguese Common Market with the African colonies, though continuous military conflict in Africa limited its development. Joining EFTA was the 'choice of non-commitment'.[2] Whilst allowing Portugal to participate in Europe's economic liberalisation, its colonial orientation could also be maintained. During the 1960s official attitudes to the EC were determined by the UK's position. Portugal asked for the opening of negotiations with the EC following the UK's membership in 1961. The second UK application led to the Portuguese addressing memoranda to the Commission to retain access to the British and Danish markets and to extend these rights to the EC as a whole, following enlargement.

After the Hague Summit's commitment to discuss post enlargement relations with EFTA non-applicants, the Portuguese met with the Council of Ministers in November 1970 to request an Association Agreement. The Special Relations Agreement came into effect on 1 January 1973, creating a free trade area between the enlarged Community and the remaining members of EFTA. The agreement provided for the elimination of all barriers on Portuguese exports to the EC by 1977, though with a longer timetable for some 'sensitive' sectors such as textiles.

THE END OF THE DICTATORSHIPS AND THE PROSPECTS FOR FULL MEMBERSHIP

The context of EC Iberian relations changed dramatically with the fall of the dictatorships in both countries in 1974/75. The possibility of full EC membership, both as an extension of the trade agreements already negotiated and as a way of reinforcing the transition to democracy, became a reality. For both countries, applying for membership was a major political move, implying a choice of a framework within which all political and economic decisions would, in future, be exercised.

SPAIN

Following the death of Franco in November 1975, King Juan Carlos committed himself, at his swearing in as the new Head of State, to the 'peaceful establishment of democratic coexistence based on respect for the law as a manifestation of the sovereignty of the people'.[3] In the light of this commitment, EC Foreign Ministers agreed in January 1976 to resume trade negotiations with Spain. Following the general election of June 1977, the Government of Adolfo Suarez submitted a formal application for EC membership in July 1977 and, in February 1978, created a new Ministry for relations with the EC.

PORTUGAL

The transition to democracy in Portugal was more convoluted than in Spain and led the EC to adopt a more cautious policy in its dealings with Portugal. Following the 'Red Carnation' revolution of April 1974, which brought down the Caetano Government, Portugal entered a period of instability. Despite the attempt of leading Portuguese politicians, including Dr Mario Soares, to obtain aid from the EC, as provided for under the 1972 Agreement, the EC was initially unsure as to where political authority lay in Portugal.

Following an abortive coup attempt in March 1975, a Supreme Revolutionary Council was established which assumed a right of veto over Cabinet decisions. During the remainder of 1975, the Portuguese Government remained unstable. This, combined with the rapid decolonisation process in Africa, created difficulties for both the Portuguese and the Community. The loss of Portugal's African colonies forced a fundamental reappraisal of its external trade policy, which led the country to focus more explicitly on the EC. For the Community, instability on its Southern flanks, at a time of wider geopolitical instability, particularly in the Middle East, led the EC to see Portugal as a higher priority than it had previously been, though any strengthening of this relationship was dependent on Portuguese progress towards democratic stability. In May 1975 the European Council in Dublin called for the strengthening of links between the EC and Portugal and, at the Brussels Council meeting in July, the EC reaffirmed that it was 'prepared to initiate discussions on close economic and financial co-operation with Portugal', but reaffirmed that 'in accordance with its historical and political traditions, the European Community can only give support to a democracy of a pluralist nature'.[4]

During 1976, the Portuguese attempted to negotiate an additional protocol to their 1972 Free Trade Agreement. Yet, despite the Community committing 200 MEUA in emergency aid, the general lack of trade concessions contained in the September 1976 Agreement, led the Portuguese Government to conclude that full membership was the best long-term option. Following a round of visits to EC capitals, the Portuguese Prime Minister, Dr Mario Soares, submitted a formal application for membership on 28 March 1977.

ECONOMIC JUSTIFICATION FOR APPLICATIONS

Both the Spanish and Portuguese applications were prompted by the belief that full integration into the EC's policy process was a necessary pre-condition of macro economic and sectoral policy management, as well as political stabilisation. First, in terms of overall trade patterns, the EC had become steadily more important for Iberian exports. Given the pivotal importance of the UK as a trading partner, the first enlargement confronted Spain and Portugal with the need to overcome the trade diverting effects of the Common External Tariff and the CAP. Given the difficulties experienced in the early to mid-1970s in negotiating through these new barriers, full membership was the most attractive option.

Second, emigration trends from Spain and Portugal to the EC argued in favour of a more active participation in EC economic policies. Third, the need to modernise and restructure economies with a, by EC standards, large agricultural sector, led both governments to conclude that membership was critical to retaining meaningful control of their economies.

ECONOMIC STRUCTURE AT APPLICATION

The critical issue for the Community's third enlargement was the challenge posed by Iberian agriculture to both the economic and political interests of the Community. These challenges covered the issues of modernity, and how far EC funds would be necessary to transform Iberian agriculture structures, agriculture's productive potential and its implications for CAP expenditure, the competitiveness of agricultural exports and their impact on particular EC member states.

At the time of application, the structure of Spanish agricultural production was roughly inverse to that of the EC. In 1980, 60 per cent of EC(9) production was in animal products, compared with 42 per cent in Spain. Fruit and vegetables made up 58 per cent of Spanish production compared with 40 per cent in the EC(9). Production concentration also varied considerably across regions, making some regions, notably the northwest, more vulnerable to the consequences of enlargement. The heterogeneity of Spanish agriculture posed major challenges to the CAP, given the propensity to produce products, such as wine and olive oil, with already favourable CAP intervention regimes. Furthermore, the competitiveness of Spain's agricultural exports of fruit and vegetables threatened existing French and Italian farmers.[5]

PORTUGAL

The productive structure of Portuguese agriculture was similar to Spain's, although, because of its smaller size, less of a threat to existing EC interests. The Portuguese primary sector posed development problems for the EC, particularly in view of the disruption involved in the land reform programme of the revolution. This meant that the negotiations on accession were conceived more as a collaborative venture between the EC and Portugal in order to restructure its economy than was to be the case with Spain, where larger economic interests were at stake.

POLITICAL ISSUES

In overall terms, both the Spanish and Portuguese applications represented an overwhelming desire by their new democratically elected governments to participate fully in the future shaping of Europe. The internal political debate in each country, however, followed different patterns.

SPAIN

There was little in terms of an internal debate concerning the desirability of EC membership, largely because of a widely held and deeply rooted consensus that full membership was the only real option for Spain. The subject was not even debated formally in the Spanish Parliament (Cortes) until June 1979, nearly two years after the application had been lodged in Brussels.[6]

Two factors contributed to this consensus. First, the 'European Option' had been chosen in 1962 when the Franco regime had requested EC Association, and had been supported by the democratic opposition, on condition that parliamentary democracy was restored. EC membership was, therefore, seen as a reward for making that peaceful transition. The second factor was the cross-party consensus in the immediate post-Franco period on all the major decisions of political development. Despite differences of emphasis, the UCD Government worked in close collaboration with the two main opposition parties on the left, the PSOE and PCE. All parts of the political spectrum saw EC membership as a catalyst for internal economic and social reforms. As Tsoukalis comments:

> The Community is something much more than the 'acquis communautaire'. It also represents a political culture and a way of thinking which, through a process of osmosis, may be transmitted to a new member country.[7]

PORTUGAL

The all-party consensus evident in Spain was absent in Portugal, largely because of the strongly anti-EC Portuguese Communist Party (PCP). The application for membership submitted by the Socialist Party, led by Mario Soares, generated little public and political debate, though this was primarily due to the indifference of public opinion in the face of the endemic political insecurity of the period. Community membership was therefore seen as a luxury rather than a basic necessity.

The lack of informed debate was also exacerbated by the lack of any detailed analysis of the effects of Portuguese EC membership on Portugal, largely due to the difficulties in establishing a functioning administrative structure in the post-revolutionary period.

Community membership became an important factor in the internal political debate over the framework for political stability. Following the defeat of the November 1975 left-wing coup, the Socialists saw EC entry as a way of averting the danger of a coup from either the right or the left. Combined with NATO membership, the European strategy was seen as a way of avoiding isolation in the post-colonial period. In terms of internal reform, the Community option meant opting for a liberal democratic system. Some aspects of the socialist constitution, such as the provision for extensive national-isation, would have been incompatible with the 'acquis communautaire', and both the PSD and the CDS sought to use this as leverage to regain some of the ground lost in the immediate post-revolutionary period.

IMPLICATIONS FOR THE CLASSICAL METHOD

Political and economic factors in the applicants and in several key member states suggested that the classical Community method of enlargement was likely to come under severe pressure. The exclusive stress on the acquis, without major EC policy adaptation was likely to place too much reliance on transitional periods as the only permissible mechanism. The impact on specific member states' economic sectors would also increase the complexity of the side deals necessary to ensure their support for enlargement.

COMMISSION OPINIONS

The 1977 applications for Community membership were followed in 1978 by the Commission Opinions. The Opinion on Spain was deliv-ered to the Council in November 1978.[8] It welcomed the Spanish application, particularly at a time when the Community was actively promoting a round of deepening through the establishment of the European Monetary System and direct elections to the European Parliament. The Commission noted that,

> It is useless to pretend, however, that Spain's accession will pose no problems. . . . Success implies that Spain's economy should be inte-grated with the economy of the Community without intolerable

strains on either side ... when the process of integration is complete, the Community should emerge strengthened and not diluted.[9]

The Opinion identified six areas of concern in making the necessary adaptations. For industry, the key issues were the dismantling of tariffs, the reduction in state aids and the introduction of VAT. The Commission argued that the dismantling of tariff and non-tariff barriers, based on the 1970 Agreement, had led to an imbalance, with reductions of 57 per cent on the Community side as against 26 per cent on the Spanish side, which effectively protected a number of Spanish firms in their domestic market.

In agriculture, the Opinion noted that Spanish accession would increase the Community's agricultural area by 30 per cent and its agricultural working population by 31 per cent. The major problem would result from the production stimulus arising from the CAP's price guarantees leading to further surpluses in some products. The Commission agreed that integration into the CAP needed to be closely connected with structural reform of farming to prevent regional imbalances being exacerbated.

In fisheries, the Opinion noted that there were problems involved in integrating the large Spanish fleet into the CFP. The propensity of the Spanish labour force to emigrate to seek employment also posed challenges in terms of the free movement of labour. Regional imbalances were also identified as causing potential problems, particularly in the French–Spanish border regions as a result of new sources of competition. Finally, the Commission noted that the integration of Spain, with its strong comparative advantage in Mediterranean produce, would have potentially negative consequences on the other non-EC Mediterranean countries. This would require the Commission to redefine its external policy in that region. Whilst accepting that some development of EC policies would result from enlargement, the Commission maintained the orthodoxy that the onus of responsibility for adaptation lay with the applicant.

PORTUGAL

The Commission's Opinion on the Portuguese application was delivered to the Council in May 1978.[10] In common with the Spanish Opinion, it welcomed the Portuguese application as an important step in the consolidation of democracy there, and as contributing to the development of the EC's external relations. However, its economic assessment differed markedly from that concerning Spain – the Opinion noted that the overall impact of Portuguese accession on the EC, would be very limited since Portugal represented only 1 per cent of total community GDP. It argued, however, that 'the problems liable to arise would stem primarily from the fact of appreciable disparities in development which would accentuate the Community's heterogeneity'. The Commission also noted 'this being so, decision making in the Community's institutions could be rendered more difficult'.[11]

The Opinion identified the overriding priority as the need to overcome the structural weaknesses in the Portuguese economy, particularly the high proportion (28 per cent) of the working population employed in agriculture, and the dominance of the industrial sector by traditional industries such as textiles. Further, by completing the process of market liberalisation started by the 1972 EC–EFTA Free Trade Agreement, some sectors of the economy could be very vulnerable to increased competition, as could some agricultural markets, faced with competition from more competitive Community produce.

The Opinion effectively envisaged a 'partnership' between the EC and Portugal in order to effect economic restructuring. Therefore, as Dominguez points out, the accession negotiations were to turn into something of a 'reconstruction plan for Portugal'. She notes that 'the policy making impasse inside the country made political leaders believe that accession into the EEC would suddenly enable them to create the correct policies to redress the economic disaster inside the country'.[12] However, she notes that this passivity also created difficulties, since the Portuguese were always waiting for the EC to arrive at negotiating positions, ever-mindful of the precedents that might be created in relation to the more complex Spanish case.

THE COMMISSION'S POSITION ON ENLARGEMENT

The Spanish and Portuguese applications inevitably confronted the EC with a set of complex issues, both in terms of specific sectoral areas such as agriculture, which would cause difficulties for the EC as a whole as well as for some member states in particular; and, more generally, in terms of further enlargement, which would affect the character of the EC. Given the level of development and heterogeneity of the enlarged Community, the Mediterranean applications again raised the need to re-examine the historic dilemmas of widening and deepening.

At the Council's request, the Commission produced a three-part study of the overall impact of enlargement in 1977. Known as the 'Fresco' Papers, it examined the institutional and transitional implications of enlargement, including the accession of Greece, as well as the economic and cultural aspects. The Commission's overall objective was to ensure that the historic mission of the Community to enlarge should not endanger the achievements of the EC to date, enshrined in the 'acquis communautaire', nor impede its capacity to deepen integration in the future. Given the widely differing views within the EC over both its historical achievements and its possible future direction, the Commission had to perform its traditional role as honest broker between the member states, whilst acting as the guardian of the 'acquis'.

The Commission opened its paper by identifying the recurrent dilemma of EC enlargement; that

> Greece, Portugal and Spain want to be part of a strong Community. If it were diluted, weakened, or became nothing more than a free trade area, or even a customs union, it would be of only limited interest to the three applicant States and to the present nine member states.[13]

The Commission identified the core economic problem as the threat posed to the cohesion of the common market and the plans for EMU by the applicants' relative share of regions and sectors in difficulty. The Commission therefore argued that co-ordinated measures to ensure economic growth in industrial sectors with potential, should be commenced before accession. The Commission envisaged utilising the EC's own budget mechanisms to achieve this, and estimated on the basis of 1978 budget figures that resources transfers would amount to 2.3 per cent of Greece's GDP, 2.5 per cent of Portugal's and 0.40 per cent of Spain's.

The paper identified the integration of the three applicants into the CAP as a major challenge. In terms of the risk of overproduction in sectors presently in oversupply, it strongly maintained that any solution should be consistent with the agricultural acquis, namely the rational use of resources, equitable producer incomes and balanced supply and demand in relation to both internal and external EC markets.

In industrial sectors, the Commission noted that enlargement would add production capacity in some sensitive sectors and that the three applicants would need to be involved as soon as possible in the development of the EC's industrial policy. The applicants were offered the possibility that they could be exempted from Community protective measures against third parties if they were to adopt Community disciplines immediately.

The paper also identified the potential aggravation of regional disparities arising from enlargement, going so far as to argue that 'in the absence of suitable corrective policies, trade liberalisation might even go so far as to jeopardise the continued development of a number of weak regions in the enlarged Community'.[14]

The Commission also addressed the issue of the enlarged Community's external relations, particularly regarding the non-EC Mediterranean regions. In economic terms, enlargement necessarily changes the terms of trade for those near neighbours not themselves involved in the enlargement process. The paper identified the potential negative effect on the Mahgreb and Mashreq countries, of Mediterranean enlargement and the need to extend ties with Turkey.

TRANSITIONAL ARRANGEMENTS

As important as the economic and sectoral aspects of enlargement were the institutional and decision-making issues raised by the prospect of a Community of Twelve. Again, the Commission had to strike a balance between the need to maintain some of the underlying principles of the Community method of enlargement whilst ensuring that the Community developed new potential for deepening, following accession.

The need also to outline a 'transitional formula' was a top priority for the Commission, given its assessment of the economic and sectoral adjustments necessary in the enlarged Community. The Commission's position was that:

> There must be a transitional period which, in view of the extent, diversity and nature of the problems it is supposed to deal with, should, while remaining a purely exceptional arrangement with a strict time limit and strict rules of application, offer enough flexibility to enable the negotiations in each case to come up with solutions capable of dealing with the particular problems of each applicant.[15]

The Commission proposed a two-stage transition strategy lasting no less than five and no more than ten years in which specific objectives and programmes would be established for both the Community and the applicants. The length of the first stage could only be extended by the Council, acting on a recommendation from the Commission.

The Commission's concern that the overall development of the

Community should not be held back during the transition period, led it to propose that, in the legal acts implementing new policies, new temporary derogations might have to be given to the new member states.

DECISION MAKING AND INSTITUTIONAL ADJUSTMENT

The Commission paper accepted that decision-making structures and processes would come under pressure in the enlarged Community, given that the institutions were designed for six countries. The principle established when the EEC and ECSC institutions were merged in 1967 and confirmed during the first enlargement, was reiterated: 'all the Member States must be represented in every Community institution and body. The Community must also remain consistent and avoid any appreciable shift in the existing balance of power between Member States'.

In the Council, the Commission proposed five votes each for Greece and Portugal, eight votes for Spain, with a qualified majority set at fifty-one out of seventy-six seats. The existing balance between large and small states would be maintained, since the four large countries from the Nine, plus Spain, would still not be able to form a qualified majority without the support of at least one smaller country. A blocking minority led by the large member states would still require the support of one smaller member state. These numerical adjustments, however, also revived the question of which issue before the Council would lead to QMV procedures being used. The Commission was careful to avoid recasting the 1966 Luxembourg Compromise, and argued for the development of the 1974 Paris Summit formula which stated that the member states 'consider it necessary to renounce the practice which consists of making agreement on all questions conditional on the unanimous consent of the Member States'.

The Commission proposed a pragmatic extension of majority voting

> based on a conviction that a more flexible approach would make it possible to eliminate the sources of hold ups, ensuing exclusively from Treaty provisions, without depriving the fundamental interests of the Member States of the full protection given by a political safety net whose raison d'etre is nowadays uncontested.[16]

The Commission therefore proposed the greater use of QMV, particularly in relation to legal approximation under Article 100, except for tax legislation, which would remain subject to unanimity.

This argument underpinned the decision-making process used in creating the Single European Market, following the 1987 Single European Act.

The Fresco Papers set out the strategic intent of the Commission regarding enlargement. They represented a compromise between the maximalist position, which saw widening as possible only if it was accompanied by a significant transfer of power and competence to Community institutions, and the minimalist position which saw enlargement as a way of preserving the intergovernmental character of the EC. They also sought to preserve the core of the classical method, that the whole of the acquis should be seen as greater than the sum of its parts, despite the strong case that could be made for selective implementation.

MEMBER STATES' ATTITUDES

More important to the pace of negotiations was the attitude of member states. Despite the overall consensus that enlargement was a 'good thing', particularly in view of the historical opening of Europe to the South, there was no agreement on the way forward. The Fresco Papers themselves reflected the delicate balance of opinion within the EC, a balance which proved very hard to maintain during the course of the negotiations.

France was pivotal in determining the way forward. The French saw themselves as forming the link between Northern and Southern Europe and therefore encouraged the Iberian applications. However, French farming interests were potentially threatened by Spanish accession and endangered the negotiations at a number of critical points. Hence, although the Commission's Opinions on Spain received Council endorsement in December 1978, the French added a proviso that substantive negotiations could not begin until both sides could agree on a common negotiating basis. Although formal negotiations were opened in February 1979, guidelines on the common negotiating basis were not adopted until September.

SPANISH NEGOTIATIONS

During 1979 and the first half of 1980, both sides set out general positions on a wide range of policy areas but, by mutual agreement, neither agriculture nor fisheries were discussed, pending Community review of the relevant parts of the agricultural acquis. The tensions concerning enlargement surfaced when the French President Valery Giscard d'Estaing made a speech to French farmers in June 1980, arguing that the consequences of the Community's first enlargement had still to be worked through before the Mediterranean enlargement could take place.

Giscard's remarks were taken to refer to concerns about the EC's budget mechanism, which had been given a higher priority by the UK, following the election of the Thatcher Conservative Government and had involved giving a commitment to introducing a new system by 1982. Underlying these concerns, however, were fears concerning the effects of enlargement on French farming interests.

The Spanish Government reacted strongly against the speech. Other EC member states, for the most part disowned the French Government position, though the West German Chancellor, Helmut Schmidt, argued that reform of agricultural and budget policy would be necessary to finance enlargement. The Portuguese Government was also concerned that its own accession negotiations might be slowed down by the Franco–Spanish problems.

Relations between Spain and the Community were very cool during the second half of 1980. The July Council of Foreign Ministers declined to endorse a Commission proposal that 1983 should be the official target date for Portuguese and Spanish accession. Both sides continued to examine non-controversial topics, whilst avoiding the agricultural issue. Negotiations were set back by the attempted coup in Madrid in February 1981. Member states were fearful that they were negotiating with an unstable Government which might revert to military rule. It brought to the surface many latent anxieties about the whole process of Mediterranean enlargement. The EC member states delayed three weeks before issuing a statement in support of the Spanish Government. This argues that the EC's oft-stated desire to enlarge in order to consolidate democracy was hollow. The Spanish internal crisis did little to speed up the negotiations. The Commission's Vice President, Lorenzo Natali, with responsibility for enlargement, declined to set a target date for Spanish accession when he visited Madrid in June.

RHETORIC AND REALITY

Community policy towards Spain was effectively being conducted on two levels. Public statements by leading EC politicians and Commission officials continued to support enlargement. Commission President, Gaston Thorn, for instance, in December 1981, reiterated the Commission's unconditional support for Spanish accession, following the December European Council meeting in London.

Yet the Community's declarations on the agriculture dossier failed to address Spanish concerns, by making substantive negotiations contingent on internal EC CAP reforms. Inevitably, this became entangled with the increasingly difficult UK budget problems, which the Thatcher Government had made a major part of its internal reform agenda. This issue linkage was very difficult for the Spanish to deal with. They argued their willingness to participate in reform discussions since their involvement would be critical to its implementation. However, this phase of the negotiations demonstrated just how rigid the barriers between existing and aspiring members, imposed by the classical method, can be. The Community gave a higher priority to its internal reforms and, hence, to the bargaining weight of members such as the UK and France, with their own agenda, than to the need to conclude the enlargement negotiations speedily. Whilst this balance of interest is hardly surprising, the Community found it extremely difficult to articulate a clear position which would allow it to run the two sets of negotiations in parallel.

The situation was further complicated by the election in March 1982 of the PASOK Government in Greece. The new Government submitted a memorandum arguing for its own Mediterranean status to be recognised, effectively introducing new preconditions into the enlargement negotiations and complicating the review of the Mediterranean acquis.

COMMISSION REVIEW

The European Council meeting in Brussels in June 1982 called on the Commission, on a French request, to prepare an inventory of the outstanding issues. The Report[17], presented by the Commission in November, was widely perceived as a way for the French to shift responsibility for their own problems with enlargement on to the Community as a whole, since there was little that was not already known and exhaustively researched in the various problem chapters.

The Commission argued this point in its opening remarks, but also stressed that the overall economic situation had deteriorated since its original enlargement paper and its Opinion had been produced, making the restructuring of some sectors such as the steel industry, more painful.

Given the protracted arguments concerning the mutual adaptation process, the Commission used the paper to revisit some of the arguments concerning policy differentiation in an enlarged Community. The Commission acknowledged that partial adoption of the acquis might seem an attractive solution to the deadlock. Yet it restated unequivocally the classical objection to this form of differentiation:

> In practice this option could, without settling the basic problem, the solution of which would merely be deferred, give rise to even greater new difficulties. If such an exception were to be made for either party, this would obviously not be done without a trade-off. Gradually, a process would be set in motion which, going beyond the principle that the problems of integration can be resolved progressively by introducing transitional measures, would considerably dilute the acquis as a whole. To this would be added the problem of the institutions' decision making capacity with regard to policies which would no longer be common.[18]

The Commission also restated its preference for the simultaneous accession of Spain and Portugal. This was in response to the difficulties created for the Portuguese by the more problematic Spanish negotiations, though the Commission argued that they both required similar solutions.

Despite these problems the Commission continued to support the classical method. In its paper, it drew a distinction between specific enlargement problems and those more underlying, internal Community problems raised by enlargement.

The EU budget and the limit on own resources was critical in this respect. Whilst the Commission argued that the final budgetary cost of enlargement was worth paying, it argued that it would increase the size of the budget by 15 to 20 per cent with the new members receiving net transfers of between 4 per cent and 6 per cent of the EU budget. This, the Commission argued, would use up the resources within the 1 per cent VAT ceiling. The Commission also argued that, enlargement apart, the ability of the Community to use the budget as a developmental tool would be severely limited without an increase in own resources.

The 'inventory' did little to break the deadlock in the negotiations, and at the December European Council in Copenhagen the heads of government again failed to fix a specific accession date. The Spanish were becoming increasingly frustrated at the gap between the rhetoric of the Community and the reality of the actual negotiations. This was doubly so given that both France and Spain had Socialist Governments, and that a shared political philosophy was not enough to override domestic sectoral interests. The new Foreign Minister in the incoming Spanish Socialist Government, and Felipe Gonzales, the Prime Minister, stated that Spain expected full membership within four years and 'concrete proof' that the Community was committed to Spain's accession.

RENEWED EFFORTS TO BREAK DEADLOCK

During 1983 the Spanish Government increased its diplomatic efforts to speed up the process in a meeting with German Chancellor Kohl, the Spanish Prime Minister securing his support for EC membership as a pre-condition of NATO membership. Gonzales also intensified bilateral contacts with the French.

The Community's agriculture declarations still proposed harsh adjustment terms for Spain and there was concern that public opinion in Spain might turn against EC membership. The negotiations were also complicated by the Greek Government, which held the Council Presidency in the second half of 1983, linking its agreement on enlargement to its demand for an Integrated Mediterranean Programme.

A negotiating breakthrough was achieved when the October Council meeting finally approved the acquis for Mediterranean products, which proposed long transition periods for fruit, vegetables and olive oil. Although the proposals pushed all the adjustment costs on to the applicants, the proposals were welcomed by the Spanish. The Athens Summit, however, failed to resolve the agriculture question, with the French still concerned about the impact of enlargement on their own agricultural interests.

ISSUE LINKAGE

By the turn of the year, the complexity of the linkage between internal reforms and enlargement threatened to precipitate a crisis in the EC. The time taken to agree on the EC's detailed negotiating position on enlargement, particularly the Mediterranean acquis, had allowed other issues, such as the UK budget rebate, Greece's special pleading on Mediterranean issues and even Spain's possible NATO membership, to become entangled with the enlargement issue. Here a critical weakness of the classical method was exposed. As the Greek accession negotiations had demonstrated, the method depends on speed, and a willingness to defer wider debates until after enlargement. This time, the Community found it more difficult to draw a clear distinction between internal and external policy considerations.

FRENCH PRESIDENCY

However, the French assumed the Council Presidency in January 1984 with a new willingness to break the deadlock. Intensive high-level bilateral contacts between the French and Spanish continued in the spring. The Fontainbleau Summit in June succeeded in solving the budget issue, by agreeing to a mechanism for the UK rebate, and agreeing to raise the maximum rate of VAT contributions to the EC budget from 1 per cent to 1.4 per cent on 1 January 1986, the date set at the summit for the accession of Spain and Portugal.

Negotiations on the agriculture chapter had reached a critical phase when, in February, the Community proposed a ten-year two-stage transition period. During the first phase, the Community proposed that Spain would adopt the acquis in full in agricultural trade with third countries, while still being treated as a third country by the Community. Only in the second phase would both sides use the 'classic' transition involving reciprocal tariff and quota reductions. The Spanish rejected the terms, fearing a backlash in domestic public opinion and, in July, sought a maximum seven-year transition programme. This again suggested that there were political limits in applicant states as to how far the classical method could be pushed.

IRISH PRESIDENCY

In the second half of 1984, under the Irish Presidency, detailed negotiations on the agriculture chapter continued, leading at the Dublin Summit, in December, to agreements on curbing home production, a key part of the agriculture negotiations. Negotiations also continued on how the Spanish fishing industry could be integrated into the Common Fisheries Policy.

At the start of 1985, when Italy took over the Council Presidency, the negotiations moved into their final stages. The Italians had committed themselves to concluding the negotiations at a special summit in March, and by this point both sides were determined to reach an agreement even if on far from ideal terms. Intensive negotiations were held right up to the March special summit, in Brussels, at which the Greek demand for an Integrated Mediterranean Programme was settled. The Accession Treaty was then signed in June with full accession scheduled to take place on 1 January 1986.

PORTUGUESE NEGOTIATIONS

Portugal's accession negotiations were intimately bound up with those of Spain. Whilst this was, to a large degree, an inevitable consequence of the Community's preference to negotiate with groups of geographically proximate countries with a roughly comparable economic and political profile, there were, nonetheless, differences in the shape of the negotiations and in the expectations that each side had of the other.

DIFFERENCES BETWEEN SPANISH AND PORTUGUESE NEGOTIATIONS

Portugal entered the negotiations as a *demandeur*. Unlike Spain, it had few, if any, industrial or agricultural sectors which posed a threat to the Community, as the Commission's Opinion had noted. Portugal's main negotiating aim was to secure Community support for the restructuring necessary for full EC membership. The Portuguese strategy of playing the supplicant also had its drawbacks, however. By taking a relatively passive line in negotiations, the Portuguese were left vulnerable to the problems encountered in the Spanish negotiations, which made it difficult to break out of this deadlock, even when its own negotiations could have been more speedily concluded. This overall strategy also constrained the Portuguese from openly criticising the Community, as the Spanish Government did on a number of occasions, when negotiations stalled. Thus, early in the negotiating process, when French President Giscard called, in June 1980, for a 'pause' in the negotiations, pending review of the agricultural acquis, the Portuguese Prime Minister, Sa Carneiro, simply reminded the Community of its decision to enlarge but, following a visit to Paris in July, received no assurances on when that was likely to happen. In adopting this overall strategy, the Portuguese were closer to the Greeks than the Spanish. However, timing and geography meant that, unlike Greece, there was no realistic possibility that Portugal could approach the EC alone.

By early 1981, it was clear to the Portuguese that accession by the original target date of January 1983 was no longer realistic and, in April, the Prime Minister, Francisco Pinto Balsemao, said that the terms of accession were more important than the accession date.

PORTUGUESE INTERNAL REFORMS

Whilst there were areas of difficulty in the negotiations specific to Portugal, such as transitional arrangements for textile exports to the Community, the main delay related to internal problems in the Community over the agricultural acquis. Those difficulties were compounded by the internal weaknesses of the Portuguese political and administrative system to embark on the reforms necessary to adapt to the acquis. These were manifest in the various position papers submitted by the Portuguese negotiators in response to the Community's agriculture declarations which only stated very general objectives and called upon the Community to set a timetable for accession before the Portuguese could embark on reforms.[19]

Portuguese strategy also sought to press the Community to consider the Portuguese application on its own merits and, if necessary, to decouple it from the Spanish negotiations. This the Community was unwilling to do, neither confirming nor denying any explicit Iberian linkage. During 1982 and the first half of 1983, the Portuguese side had considerable difficulty in articulating clear and credible responses to EC declarations, due to internal instability.

CHANGE OF GOVERNMENT

In June 1983, a Socialist/Social Democrat coalition, led by Dr Mario Soares, took office, leading to a period of relative stability in Portugal. Portuguese Ministers pressed hard to get the Community to accept 1 January 1986 as a realistic accession target. The detailed phase of the negotiations which started in October, after the Community had finally managed to agree on the Mediterranean acquis, differed in several respects from the Spanish negotiations. Because of the relative apathy of public opinion in Portugal, negotiators were under less pressure than in Spain. Also the low level of public respect for democratic government meant that accession to the Community, even on less than 'equal' terms, as was being demanded by the Spanish, would increase governmental legitimacy.

At this stage, latent tensions in Spanish–Portuguese relations started to surface. At the summit meeting in November between Soares and Gonzales, the Portuguese Prime Minister rejected Gonzales' offer of a joint negotiating approach to the EC, claiming that the Spanish negotiations threatened to delay their own.[20] By late 1983 negotiations were focusing on the key issue for Portugal: how its agricultural section could be protected from serious disruption on accession, and how transitional arrangements could be linked to specific development programmes for Portugal. This issue was largely settled in April 1984 when the Community indicated its willingness to allocate a total of 700 million ecu to Portuguese agricultural development over a ten-year period.

The second half of 1984 saw few negotiations of any substance over Portuguese accession. The key chapters had already been closed but conclusions were delayed because of difficulties in the Spanish negotiations. Portuguese politicians continued to exhort the Community to accept that Portugal could, if necessary, accede before Spain, whilst key Community actors, such as the President of the Council, the Irish Prime Minister, Garret Fitzgerald, declared publicly the irreversibility of the process of Portuguese integration into the EC despite the complex issue of linkage hampering the negotiations.

As with the Spanish case, the Italian Presidency pushed to conclude the negotiations at a special summit in Brussels in March. Following this meeting, the Spanish and Portuguese concluded a bilateral agreement in April, regulating their own relations mainly concerning fisheries policy, during the 10-year transition period. The Agreement considerably improved Spanish–Portuguese relations, which had become strained during the enlargement negotiations.

THE TERMS OF ACCESSION FOR SPAIN AND PORTUGAL

The negotiations led to the implementation of a 'dual transition' model to cope with the complexities uncovered during the negotiations. The terms eventually agreed incorporated elements of the 'classic' transition, extending for seven years, and involving reciprocal tariff and quota reductions and a more complex two-stage transition extending in total for ten years, covering 'sensitive' (i.e. mainly Mediterranean agricultural) products. The 'classic' transition applied primarily to customs duties on industrial goods, which, after three years, would be reduced by at least 50 per cent in both countries and completely abolished after a further four. Quantitative restrictions were in general abolished immediately on accession.

AGRICULTURE

For Spain, the ten-year transitional period applied to oil seeds and olive oil, fresh fruit and vegetables, on which import controls would remain for three to five years whilst alignment to EC market mechanisms took place.

In Portugal, about 85 per cent of agricultural production was included in the ten-year transitional period, with the first five-year period being devoted to the setting up of marketing structures, and the second to the alignment of prices and opening of markets. The Community pledged 700 million ecu during the transitional period for agricultural restructuring. For fisheries, the alignment of price differences and dismantling of custom duties was to take place over a ten-year period. Spain and Portugal's external tariffs were also to be aligned with the Community's CET over the seven-year period. Contributions to, and receipts from, the EC budget were regulated so that over a six-year period, Spanish receipts and contributions would be neutral, whereas Portugal would be a net beneficiary.

The differences in the accession terms granted to Spain and Portugal reflected the different impact that each applicant was calculated to make on the Community's 'sensitive' economic sectors and, by implication, its domestic producer interest groups. It has been noted that the dual transition was used as a device 'to protect the EC from Spain and to protect Portugal from the EC'.[21]

For Spain, the lengthiest transitions occurred in the fruit and vegetable sectors where Spanish exports were strongest, and shortest in its weaker 'northern' dairy, livestock and grain sectors. For Portugal, almost the exact opposite was the case with the transitional measures oriented towards allowing EC aid to ensure that Portugal's primary sector could survive in the enlarged Community. However, even in the Portuguese case, it has been argued that in some sectors (such as oils and wine) the lengthy transition period was still geared more to Community fears about Spanish agriculture than to issues specific to Portugal.[22]

INTEGRATED MEDITERRANEAN PROGRAMMES

The additional aid that Greece, France and Italy extracted from the EC through the seven-year Integrated Mediterranean Programme for their own Mediterranean regions, demonstrates the inherent bias in the Community's bargaining system towards insiders. Against Portugal's 700 million ecu in transitional aid, Greece's primary sector received 2000 million ecu, ostensibly for restructuring to meet increased competition in an enlarged Community, but in reality, the price extracted by the Papandreou Government late in the negotiations for its agreement to enlargement. The implications of this kind of bargaining strategy were not lost on the Iberians who were to deploy similar strategies over the SEA and the EEA and EFTA enlargement negotiations.

CONCLUSION

The Iberian accession negotiations have been the most protracted and, arguably, the most acrimonious to date, with the possible exception of the British negotiations. Yet, unlike the British case, accession quickly led to the active involvement of Spain and Portugal in the development of European integration without either party seriously questioning its commitment to the EC. Both the economic and political factors were important in this. Whilst the Spanish economy had some 'crisis sectors' (e.g. steel) and some major adjustment problems, for instance in fisheries, overall the Spanish economy was strong and diversified enough to make the necessary adaptation to the acquis. The buoyant economic conditions of the mid-1980s led to a large inflow of foreign investment, in anticipation of membership. This greatly smoothed the rough edges of the accession terms. Spanish public opinion was also behind the elite consensus that Spain should be a leading player within the EC. Whilst Community behaviour towards Spain sometimes contradicted their statements in support of democracy, the Spanish themselves saw Community membership as vital to their national political self-respect. Portugal, once inside the EC, pursued a strategy similar to that of Greece or Ireland, in which its agreement to further integration could be bought for relatively small sums.

The Spanish position had been more complex. Spain approached the negotiations with a strong belief that it has a self evident right to be treated as an equal by the Community. Thus, a key negotiating objective for the Spanish was to gain recognition of Spain's legitimate interests. As Dominguez has written:

> All the Spanish delegations felt that the size and developed nature of Spain's economy and society merited equal treatment. The assumption on both sides, that Spain would return two Commissioners to Brussels befitting Spanish importance in Europe, supported this. Secondly the delegations pointed to the well tried notion of reciprocity in international negotiations. Thirdly, they pointed to the wide and varied nature of Spanish foreign policy interests which, in their view, reinforced their (newly recognised) identity as a middle ranking power.[23]

Spanish optimism was soon disabused as they were faced with the reality of Community negotiations with its gridlock of domestic interest groups. In demanding equality of respect, the Spanish arguably expected too much. The asymmetrical bargaining inherent in the Community method was already long established and had been most clearly seen in the British case. The notion of reciprocity is thereby strongly qualified by the expectation on both sides that hard bargaining will continue, albeit focused on different issues, once the new member has acceded. In this sense accession negotiations should be seen as one stage, albeit a critical one, in the mutual adjustment process of an enlarging Community.

The seeming inflexibility of the Community side is only palatable to the applicants on the implicit understanding that they will, before long, have the voting rights of full members. This is one of the most enduring features of the Community method of enlargement and is a strategy that the Community uses to close negotiations when they threaten to reach an impasse. The large number of individually small items noted in the Treaty of Accession 'to be decided later' bears this out. The Iberian negotiations demonstrated these principles in action. The difficulties experienced by the Spanish in achieving the equality of respect that they expected caused them to focus more explicitly on a more limited range of objectives likely to facilitate their entry to the EC. Even this proved difficult, given the internal problems the EC experienced in developing its Mediterranean agricultural acquis.

Although the Community method is strongly biased in favour of the interests of existing members, applicants can find points of leverage in the process. Having agreed to open accession negotiations, the Community, more specifically key member states, can be leaned upon to substantiate their commitments. Both the Spanish and Portuguese focused much diplomatic effort on bilateral diplomacy, particularly with the French.

Yet a key lesson of the Iberian enlargement negotiations was that EC policy reform needs to be confronted before enlargement can proceed if the classical method is to retain credibility. Though the prospect of obtaining full membership decision making rights hastened the closure of negotiations, once the point of exhaustion had been reached, the whole process demonstrated systemic weaknesses on the EC side. The vulnerability of negotiations to sectoral lobbying was disproportionate to the wider geopolitical interests at stake. These were issues that were to reappear in the 1990s.

5 The fourth enlargement
Austria, Sweden and Finland

INTRODUCTION

The fourth enlargement of the Community, bringing in Austria, Sweden and Finland in January 1995 was also, following the ratification of the Treaty on European Union, the first enlargement of the EU. The fact that these countries were acceding to a Union rather than a Community, however, did not markedly affect the accession negotiations. The EFTA enlargement, however, was a watershed in the development of the EC, since it represented the resolution, in the EC's favour, of the tension that had existed for nearly forty years between the EC and EFTA models of economic development.

The fourth enlargement was, in important respects, the last classical enlargement. As a relatively homogeneous group of small, wealthy, open trading nations with long traditions of democracy, the EFTA countries were well able to adopt the acquis. None of them threatened major EU domestic interest groups. However, this did not mean that the development of EC–EFTA relations was easy, nor that the enlargement negotiations proceeded smoothly. All the EFTA applicants had sensitive domestic political interests at stake which, in several cases, eventually proved to be incompatible with EU membership.

This chapter therefore covers the EC's relations with EFTA in three phases. The first, from 1960 to 1989, was marked by the desire of both groups to pursue their own agenda of economic development, whilst improving co-operation. The second, from 1989 to 1993, signalled an attempt, through the European Economic Area (EEA), to reconcile these two models. The third, from 1993 to 1995, saw the accession negotiations which led to three EFTA members acceding.

EC–EFTA RELATIONS 1960–89

Since its inception, EFTA's relations with the EC had been characterised by its desire to develop close economic ties whilst avoiding political engagement that might compromise its members' explicit neutrality policies or, at least, their own notions of political sovereignty.

DEVELOPING TRADE RELATIONS

In terms of trade patterns, the EC and EFTA have been strongly interdependent since the early 1960s. The completion of the EC's customs union in 1969, therefore led the EC and EFTA to seek a Free Trade Agreement. Signed in 1972 it ensured the elimination of duties on all industrial goods traded between the two groups by 1977. Its implementation was achieved on time, and created a *de facto* free trade area, under the GATT umbrella across the whole of Western Europe. The success of the Agreement led to a willingness to intensify and formalise co-operation. In April 1984, the Luxembourg Declaration set out a common intention to improve co-operation on the harmonisation of standards, the removal of technical barriers and the simplification of border formalities. It further created co-operation in research and development, and environmental issues, with the broad aim of creating a dynamic European Economic Area.

LUXEMBOURG PROCESS

The Luxembourg process led to a large number of agreements between the EC and EFTA states, such as common rules of origin with the aim of reducing the trade-diverting effects of having two trade regimes in Europe. The effect of these agreements was to facilitate the creation of inter-bloc trade but also to strengthen Europe's economic core, centred on West Germany. This led to an economic asymmetry between the two groups which led to a more fundamental reappraisal of EFTA's purpose. This asymmetry was intensified by the 1987 'Interlaken Principles' proposed by the European Commission. Although accepting that a balance of advantages and obligations had to be maintained on both sides in further negotiations, the Commission nevertheless confirmed that priority should be given to the Community's own internal integration and that the Community's decision-making autonomy should be preserved.[1]

Faced with the intensification of the integration process presaged by the Single European Act and the commitment to complete the Internal Market by 1992, the piecemeal Luxembourg process came under increasing pressure. The EFTA countries were increasingly faced with the dilemma of adapting to a process in which they were economically engaged but politically excluded.

EFTA INVESTMENT IN THE EC

The major consequence of this was to increase direct investment by EFTA-based companies in the core economies of the EC, in part to take advantage of new market opportunities opened up as a result of the Single European Market (SEM) deregulation process, and partly a prudential move should the process of internal deregulation lead to higher external barriers and a 'Fortress Europe'. EFTA's outward investment flows increased markedly during the 1980s.[2]

These economic factors underpinned the desire of the EFTA countries to engage in a more structured relationship with the EC than was possible within the Luxembourg process. From the Community's perspective, EFTA was recognised as a significant trading partner, although, with priority given to the Internal Market process, EC–EFTA relations were not, during this period, regarded as critical.

DELORS INITIATIVE

The situation changed considerably, however, when Commission President Jacques Delors spoke to the European Parliament in January 1989 and argued in favour of a more 'structured partnership' involving a formalised institutional framework.[3] In response to prompting from the Norwegian Prime Minister, Gro Harlem Bruntlund, he proposed a 'two pillar' approach in which the EFTA countries would reach common positions in negotiations mirroring, to a large degree, the process on the EC side. Delors argued that the objective of these negotiations should be the creation of an 'economic space', encompassing the EC and EFTA in which the 'four freedoms' of the Community's Internal Market would apply.

The Delors initiative was widely seen as a way of meeting EFTA's desire for closer engagement with the EC without raising the politically sensitive issue of enlargement at a time when the EC's agenda were in danger of becoming overcrowded.[4] From the Commission's perspective, the proposal provided for the management of the 'spillover' effects of the Single Market but without increasing its political salience too far. The expectation was that a 'technocratic consensus' could be formed on the key parts of the single Market process.

MEMBER STATES' ATTITUDES

The attitude of the individual EC member states varied considerably. During the late 1980s, EC–EFTA relations were not regarded as a high priority on the Community agenda dominated by the construction of the Internal Market and the possibility of moving thereafter in stages towards full economic and monetary union. The former founder EFTA members in the Community, Denmark and the UK were in favour of closer ties with EFTA, as was West Germany in view of the expanded trade opportunities. Yet elsewhere in the Community, there was little real enthusiasm for the EEA proposal, at a time when the deepening agenda were pre-eminent.

EEA NEGOTIATIONS OPEN

Following a long delay whilst the EC came to internal consensus over the EEA concept, in December 1989 both sides agreed to start formal negotiations. In May 1990, the Council agreed the Commission's mandate with particular stress being put on the two-pillar approach, and the need to maintain the autonomy of the two sides' institutions, an issue that was to become particularly problematic in the later stages of the negotiations.

The start of negotiations marked the desire of both the EC and EFTA to explore the possibility of a new partnership, though in contrast with full enlargement negotiations, the shape of that partnership was not predetermined. The late 1980s were a period of considerable flux and uncertainty in the debate about the future shape of Europe. Internally, the process of implementing the provisions of the White Paper on the Internal Market triggered a debate about how far complementary policies in the social sphere were necessary for completion of the SEM, together with a debate about the future of economic and monetary union. Externally, the loosening of the USSR's domination of Eastern Europe opened up the need to reconsider the EC's relations to the East.[5]

The closer approach to EC–EFTA relations necessitated convergence in the negotiating positions of the individual EFTA countries. Yet despite this, there were differences in the underlying positions and perspectives of EFTA members. Whilst all shared a fear of exclusion from the Single European Market, they varied as to how far the multi-lateral approach would serve their interest, and how far their own notions of sovereignty would be compromised by the development of the EEA negotiations. For Norway, Sweden, Finland and Switzerland, the EEA concept allowed them to pursue an integration strategy without raising sensitive domestic political issues.

NORWAY

In Norway, the debate was largely shaped by the traumatic experience of 1972. Official Norwegian policy was therefore very cautious, and mindful of the need to maintain unity in the governing Labour Party. The key policy document, the May 1987 Government 'European Report' stated the intention to adapt to the development of the Internal Market 'as far as possible'. Developing the argument in Parliament in 1988, the Prime Minister, Gro Harlem Bruntlund, stated that 'it is important that Norwegian society should be ready and able to discuss these challenges without being eclipsed by a new and premature debate on Norwegian membership of the Community'[6], given the lack of public support for membership revealed in opinion polls at the time.[7] Whilst Norway's NATO membership meant that there were no political obstacles to eventual EC membership, the focus on Internal Market issues and the strong preference for pursuing a multilateral EFTA-focused strategy, drew attention away from the political aspect of European integration.

SWEDEN

Swedish policy towards the EC during this period was set out in a policy paper presented to the Swedish Parliament in 1987. The paper stressed the economic impact of the SEM on Sweden and argued that, unilateral alignment with Single Market rules might be necessary.[8] Yet, given the lack of consensus in the Rikstag on the issue of membership, the debate's conclusion, endorsed by the Foreign Affairs Committee, was that 'membership of the Community is not an objective for the negotiations which are now starting'. The possibility of EC membership, however, was not excluded so long as any foreign policy requirements did not compromise the credibility of Sweden's neutrality policy.[9]

FINLAND

Finnish policy towards the EC was centred on the need to pursue closer economic ties with the EC without compromising its trade and strategic relationship with the USSR, as defined by the 1948 Treaty of Friendship, Co-operation and Mutual Assistance. Whilst Finland's trade links with the USSR served to cushion its economy more than in Sweden's case, the economic rationale for closer engagement in the Internal Market process was similar. The Finns were, therefore, strongly in favour of the Luxembourg process which suited their cautious, pragmatic approach. Government policy towards the EC was set out in the November 1988 White Paper which categorically rejected EC membership as incompatible with neutrality. Two subsequent White Papers, in November 1989 and 1990, though less categorical, effectively ruled out membership into the foreseeable future.[10]

ICELAND

Iceland's policy towards the EC was also cautious. However, given its full participation in NATO, this was largely due to sovereignty and economic issues, particularly its dependence on fish exports which, in the postwar period, have constituted between 70 per cent and 90 per cent of the total value of its exports. The question of exchanging access to resources for access to market, implicit in EC membership, had little attraction for Iceland whilst the development of the EC's Common Fisheries Policy during the 1980s hardened attitudes. Successive governments made it clear that EC membership was not an option.[11]

AUSTRIA

Austrian policy towards the EC was largely shaped by its policy of permanent neutrality, enshrined in Article I of the 1955 State Treaty. However, by the late 1980s, the economic arguments in favour of closer integration with the EC became more pressing, given Austria's central position, its very high trade dependence on the EC – 68 per cent of imports and 64 per cent of exports – and its close ties with Germany. The Austrians openly considered the possibility of membership before the other members of EFTA, largely because of their belief that only full participation in EC decision making would secure their economic interests. The Austrian economy was also widely perceived as being over-protected, and in need of an 'external shock'.

In 1988, Chancellor Vranitsky announced that the Government would decide on the EC question in 1989, and that a membership application had not been ruled out. The Delors speech setting out the EEA option, although interpreted in some quarters as a way of heading off an Austrian application, did not deflect the Austrian Government which, in July 1989, submitted a formal application for EC membership. The application assumed that Austrian neutrality would not be compromised by its application.[12] From that point, the Austrians effectively pursued a 'twin-track' approach to the EC since they also supported the multilateral EEA negotiation, regarding the EEA as a fall-back position should the full membership option not work out.

SWITZERLAND

Swiss policy towards the EC had been largely determined by the need to sustain its neutrality policy whilst ensuring market access to the EC, given its high level of trade dependency on the EC (80 per cent of imports and 60.4 per cent of exports), the highest in EFTA. Its central position, controlling a large proportion of the EC's transalpine traffic, gave it a strong interest in the Internal Market, whilst also reinforcing its determination to protect its own environmental interests.[13]

The Swiss approach had shown a preference for bilateral negotiations with the EC in which detailed reciprocal rights and duties could be specified. By the late 1980s, Switzerland had some 150 such agreements with the EC. The Swiss were willing to participate in the EEA negotiations, though the possibility of EC membership was not considered feasible because of its effect on Swiss sovereignty and the incompatibility, as the Swiss saw it, of the EU's decision-making processes with their own federal, decentralised system of government.[14]

THE EEA NEGOTIATIONS

At the start of the EEA negotiations, the overall framework served the needs of all the participants well enough to keep the process moving forward. For the EFTA countries, it allowed them to retain coherence as a group whilst reserving their individual positions on matters of vital national interests. For the EC, it allowed for closer engagement with EFTA whilst reserving its position on further enlargement. At this stage, the Austrian application did not indicate a general preference in EFTA for this option. Yet even at the outset of negotiations in early 1990 there was concern about aspects of the process that were to become problematic. These fell into three areas, derogations from the 'acquis communautaire', institutional arrangements for the EEA and legal issues.

DEROGATIONS FROM THE ACQUIS

The December 1989 Joint Declaration recognised that derogations could be justified by considerations of fundamental interests, though no guidance was forthcoming on how this might be interpreted. Given free trade in goods established in 1972, the possibility of EFTA having to conform to lower EC environmental standards was potentially problematic, particularly in Sweden. The extension of free trade in goods to cover agricultural and fish products caused difficulties in Iceland, where access to territorial waters was regarded as non-negotiable.

Some derogations and transitional arrangements from the free movement of services and capital were requested. Foreign ownership of national resources of fundamental national interest (e.g. forests in Finland and the fishing industry in Iceland) were considered highly sensitive, as was land ownership in Switzerland. The free movement of people was predicted to be very difficult, particularly in Switzerland which traditionally retained tight controls on foreigners.[15]

INSTITUTIONAL ISSUES

Whilst some of the above issues were to prove difficult in the negotiations for the scope of an eventual agreement, the institutional and decision-making arrangements were to prove even more so. At the outset of the negotiations, the objectives were unclear. The Joint Declaration stated that the goal should be 'procedures which effectively ensure that both parties' views are taken into account, so as to facilitate the reaching of a consensus in decisions relating to the European Economic Area'. Yet the 1987 Interlaken principles stated that the decision-making autonomy of the Community should not be compromised. Much of the EEA negotiations focused on trying to reconcile these two positions.

LEGAL ISSUES

The third area of concern was with implementation and enforcement procedures. Within the EC, enforcement of the acquis and legal homogeneity is ensured by the supremacy of the European Court of Justice (ECJ), complemented by the Commission's power of monitoring and inspection (particularly in relation to competition policy). Several options for ensuring equally rigorous enforcement throughout the EEA were considered, including the extension of the jurisdiction of the ECJ into the EFTA states when dealing with EEA legislation, joint hearings with EFTA judges on EEA cases, and the creation of a new EEA Court with judges from both the EC and EFTA hearing cases being brought from both sides. Assuming the reluctance of EFTA states to accept the direct authority of the Commission, a parallel EFTA Surveillance Body with similar powers was proposed.

During 1990 and early 1991, it became progressively clear in the EFTA countries that the EEA would be unlikely to provide them with the relatively low-cost benefits that they had hoped. Far from diverting attention from the issue of full Community membership, the EEA negotiations were bringing the issue into sharper focus. The Community took a tough stand on the EFTA states' request for permanent derogations from the acquis, particularly relating to the free movement of capital and the foreign ownership of shares. The free movement of persons also proved difficult, particularly for Switzerland. In terms of policy scope, therefore, the EEA negotiations closely resembled those of full accession negotiations, a scenario the EFTA countries had earlier hoped to avoid. It also became clearer that the institutional/legal issues would lead to complex formulae which did not give the EFTA countries decisive policy-making input, and did not give other actors, particularly corporate interests, a clear framework within which to operate.[16]

EVOLVING DEBATE ON MEMBERSHIP IN EFTA COUNTRIES

These concerns led to a more general debate in the EFTA countries about the real costs and benefits of full membership. The structural weaknesses, particularly in the Scandinavian economies, exposed by the recession, compounded by the dynamic effects of the developing Single European Market, led EFTA's industrial lobbies to argue strongly in favour of full membership.

Changes in the external security environment also led to a reappraisal of the concept of neutrality. The disintegration of the Communist regimes in Eastern Europe, the unification of Germany in 1990 and the collapse of the USSR in 1991, resulting in the collapse of the bipolar military balance, led to the possibility that neutrality might be compatible with EC membership. In Scandinavia, these debates proceeded fastest in Sweden, where the Parliament, as early as December 1990, had approved the Government's decision to seek EC membership. Its formal application for membership was lodged in July 1991.[17]

Given the value placed on Nordic co-operation the Swedish decision to apply put pressure on the Finns and Norwegians. In January 1992 the Finnish Government sought approval from the Parliament and, in February 1992, submitted an application for full membership. The Norwegians were more cautious still, given the experience of the 1972 referendum and did not apply until November 1992 after careful consultation processes inside the Labour Party.

EUROPEAN COURT OF JUSTICE OPINION

Despite the preference of the EFTA side, with the exception of Iceland, for full accession, the EEA negotiations continued. However, they received a severe blow in December 1991 when the European Court of Justice delivered its opinion on the draft EEA Agreement.[18] The ECJ judgement stated that the powers given to the EEA Court were incompatible with the EC Treaties since its interpretation of EEA legislation might differ from that of the EC Treaties, given that the objectives of the EC and EEA were different.

Eventually a political compromise was reached in which the EEA Joint Committee, comprised of senior officials of the EC and EFTA, would closely monitor the decision of both the EC and the separately constituted EFTA Court to ensure as much legal homogeneity as possible. Whilst satisfying the ECJ, the redrafted proposals did not ensure legal homogeneity in the EEA, and reinforced the view in EFTA that there was no credible long-term half-way house between being an outsider and a full insider. The judgement can be seen as a restatement of the inviolability of the acquis which underpinned the classical method. It was also critical in leading the Swiss to apply for full membership in May 1992.

DEVELOPMENTS WITHIN THE COMMUNITY

From the Community's perspective, these issues were raised at a time when the EC was preoccupied with negotiating and ratifying the Maastricht Treaty of European Union (TEU). By setting out a timetable for the achievement of EMU and of establishing two non-Community pillars, for the Common Foreign and Security Policy –

second pillar – and enhanced co-operation in Justice and Home Affairs – third pillar – the existing EC member states moved forward strongly on the deepening agenda. Yet the Maastricht Summit of December 1991 also prepared the ground for further widening. The Presidency's conclusions stated that 'negotiations on accession to the European Union on the basis of the Treaty now agreed, can start as soon as the Community has terminated its negotiations on Own Resources and related issues in 1992'. This suggested that the widening process could commence in January 1993, following the implementation of the Delors 2 package. The Summit also requested that the Commission prepare a Report for the June 1992 Lisbon Summit on the implications of enlargement for the Union's future.

The Maastricht agreement can be seen as a typical Community package making widening, conditional on further deepening, similar to the Hague Summit of 1969.

IMPLICATIONS FOR APPLICANTS

The TEU's commitment to the EMU timetable did not present the EFTA applicants with major difficulties, given that it was predicted that they could meet the convergence criteria as well as any of the existing member states. The strengthening of policy areas such as the environment and the social dimension also played to their existing preferences and strengths.

RE-EVALUATION OF NEUTRALITY

However, since the rapidly changing geopolitical changes started in the late 1980s, all three countries had been engaged in a reassessment and redefinition of neutrality. The Swedish application to the EC supported the plan towards the CFSP and, in 1992, the Foreign Affairs Committee of the Parliament adopted new guidelines for Swedish neutrality policy stating that, in having a true European identity, Sweden wished to play an active part in building the new security structure for Europe. Neutrality was therefore redefined as 'non alignment to military organisations'. The Finnish application for membership entered no reservation on the neutrality issue and adopted essentially the same pragmatic approach to the development of the CFSP as the Swedes.[19]

Austrian neutrality was perceived to be potentially more contentious, given its permanent nature, enshrined in its constitution and deemed binding in international law, which led to its reservation entered in its membership application. The Commission's Opinion on the Austrian application, produced in August 1991, that this might create difficulties, both with the existing EC Treaties, and the possible development of the CFSP, required the Community to 'seek specific assurances from the Austrian authorities with regard to their legal capacity to undertake obligations entailed by the future CFSP'.[20]

THE LISBON SUMMIT

The Lisbon Summit in June 1992 was critical in setting out the principles upon which the next phase of EU enlargement would be based, particularly given the additional pressures starting to build for a more active policy towards the Central and East European countries. In its conclusions the Presidency noted that the EEA Agreement (finally reached in May 1992) paved the way for the opening of negotiations 'with a view to an early conclusion' with the EFTA countries. The Commission was asked to prepare a general negotiating framework for the Edinburgh Summit in December 1992.

The Council also accepted that enlargement should be possible on the basis of the constitutional provisions contained in the Treaty on the Union and attached declarations, implying that an EFTA enlargement could take place before the major institutional reforms predicted for the next IGC. In this respect, the classical method of enlargement was reiterated. Only limited incremental adaptation was considered necessary for accession, despite the pressures for a more fundamental review of EC structures and processes.

THE COMMISSION'S PAPER: 'THE CHALLENGE OF ENLARGEMENT'

Many of these issues were taken up in the Commission paper 'The Challenge of Enlargement' presented to the Lisbon Summit.[21] The paper attempted to map out the issues that needed to be considered if the Community was to enlarge to twenty or more members, now that countries in Central and Eastern Europe were also expressing interest in EU membership in the long term.

The Commission acknowledged that the context of enlargement had changed. Yet, as was the case in the Commission's 1978 papers on the Mediterranean enlargement, the Commission restated the orthodox classical position:

The accession negotiations ... must be conducted in such a way as to contribute to the strengthening of the Union. The accession of new members will increase its diversity and heterogeneity. But widening must not be at the expense of deepening. Enlargement must not be a dilution of the community's achievements. On this point there should be absolute clarity, on the part of the member states and of the applicants.

(Para. 6)[22]

The Commission was also more explicit than it had been in previous papers about the definition of the acquis that new members would have to take on. It was defined as

- the contents, principles and political objectives of the Treaties including the Maastrict Treaty
- the legislation adopted in implementation of the Treaties and the jurisprudence of the Court
- the declaration and resolutions adopted in the Community framework
- the international agreements and the agreements between member states connected with the Community's activities.

(Para. 11)

The Commission accepted the need to 'show comprehension for the problems of adjustment which may be posed for new members and will seek adequate solutions', whilst retaining acceptance of the acquis.

As in the 1978 papers, the Commission paid considerable attention to 'governance' issues, to ensure that the Community retained both its effectiveness and its democratic credibility. The Commission called for a more rigorous application of the principle of subsidiarity which would lead to:

- a less comprehensive and detailed legislative programme for the Council and Parliament
- a more balanced attribution of tasks, to the appropriate bodies at the appropriate levels (regional, national or Community levels)
- a clearer distinction between responsibility for decision and responsibility for implementation, which can often be decentralised.[23]

Many of the issues addressed in the Commission's paper were clearly fundamental to Community governance and therefore could have over-complicated the proposed accession negotiations with the EFTA applicants. The Commission therefore advised that institutional adaptations should be limited to those necessary under Article O of the

TEU. Compared with the extensive review that Delors had hinted might be produced, the Commission's paper was cautious and, in restating Community orthodoxy, ensured that the EFTA enlargement would proceed along classical lines.

COMMISSION OPINIONS

The Commission's Opinion on the Swedish application was produced in August 1992,[24] and the Opinion on Finland in November 1992[2-5] and the Opinion on Norway in March 1993.[26] They identified the areas of likely concern in the negotiations.

AGRICULTURE

Of these, by far the most sensitive was agriculture which, in Scandinavia, had traditionally been subsidised to an even greater degree than was the case in the EC. This reflected a deliberate and widely accepted policy of ensuring that peripheral northern regions remained populated. In Finland, in particular, this was linked to security considerations in relation to Russia. It was also linked to the issue of the special problems of arctic and subarctic agriculture with short growing seasons and low yields. Self-sufficiency in Finland, for historical reasons, was also an important policy goal. These factors led to a level of price support in Finland between one-and-a-half and two times higher than the EC average.[27] In Sweden, agriculture policy reforms started in 1991 led to a reduction in average levels of price support for most products, though by 1992 they were still 15 to 20 per cent higher than the EC average.[28]

FISHERIES

This for Norway was the critical issue in its application for membership. It had caused problems both during the 1972 negotiations and in the EEA negotiations and had led to a separate bilateral agreement. The key issue for Norway was that of reciprocal access and whether membership would mean accepting the limited twelve-mile exclusive zone of the Common Fisheries Policy (CFP). Domestic opinion constrained the Norwegian Government's room for manoeuvre on this matter and was to become the defining issue in the later stages of the negotiations.

With all the Scandinavian applicants, agriculture and fisheries was closely linked to regional policy and, therefore, economic and social cohesion issues. With average GDP per capita near or above EC levels, no regions at all in Sweden and Finland, and few in Norway would qualify for Objective 1 Structural Fund aid, though some regions might qualify for Objective 2 aid. The issue for the negotiations, therefore, was how to adapt regional policy instruments in Scandinavia to make them compatible in the EC regional policy, and how far EC policy could be adapted for arctic regions.

CFSP

For Finland, Sweden and Austria, the Commission's Opinions noted that the CFSP might create difficulties if it were to evolve quickly into a Common Defence Policy. In their declaration at Maastricht, the member states of the EC invited EU members to join the WEU. However, both the Finnish and Swedish Governments reserved their position on WEU membership until they were accepted as members of the EU. In a statement to the Swedish Parliament on 8 October 1992, outlining Sweden's negotiation objectives, the European Affairs Minister, Ulf Dinkelspiel, stated the Swedish Government's assumption that no additional commitments would be required of it beyond those agreed by the member countries at Maastricht. The negotiating framework for enlargement in relation to the CFSP was agreed in November 1992, when the following principles were established:

> Enlargement should strengthen the internal coherence of the Union and its capacity to act effectively in foreign and security policy.
>
> Applicants must, from the time of their accession, be ready and able to participate fully and actively in the CFSP as defined in the TEU.
>
> Applicants must, on accession, take on, in their entirety and without reservation, the objectives of the Treaty, the Provisions of its Title V and the relevant declarations attached to it.
>
> Applicants should be ready and able to support the specific policies of the Union in force at the time of their accession.
>
> In order to assist applicants before their accession, to bring their policies in the field of foreign and security affairs close to those of the Union, there should be an intensified dialogue on these policies during accession negotiations between the Union and applicants.[29]

EDINBURGH COUNCIL

The Edinburgh Summit of 12 December 1992 confirmed the general negotiations framework for enlargement. Following ratification of the Delors 2 package on the EC budget, the Council agreed that negotiations could commence with Austria, Sweden and Finland at the beginning of 1993. Following the rejection of the EEA Treaty by the Swiss referendum on 6 December, the Swiss application effectively lapsed, though it was never formally withdrawn. The Lisbon Council condition that the TEU should be ratified before negotiations started was relaxed at Edinburgh so that the TEU should be ratified before the accession negotiations were concluded.

Opinions varied as to how long the negotiations need take. The Swedes hoped to conclude in 1993 so that the constitutional amendment necessary for accession could pass the Parliament twice (before and after the election scheduled for September 1994). Austria, Norway and Finland had no pressing constitutional hurdles to clear, though the desire to become full members in time to participate in the 1996 IGC was the key factor. This was considered to be a realistic negotiating timetable, given that the candidates had accepted 60 per cent of the acquis during the EEA negotiations. In addition, in contrast with the third enlargement negotiations with Spain, the Community had no sensitive sectors to protect, and therefore could come to 'common positions' on the various chapters of the Treaties relatively easily. However, it was also acknowledged that sensitive sectors such as agriculture and fisheries could present problems later in the negotiations. Public opinion difficulties and referenda on the accession terms could also be difficult. Thus, while the principle of the classical method was accepted by the applicants, its practicalities were expected to be challenging.

NEGOTIATIONS OPEN

Following the opening of negotiations in February 1993, under the Danish Presidency, the process started with the 'screening' of all the Community's secondary legislation to identify areas where problems might arise. This process continued throughout the Danish Presidency, which was largely preoccupied with ensuring that the TEU could be ratified in Denmark, though the Copenhagen Summit in June set the target date for accession as 1 January 1995.

ALCOHOL MONOPOLIES

The negotiations started to tackle substantive issues only during the Belgian Presidency in the autumn of 1993. A key issue for Sweden and Finland was the state alcohol monopoly, traditionally defended on the grounds of public health. The Commission's Opinion argued that these monopolies contravened Article 37 of the EC Treaty. The ECJ had ruled in 1987 that the protection of public health should only entail barriers to free trade if absolutely necessary.

> The Commission is of the opinion that the health objective of the alcohol monopoly could be achieved by means which were less obstructive of competition. In general, the granting of exclusive rights and concessions must respect the basic principle of equal opportunities for all economic operators whether domestic, or from other member states ... [30]

In December, a compromise was reached in which both countries agreed to abolish their monopolies on the import, production and wholesaling of alcohol, but would be allowed to maintain their monopolies on its retail, thereby ensuring consistency with the view of Article 37 above.

FREE TRADE AGREEMENTS WITH THE BALTIC STATES

The Free Trade Agreements (FTAs) between Sweden and Finland and Estonia, Latvia and Lithuania were seen as important components in the framework for stabilisation in the Baltic region. Strictly interpreted, these FTAs fell outside the scope of the acquis. If forced to relinquish them, the Baltic States would have received mixed messages about the EU's concern for stability in the region. Following the election of extreme nationalists to the Russian Parliament in the autumn of 1993, the EU upgraded the importance of developing formal links in the region. In December, the General Affairs Council concluded that the scope of the Trade Agreements to be negotiated between the EU and the Baltic States should be extended and that their implementation should coincide with Sweden and Finland's accession to the Union.

ENVIRONMENTAL STANDARDS

Of major concern to the applicants was the issue of environmental standards. The EEA negotiations had side-stepped the issue of whether some of EFTA's product standards, considered to be higher than the EU's, might constitute barriers to the free movement of goods. Following lengthy negotiations in the autumn, both sides agreed on a compromise known as an Option 3 solution. The applicants were allowed to maintain their own rules for a four-year period during which time the enlarged EU would review its provisions in this area, leading (hopefully, from the applicants' point of view) to upwards harmonisation.[31]

REGIONAL POLICY

Regional policy also touched on sensitive political nerves, particularly in the Nordic countries. The applicants wanted to continue with the main elements of their regional policy and enjoy Objective 1 status. However, only Burgenland, Austria, satisfied the economic criteria for Objective 1 status. The Union recognised the political and economic sensitivity of this issue and eventually agreed to the creation of new Objective '6' regions with a population density below eight persons per square kilometre. Given that substantial parts of the Nordic countries would be eligible for Structural Fund monies, this represented a concession from the EU side, though it was only acceptable to the existing member states as a transitional arrangement to be re-evaluated when the Structural Funds framework regulation is reviewed in 1999.[32]

GREEK PRESIDENCY

Whilst the Belgian Presidency closed most of the chapters in the negotiations, the most contentious issues, relating to agriculture, fishing and QMV in the Council were left until the Greek Presidency. The Greeks were determined to conclude the negotiations during their Presidency, particularly in view of the timescales necessary for domestic ratification procedures to achieve accession by January 1995, and they proposed a special accession conference for March 1994.

AGRICULTURE

In previous enlargement rounds, integration into the Common Agricultural Policy had been achieved by gradual price approximation over the transitional period and the use of Agriculture Compensation Amounts (ACAs) to facilitate the process. However, in view of the implementation of the Single European Market and the removal of border controls, this option was not available for the EFTA states. The solution eventually agreed was that common EU prices would extend across the whole of the EU from accession, but that degressive aids, in the form of direct payments to farmers over a five-year transition period, would be made to compensate for income loss. A special package was agreed with Finland in order to take into account its specific concerns.

FISHERIES

The fisheries issue proved highly contentious for Norway and delayed the conclusion of Norway's negotiations until two weeks after those of the other three. The negotiators had the difficult task of reconciling the Norwegian approach to the sustainable management of resources with the EU's policy of ensuring equal access to waters under the CFP. The conclusion reached on 16 March allowed for a transitional regime, granting restricted access, similar to that applied to Portugal and Spain which would apply until January 1996 when a single access regime would apply. The Spanish, who had lingering resentments about the terms of their own integration into the CFP, also made their agreement to enlargement conditional on their full integration into the CFP at the same time as Norway's proposed accession. The negotiators showed great ingenuity in allocating catch quotas to ensure that the existing member states, in particular the Spanish, supported the package deal that involved consolidating the quotas in the EEA Agreement with 'certain additional fishing possibilities'.

The resolution of these sensitive issues demonstrated the extent to which policy innovation could be incorporated into the classical method without breaching its underlying principles. These chapters were closed on the basis of using transition periods, and specific time-limited derogations, with the agreement of both sides to reconsider these issues at a later date.

INSTITUTIONAL ISSUES

Despite agreement on the policy issues, the key institutional question of the level of the blocking minority for Council decisions using QMV had still to be settled. Britain, supported by Spain, argued that raising the number of votes needed for a blocking minority from twenty-three to twenty-seven further distorted the bias in favour of small states, since two large countries and one small, would no longer be able to block Council decisions. The change would also further distort the relationship between a country's voting strength and its population, since large states, representing 40 per cent of the EU's population, could be outvoted by a combination of small states.

Spanish concerns surrounded the possible effects of a shift of influence within the EU to the North. In the event, Spain's interests proved to be less intractable than those of Britain who, in the final negotiating session of 14–15 March, maintained that retaining the block at twenty-three votes was consistent with the Lisbon Summit's commitment to complete the EFTA enlargement before the institutional balance in the Union was reviewed. Given that the other ten member states were adamant that raising the threshold to twenty-seven votes was consistent with this institutional balance, by maintaining the blocking minority at roughly 30 per cent of the available votes, Spain and Britain were isolated and risked squandering political credibility at the eleventh hour of the enlargement negotiations. The British position was strongly shaped by domestic political factors, in particular the Government's fear of a further intensified 'Euro-Sceptic' backlash threatening its small Parliamentary majority.

IOANNINA COMPROMISE

This brinkmanship led to the 'Ioannina compromise' on 30 March. It was agreed that the compromise would come into force if a dispute arose and a veto block of between twenty-three and twenty-seven votes were achieved. The measure would then be subject to a 'reasonable delay', during which time the Council Presidency would attempt to find a solution. The compromise was an interim solution before the whole issue of institutional reform was tackled in the 1996 IGC, and again demonstrated the reluctance of the EC to undertake reform during accession negotiations, a key feature of the classical enlargement method.

RATIFICATION BY EUROPEAN PARLIAMENT

The Ioannina compromise opened the way for the ratification of the draft accession Treaty by the European Parliament (EP). Under the procedures agreed at Maastricht, the EP had to give its own assent before the Council could ratify the Treaty. Although in favour of enlargement in principle, the Parliament had consistently called for further institutional reform, in particular the more extensive use of majority voting in the Council as a precondition of enlargement. Concern was expressed that the Parliament might reject the draft Treaties as presented, though in the event they were passed in May.

The Treaty of Accession was signed by the four applicants at the European Council Summit in Corfu on 24–25 June, leaving domestic ratification procedures as the only substantive hurdles to be cleared prior to accession.

REFERENDA IN APPLICANT COUNTRIES

The Austrian referendum took place on 12 June and saw a 66.6 per cent vote in favour of joining the EU on the terms negotiated.[33] Public opinion in Scandinavia was more finely balanced and the three referenda were scheduled to take place in order of public popularity of membership. Finland held its referendum on 16 October, and this resulted in a vote in favour of 56.9 per cent (with 43.1 per cent voting against). The Swedish referendum was held on 13 November, and resulted in a 52.2 per cent vote for membership (with 46.9 per cent voting against). In both countries the Yes vote was heavily concentrated in the main urban centres, with the rural, mainly Northern areas firmly voting No.

The Norwegian referendum was scheduled last, following a judgement by the Norwegian Government that positive votes in Finland and Sweden might be decisive in overcoming the majority against membership. In the event, the referendum, held on 28 November, resulted in a rejection of EU membership by 52.3 per cent to 47.7 per cent in favour, with a similar regional pattern of voting as in the other Scandinavian countries. The vote in favour of membership was only 0.6 per cent higher than in 1972, demonstrating consistent public opposition to European integration despite the evolution of the Community in the mean time, the changing external political and economic environment and the greater risk of isolation following the accession of the other three members of EFTA. The Norwegian vote also demonstrated the limitations of compromises struck by officials. Despite the ingenuity of the deal concerning fish, the Norwegian Government was unable to overcome more deepseated anxieties in Norwegian society about the possible impact of membership on Norwegian identity.[34]

CONCLUSION

Overall, the fourth enlargement negotiations were conducted more speedily and more effectively than the third Iberian enlargement negotiations. The average duration of the EFTA accession negotiations, at thirteen months, was the shortest in the Community's history. Even allowing for Austria's three-and-a-half-year wait from application to the start of negotiations, it compares favourably with earlier applicants.

A number of reasons explain this. First, the EFTA countries enjoyed closer ties with the Community than was the case with previous applicants. About 60 per cent of the acquis had already been accepted by the applicants as part of the EEA process. At both the technical level, in terms of pre-existing structures for implementing and enforcing the acquis, and at the substantive level, in terms of overall policy alignment, there was already a high degree of convergence before negotiations started. The actual negotiations, therefore, focused on the relatively confined areas where the applicants had important national and sectoral interests to defend. The experience of previous enlargement rounds and of the early phase of the EEA negotiations led the applicants to confine these as much as possible.

The EU side also showed more flexibility in the interpretation of the acquis than was the case in previous rounds. The adaptation of the Structural Funds, the acceptance of EFTA's environmental standards, the continuation of Austria's control on heavy lorries in transit, and the continuation of the retail monopoly on sales of alcohol, all met the essential negotiating position put forward by the applicants, though these agreements were all worded in ways that the Commission and member states felt preserved the essential integrity of the acquis and, therefore, the classical method of enlargement.

This flexibility was largely due to the fact that none of these compromises affected any major existing EU interests. In marked contrast to the third enlargement, when the negotiation of the Mediterranean agricultural acquis created a deadlock, few existing sectoral interests, with the exception of the Spanish fishing industry, threatened to block a deal. As net contributors to the budget, the EFTA countries were also more warmly welcomed than previous applications.

Unlike in the Iberian case, the linkage forged between the four EFTA applications facilitated the negotiating process. The 'twin pillars' approach of the EEA method led to convergence in EFTA's negotiating positions, in particular accelerating the Norwegian negotiations following their later start and helping to conclude them in March 1994. It is unlikely that any further negotiations would have made any difference to the final outcome of the referendum.

The EFTA negotiations also became less entangled in negotiations over the future structure of the EU than was the case in the past. Fears that the TEU's commitment to a *finalite politique*, incorporating a Common Foreign and Security Policy that might lead to a common defence policy, would prove difficult for the EFTA neutrals to accept, never materialised. The geopolitical situation had changed enough by 1993 that the traditional concept of neutrality in a bipolar world no longer carried such weight.

The time taken to negotiate the Mediterranean acquis ensnared the Iberian negotiations in wider debates about the future of the EC and particularly the British budget problem which was not settled until the Fontainbleau Summit of 1984. Moreover, the Commission's papers of 1978, on the implications of enlargement, floated a wide range of options as to how widening and deepening could be developed together. By contrast, the EU avoided conflating these two sets of issues during the fourth enlargement negotiations. Although the Maastricht Treaty ratification difficulties threatened to 'spill over' into the EFTA negotiations, the original requirement (of the Lisbon Summit) that the TEU should be ratified prior to negotiations starting was relaxed at the Edinburgh Summit, so that the TEU was to be ratified before their conclusion. The Lisbon Summit's decision to undertake enlargement before reforming the institutional and decision-making process despite the preference of some EU actors, in particular the European Parliament, to consider them in parallel, clearly facilitated the negotiations by focusing on a more limited set of objectives and adhering closely to the classical model.

The fourth enlargement was also likely to be the last to use the pure classical method. With the exception of Iceland, Liechtenstein, Norway and Switzerland, who have chosen for domestic political reasons to stay outside the EU, all the former members of EFTA have been absorbed into the EU. To the East lies a group of potential applicants that poses more fundamental challenges to the EU and the classical method of enlargement.

Part II

The effects of enlargement

6　The impact of membership on new members

INTRODUCTION

The four enlargement rounds to date have brought into the Community groups of states with a wide range of political and economic interests who have very different expectations of membership. These expectations and interests, in turn, shape the development of the EC/EU itself. The classical method of enlargement is also characterised by very rapid transition from the hard bargaining of the accession conference to the, normally, more subtle and complex intergovernmental bargaining within the EC's decision-making machinery. The specific gains and losses calculated during the accession process inevitably become modified as new patterns of issue linkage develop with full membership.

Yet an applicant state's experience of the accession negotiations, and of the final terms agreed in the accession Treaty, can have a strong effect on how it views its rights and responsibilities as a full member. Terms and conditions perceived as unfair, by imposing heavy adjustment costs or budgetary burdens on particular groups can lead to lingering resentments. Once internalised in the Community's system, these can lead to new demands for compensation and even, in the UK's case, for 'renegotiation' of the entry terms. At the very least, a new member state which considers itself 'hard done by' is likely to prove a difficult partner.

This chapter therefore looks at how new members are integrated into the EC, how far and how quickly they have adapted to the acquis, and what longer term structural and economic changes have taken place. This focus on new members underpins further chapters in Part 2, which examine how these issues have, in turn, affected the character of the EC/EU. The first part of this chapter examines the direct and indirect

Figure 1: Impact of EC membership on new member states

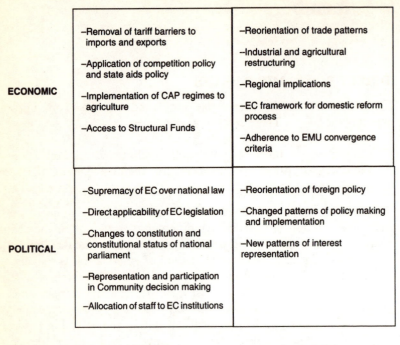

	DIRECT	INDIRECT
ECONOMIC	–Removal of tariff barriers to imports and exports –Application of competition policy and state aids policy –Implementation of CAP regimes to agriculture –Access to Structural Funds	–Reorientation of trade patterns –Industrial and agricultural restructuring –Regional implications –EC framework for domestic reform process –Adherence to EMU convergence criteria
POLITICAL	–Supremacy of EC over national law –Direct applicability of EC legislation –Changes to constitution and constitutional status of national parliament –Representation and participation in Community decision making –Allocation of staff to EC institutions	–Reorientation of foreign policy –Changed patterns of policy making and implementation –New patterns of interest representation

political and economic impacts of accession. The second part evaluates these issues in the context of each enlargement round to date.

IMPLEMENTING THE ACQUIS

The potential scope of the impact of Community membership on a new member state is very wide, and encompasses economic and political, direct and indirect effects, many of which may be difficult to quantify, and take many years to manifest themselves. Figure 1 summarises these effects. The direct political and economic effects are those that arise explicitly from the implementation of the acquis. These are usually dealt with in some detail in the Commission's Opinion and form the substance of the actual accession negotiations, leading to the specific terms of the accession Treaty. The indirect effects form both the context of the negotiations, informing the

negotiators' overall evaluation of the costs and benefits of membership, and setting the agenda for the longer term economic
restructuring and political orientation that membership brings. All the
components of this process are closely linked, though some may be of
more importance to some member states than others.

DIRECT ECONOMIC IMPACTS

These encompass the identifiable costs and benefits from implementing the acquis. There are several key issues:

* The removal of tariff barriers, quotas and other trade restrictions.
  The core commitment of membership is the liberalisation of trade
  in goods and services with other members of the Community. This
  involves the dismantling of tariffs on imports from the Community
  and exports to it, and the abolition of quotas and other measures
  'having equivalent effect' falling within the scope of Article 30,
  such as discriminatory technical barriers. The same applies to
  barriers to the service section, such as restrictions on the banking
  and insurance sectors, capital mobility and the free movement of
  workers.
* The application of the Community's Common External Tariff
  (CET). Tariffs on third-country imports are aligned with the CET.
  Preferential trade agreements have to be superseded and integrated
  into the Community's framework.
* The application of competition and state aids policy. The provisions
  of Articles 85/86 (rules applicable to undertakings) and Article 92
  (State aids) may involve the removal of direct support from some
  sectors (for instance steel and shipbuilding).
* The implementation of Common Agricultural Policy regimes in
  agriculture. This involves aligning market support mechanisms with
  the CAP, and setting up new regimes for products previously not
  covered by intervention mechanisms. These are likely to result in the
  redistribution of farming incomes and have implications for
  consumers.
* Access to the Structural Funds. New member states receive some
  benefits from the ERDF, ESF and FEOGA.

All new member states undertake a cost-benefit analysis of implementing these provisions in order to arrive at a net budgetary balance.
Losses in one area are expected to be made up in other areas, so that

the benefits of membership can be sold to domestic public opinion which will include groups of specific gainers and losers.

DIRECT POLITICAL IMPACT

Implementing the acquis inevitably leads to political and legal implications.

- Accepting the supremacy of EC over national laws. Accepting the Treaty obligations of full membership, for instance in such areas as external trade policy, the imposition of economic sanctions, the adoption of common positions, etc., involves restrictions on unilateral policies and actions which some member states have found more difficult to accept than others. The enormous expansion in the size of the acquis over the course of the four enlargements has itself increased this burden.
- The direct applicability of EC legislation means that national legal systems must absorb and integrate the EC's case law, establish mechanisms for monitoring and evaluating EC directives and transposing them into national law.
- Change to constitutional status of national parliaments. The supranationality of the EC Treaties means that any future national legislation passed must be compatible with EC law. The extent to which this affects the sovereignty of national parliaments has been much debated with different doctrines of sovereignty applying in different member states.
- Representation and participation in Community decision making. Membership immediately gives the new member state 'a microphone and a nameplate', and the opportunity to affect, if not always decisively, the shape of Community policies. As seen, this is usually perceived as the most important benefit of membership and, during accession negotiations, usually overrides fears about compromising national independence. This also requires changes to internal administrative structures, and a reorientation of attitudes towards multilateral bargaining on the part of officials and politicians.
- Staffing of EC institutions. Membership involves the substantial allocation of human resources, both recruiting to the main Community institutions, and to redirecting national officials towards EC policy work.

The impact that all of these factors have on a new member state involves complex calculations of the capabilities and commitment of its government, the key interest groups likely to be affected, and the overall level of public opinion support for membership. The extent to which these factors suddenly hit the new member state on accession is also dependent on the nature of their pre-accession relationship. A large measure of tariff alignment and other forms of policy convergence takes place within the framework of an Association Agreement, EFTA membership or participation in the European Economic Area, though there is still a qualitative change in reaching the accession threshold and assuming the obligations of full membership.

INDIRECT IMPACT

The position that a new member state takes of the direct economic and political impact is shaped by its view of the longer term 'dynamic' effects of integration. Whilst these may be difficult to quantify and subject to different political interpretations, they are critical in a new member state's overall evaluation of membership. Even if membership imposes net budgetary burdens (as in the UK's case) or is perceived to discriminate against some domestic groups (as in the case of Spain's Mediterranean farmers), the promise of longer term gains may be enough to overcome resistance to membership.

INDIRECT ECONOMIC IMPACT: RE-ORIENTATION OF TRADE PATTERNS

The key issue here is how the removal of tariff and other barriers, within an expanded customs union, will affect the new member's overall trade structure. The concepts of trade creation and trade diversion are used to model these effects, i.e. whether the expanded customs union leads to a better or less efficient allocation of resources and an increase or reduction in welfare.

Lintner notes three sets of factors likely to affect the outcome of these trade effects. First, whether the new entrant's traded goods and services sector is competitive (overlapping) or complementary (dissimilar) to that of existing members. He argues that competitive structures are more likely to be trade creating, since inefficiently produced expensive domestic products will be replaced by cheaper, more efficiently produced products from a customs union partner. Complementary structures, by displacing cheap third-country products with more expensive partner products, are more likely to be trade diverting, though the net effect depends on the tariff structure, both before and after enlargement. Where tariffs rise on enlargement, trade diversion is more likely to occur, with trade creation occurring where they fall.[1]

INDUSTRY RESTRUCTURING

Second, gains may also arise from the dynamic effects of customs union by allowing firms to exploit economies of scale in the enlarged market. However, the size of these gains will depend on how far they were previously excluded from the customs union, and how far the industrial structure of the enlarged union is internationally competitive. Lintner argues that enlargements are more likely to be trade and welfare enhancing when they incorporate countries whose economics are broadly similar to those of existing member states. The integration of dissimilar economies will impose adjustment burdens on existing and new members.

From the new member's perspective, the overall impact of these effects depends on how far accession gives it access to new markets previously protected, whether it has enough competitive firms to take advantage of new opportunities and how far its own previously protected sectors can withstand increased competition.

Third, Lintner argues that, from the neo-classical perspective, increased factor mobility is welfare enhancing, since labour and capital will move to where they are most productive. This could lead to a net labour and capital outflow from the new member. Neo-classical theory argues that over time these factors will tend to equalise and lead to economic convergence between existing and new members. However, alternative theories posit a polarisation process whereby the attractiveness of dynamic regions is reinforced at the expense of less dynamic ones, leading to ever-wider income and wealth disparities in an enlarging EC.[2] Although empirical testing of these rival theories is inconclusive, the fear of increased regional disparities underpins the demands from poorer acceding and existing member states for increased structural spending as a consequence of enlargement.

The longer term economic impact of membership extends beyond the trade effects predicted by customs union theory. Implementing the acquis also triggers a wider economic reform programme in the new member, involving deregulation in areas such as public procurement, accepting the principle of mutual recognition, foreign ownership of domestic companies and so on. More recently, adherence to the EMU convergence criteria has also imposed new external constraints on domestic macroeconomic policies. As the acquis has expanded, so new members at each enlargement must accept a more explicit and comprehensive EC framework for their domestic economic policies.

POLITICAL IMPACT

The longer term, indirect, political effects of membership are the most difficult to quantify. Yet they represent, in many respects, the most important reasons for accession, and are often invoked when the more tangible consequences of membership are more finely balanced. In countries recently returned to democracy from dictatorship, EC membership is seen as a stabilising influence on political parties and the internal democratic process.

REORIENTATION OF FOREIGN POLICY

Applicant states seek the benefits (as they see them) of membership of a larger political and economic bloc. The lure of gaining more influence in international affairs within an EC/EU framework is perceived to outweigh the freedom of unilateral action. How far a new member reorientates its foreign policy depends on a multiplicity of factors but, most importantly, on an evaluation of how far adaptation is necessary in order to promote vital national interests. For members, in particular the UK, with an historical experience of regional or even global influence, this can be a painful process.

However, for many new members, this change is motivated by a desire to escape from an undemocratic past, as was the case for Greece, Spain and Portugal, and/or to capitalise on the new geopolitical flexibility following the collapse of the USSR, as was the case for Austria, Sweden and Finland. Even those EC countries in less vulnerable positions, such as Ireland and Denmark, acceded partly in order to lessen dependency on, and to manage their relations with, their larger neighbours (the UK and Germany respectively) within a pan-European framework.

CHANGED PATTERNS OF POLICY MAKING AND IMPLEMENTATION

The EC framework also affects the structures, processes and content of domestic policy making. Lines dividing strictly domestic from foreign-policy issues become blurred as national policy makers increasingly interact with European and other member states' officials. The issue linkage and coalition building inherent in the Community method of policy making over a period of time is internalised into the new member state's policy process.

NEW PATTERNS OF INTEREST REPRESENTATION

Participation in Community institutions opens up new channels of communication for corporate and other interests. Whilst national governments continue to shape overall national policies, the complexity of the EC policy process provides multiple points of contact and influence. As the source of research, development and structural fund monies, Community institutions have also become a magnet for local and regional authorities. Membership may therefore involve some recasting of the relationship between national and subnational levels of government.

Many of these economic and political effects can be predicted and, indeed, form the basis of accession negotiations themselves, for instance, in the requests made for derogations and transition periods, and for technical assistance in sectoral restructuring. Yet the dynamic effects of enlargement means that more has to be taken on trust. The extent to which the predicted effects actually materialised can only be analysed retrospectively.

THE FIRST ENLARGEMENT: THE IMPACT OF MEMBERSHIP ON THE UK, IRELAND AND DENMARK

From the perspective of customs union theory, the first enlargement should have been welfare enhancing, since it brought into the Community at least two countries (UK and Denmark) at similar levels of economic development to the existing members, with competitive economic structures likely to lead to trade creation.

The economic impact of Community membership on the UK economy has been the subject of much academic research and partisan political debate since 1973.[3] Most attention has focused on the direct economic costs of the CAP and the UK's budget contributions. These were largely predicted during the accession negotiations (see Chapter 2), although their political importance remained high for many years. The abandonment of the cheap food policy undoubtedly resulted in trade diversion from lower cost, largely Commonwealth producers, to EC producers. Between 1971 and 1981, food prices in the UK increased by almost 300 per cent. The extent to which the CAP is directly responsible for this is debatable. The European Commission only attributes about 10 per cent of the increase directly to the CAP, the rest coming from worldwide increases in food prices.[4] However, as Lintner argues, as a major world food producer, the Community, through the CAP, itself contributes to high world food prices.[5] Studies of other resource costs of the CAP estimate job losses of about 860,000 in the four largest EC countries, with the UK and Germany suffering the most, as the result of the loss of potential gross output of between 1.1 per cent and 2.5 per cent (and 4.4 per cent to 6.2 per cent of manufacturing exports). Further costs result from the small size of Britain's agricultural population (2.5 per cent of the total population) leading her to get relatively small receipts from the CAP.[6]

The net budgetary burden on the UK led to the Labour Government's renegotiation of 1975, and remained a major factor in British politics into the early 1980s.[7] The Conservative Government led by Mrs Thatcher pledged to 'get our money back', which eventually led to an agreement at the 1984 Fontainbleau Summit on a formula for reducing the UK's contributions. Despite this, as Lintner points out

> the amounts involved in budgetary contributions are still relatively small, for EC contributions have not constituted as much as 1% of government expenditure since 1980. The UK's economic performance would not be transformed even by their complete curtailment.[8]

Arguably of more significance has been the overall reorientation of UK trade towards the EC over the last twenty years. In 1972, visible trade with the EC accounted for 31 per cent of the UK's total world exports but by 1988 this had risen to 49.8 per cent. The UK's total imports from the EC rose from 31.8 per cent in 1972 to 49.2 per cent in 1988. Whilst trade flow in both directions has increased, imports have risen quicker, leaving the UK with a trade deficit with the rest of the EC.[9]

Attributing this solely to the effects of intra-EC tariff removal is problematic. Many of these effects might have occurred anyway, given the structural weaknesses during that period in the UK economy, particularly in the manufacturing sector. Nevertheless the competitive shock of EC market entry undoubtedly affected the UK economy. Winters estimates that the gross loss of output resulting from accession was at least £3 billion (1.5 per cent of GNP), though these losses might have been affected by welfare gains by UK consumers benefiting from cheaper EC imports.[10] Arguably, the UK also benefited from the inflow of Japanese and US direct investment during the 1980s, stimulated by the desire to gain access to the Single European Market before the 1992 deadline. The decline of manufacturing and the restructuring of UK industry has also had marked regional consequences, with regions such as the North East of England, South Wales, West Central Scotland and North of Ireland, witnessing accelerated relative decline in the 1970s and 1980s.

POLITICAL EFFECTS

The political impact of membership has affected both constitutional issues and broader issues of the UK's political orientation. Constitutional convention in the UK had traditionally held that Parliament was sovereign and the ultimate source of all legislation. The 1972 European Communities Act, in enshrining the supremacy of EC legislation over UK law effectively overrode Parliament's right and the convention that no Parliament could bind its successor. The concept of sovereignty was exhaustively, though inconclusively, debated during the passage of UK legislation in 1972.[11] As well as strict legal/constitutional issues, much concern focused on Parliamentary scrutiny of the executive. The European Commission's right to initiate legislation, together with the possibility that a UK minister could be outvoted in the Council of Ministers and the difficulty of adequately scrutinising Community legislation were deemed problematic. Both the Commons and the Lords established Scrutiny Committees to deal with these problems. The Commons' European Legislation Committee concentrated on monitoring the output of the Community's legislative process in order to identify any which may have constitutional implications. The Lord's Select Committee on the European Communities undertook more evaluative work and its reports are widely circulated and well respected throughout the EC.

IMPACT ON ADMINISTRATION

Following accession, the UK adapted its administrative structures in order to manage the more complex processes of the EC's intergovernmental system.[12] The Foreign and Commonwealth Office retained its overall responsibility for the strategic direction of UK policy in the EC, dividing its EC work into two sections, internal and external. Individual functional departments lead in their own policy areas with operational co-ordination centred on the European Secretariat of the

Cabinet Office. Direct interface with the European institutions is managed by the UK's Representation in Brussels (UKREP). Over the years, the UK machinery of government has become increasingly interlocked with the EC's policy process. More domestically based officials in a wider range of departments now deal with EC issues as the EC has gradually increased its policy domain. Patterns of interest representation have also adapted to Community membership. UK corporate interests and trade unions have increasingly focused their attention on Brussels, and have participated in pan-European industry and union groups.[13] UK local authorities have also become more actively involved in the EC policy process, both as an alternative source of funds as public expenditure has been increasingly cut, and as participants in initiatives such as trans-European networks.[14]

From an administrative/legal perspective the UK has fully adapted to EC membership. The UK Government has only rarely been taken before the ECJ for failure to comply with Treaty obligations. The assumption is that agreement to EC legislation in the Council of Ministers will result in proper implementation and transposition into national law. Yet the wider political impact of EC membership on the UK has been a more mixed experience. Whilst there has been an increasing, though by no means universal, acceptance that the UK's key national, political and economic interests can be best dealt with in an EC framework, many sectors of both elite and popular opinion are still cautious about further integration. The extent of this caution depends initially on domestic political priorities. For the Conservative Government during the 1980s, the Community's plans to implement the Single European Market were consistent with its own agenda of economic liberalisation and deregulation. To ensure its effective implementation Mrs Thatcher agreed to the Single European Act, which, by extending qualified majority voting, arguably further compromised UK sovereignty. Yet the Government's hostility to EC social legislation led to the opt-out from the Social Chapter of the Maastricht Treaty in 1991. Resistance to specific directives (such as limitations on working time) was severe despite their being brought forward under pre-existing decision-making procedures. More recently the growth of 'Euroscepticism' within the Conservative Party has raised more fundamental questions about UK membership.

Conversely, for the Labour Party, hostility to the EC was highest during the early 1980s, when the UK's Treaty obligations would have constrained its ability to pursue an 'alternative economic strategy' of import control and state intervention. Yet by the early 1990s, its support for EC social legislation, largely to regain rights and powers lost under the Conservative Government, led it to be much more favourable towards further integration. Whilst most member states have elements of anti-integration opinion, and may, over particular issues, display truculence and a lack of 'communautaire' spirit, the impact of EC membership on the UK remains problematic. As a large member state with significant economic and political interests beyond Europe, UK governments have often been ambivalent about how far the EC's policy priorities are compatible with these interests. Evidently there is still validity in De Gaulle's 1961 judgement on the UK.

DENMARK

Denmark's motivation for joining the EC was primarily economic, in order to safeguard its trade, predominantly with the UK and Germany. Thus, whilst Danish politicians were fully aware of the political implications of full EC membership, these were usually downplayed, given the sizeable anti-EC vote (33 per cent in the 1972 membership referendum) and the general Nordic suspicion of grand political designs.

Denmark had few difficulties in technical adjustment to the acquis, given its high level of administrative capability. Danish farmers have benefited from the CAP, because of its high level of support for dairy and pigmeat products, and Denmark has been a net recipient from the EC budget.

Nordic democratic traditions have influenced the way in which Denmark has approached the EC decision making-system. The main instrument of Danish EC policy making is the parliamentary market committee (Folketingets Markedsudvalg FMU) which effectively mandates individual Ministers in EC Council meetings. These have even been delayed while Danish ministers consult with the FMU. This is largely a result of the constraints imposed by Danish coalition politics which demand a carefully constructed consensus on individual issues.[15]

Despite the original preference for the EFTA model of intergovernmental co-operation, as a full EC member Denmark has taken a pragmatic view of sovereignty.[16] Thus Denmark has been willing to support the extension of Community powers in areas such as environmental and social policy where it believes that it has important political and economic interests at stake. The advisory referendum in February 1986 on the Single European Act, though carried by 56 per cent, was presented as a package of reforms necessary to keep the EC functioning efficiently. The Maastricht Treaty, however, proved too integrationist, and at the 2 June 1992 referendum, the TEU was rejected by a small majority of 50.7 per cent despite the recommendation of a Yes vote by all the main political parties, interest groups and newspapers.[17] The vote precipitated a crisis in the EC and led to a series of opt outs being negotiated. A revised draft Treaty was presented to the Danish electorate in May 1993 and was carried by 57 per cent.[18] Nevertheless, Danish political and public opinion has remained sceptical towards maximalist interpretation of political union. Following the accession of Sweden and Finland, the Nordic perspective is more strongly represented in the EC and has reduced Denmark's occasional sense of isolation.

IRELAND

Ireland's political and economic position on accession was very different from that of the UK and Denmark. As a small geographically peripheral state with a large agricultural sector, Ireland's accession brought to the fore issues of economic and political cohesion. Whilst regions in the Community of Six, particularly Italy's Mezzogiorno, exhibited similar characteristics, Ireland's membership highlighted the political consequences of their concentration in one member state. In addition to a heavy dependence on the UK economy, the Irish used grant and tax incentives to attract foreign, particularly US, investment. The Special Protocol, included alongside the Treaty of Accession, allowed Ireland to continue these incentives, which would otherwise have counted as trade-distorting aids, illegal under EC law.

Participation in the CAP led to higher prices for agricultural exports which led to a short-term bonanza for Irish farmers, before attempts to control the CAP were implemented.[19] Ireland has also been one of the largest per capita net beneficiary of EC funds, and has received substantial amounts from the Regional and Social Funds in addition to CAP support. The inflows have contributed to the improvement in Ireland's position in the EC income league over its period of EC membership. The structure of the Irish economy has also changed as a result of becoming an EC member. Tsoukalis notes that the effect of increasing competition on the domestic economy has been to strengthen its 'dualistic' character.[20] High-technology, capital-intensive sectors have become dominated by the subsidiaries of multinationals, who have also been mainly responsible for the internationalisation of Ireland's trade and the diversification of its markets. In 1989, exports of foreign-owned firms accounted for 30 per cent of

Irish GNP. Linkages with the domestic economy have been weak, with traditional sectors experiencing continuous decline, and foreign multinationals depending on imported inputs, further reducing the balance of payments contributions of these firms.

EC membership has led to the internationalisation of the Irish economy, with exports of goods and services increasing from 38 per cent to 67 per cent of GDP between 1973 and 1989. During the 1970s, this restructuring and its attendant growth rates produced inflationary pressures and a large increase in the public deficit. Yet the stabilisation policies adopted in the 1980s, to ensure participation in the ERM and to meet the Maastricht convergence criteria, resulted in a considerable reduction in inflation. Stabilisation has, however, been at the expense of high levels of unemployment, which has been compounded by the EC's highest birth rate. Ireland's experience demonstrates the vulnerability of a small open economy to the effects of economic integration. Whilst macroeconomic policies have, since the 1980s, been more rigorous, the Irish economy remains over-dependent on foreign firms and on EC Funds. Pressures on structural spending in preparation for an Eastern enlargement are likely to be particularly keen felt in Ireland.

Although economic factors dominated the accession negotiations and the public debate on membership, EC membership has also led to the evolution of Ireland's political system and its overall foreign policy perspective. Like all new members, Ireland had to adapt its administrative structures to cope with the demands of EC business. The Irish approach has been less institutionalised than in other large member states. Administrative adaptation has been pragmatic and ad hoc. Thus a European Communities Committee was established at senior official level to co-ordinate inter-departmental policy. However, Laffan argues that it has lacked a strategic perspective during critical periods of EC development, such as 1984–85.[21]

Sovereignty issues were raised during the referendum on the ratification of the Single European Act in 1987, necessitated by a challenge to its constitutionality in the Supreme Court. This was an embarrassment to the Government and suggested that, despite the absence of a highly politicised debate over sovereignty, as seen in the UK and Denmark, political and constitutional issues could still, from time to time, excite public concern.

More broadly, however, EC membership has allowed Ireland to break out of the limitations imposed by its traditional bilateral links with Britain, and to play a more self-confident role in European developments.

SECOND AND THIRD ENLARGEMENTS: GREECE, SPAIN AND PORTUGAL

The Mediterranean enlargement brought into the Community a group of countries with below average EC levels of GDP, who all needed to make significant structural adjustments to adapt to the acquis. The long transition periods and derogations reflected this. Yet the experience of the three countries as full members differs markedly.

GREECE

The haste with which Greece was brought into the EC meant that many of the more painful political choices resulting from full membership were deferred until Greece was a full member. In October 1981, the anti EC PASOK Party came to power, with a formal commitment to renegotiate Greece's entry terms. Realising the difficulties of this, the Socialist Government softened its line, eventually submitting a Memorandum to the EC in March 1982, highlighting the structural weaknesses of the Greek economy, identifying where the membership terms had failed to recognise them. As a result, Greece was allowed to retain protection for her industry through the introduction of a 'regulatory tax' replacing indirect taxes on imports, to be phased out by 1989. Requests for increased structural spending became part of the Integrated Mediterranean Programmes, agreed in 1984, which Greece made a precondition for agreeing to the Iberian enlargement. Arguably, the Memorandum diverted the Government's attention away from dealing with the domestic adjustments demanded by full EC membership.[22] The 1983–87 five-year plan for economic and social development completely ignored the Community dimension.

The PASOK Government largely ignored the external constraints of a small, open economy, and pursued expansionary policies, running up large public deficits, and stimulating inflation. Attempts were made in the mid-1980s to control this, but political factors led to the cycle being repeated in the late 1980s.

As tariff and non-tariff barriers have been removed, so import penetration of the Greek market has increased, though Greek exporters have not increased their share of EC markets, leading to a widening trade deficit. There is evidence that Greek companies have actually shifted back to traditional activities such as food and textiles manufacture, competing with low wage cost Third World countries, thereby increasing the inter-industry division of labour in the EC.[23]

Unlike Ireland, however, Greece has not attracted significant inflows of foreign investment. This can be attributed both to Greece's peripheral location in a region, since the early 1990s, of intense political instability, and a lack of investor confidence in its domestic reform process.

Greece has been a large net beneficiary of the EC budget, both in terms of agricultural price support and Structural Funds. However, it is arguable how far these have speeded up the process of structural adjustment. Successive Greek governments have been unwilling to undertake the necessary reforms, particularly in relation to the public sector, though, in the early 1990s, the Greek Conservative Government embarked on a major economic reform and privatisation programme.

The reorientation of Greek foreign policy was also problematic. Under the PASOK Governments, Greek positions in EPC were frequently at odds with Community policies, for instance over the Middle East. Greece also used its position as an EC member to block the development of EC policy towards Turkey. More recently, however, apart from Greece's refusal in 1993 to recognise the independence of Macedonia, Greek policy has converged with the Community's, given that the prospects for further Mediterranean enlargement, particularly Cyprus, have taken a higher position on the EC's agenda.

SPAIN

Spain's accession negotiations were characterised by EC fears that the size and structure of the Spanish economy would prove difficult to integrate. The Spanish were concerned that removal of their trade barriers would lead to very high levels of import penetration. Both concerns were reflected in the terms of accession which provided for a longer seven-year general transition period, a ten-year transition for fruit and vegetables with a four year standstill, and the careful monitoring of trade through 'indicative import ceilings'.

For the ten years prior to accession, the Spanish economy stagnated, accompanied by very high levels of unemployment (22 per cent in 1985). However, the extended period during which Spain waited for accession allowed the governments of the early 1980s to implement domestic reform programmes in preparation for membership.

The first three to four years of EC membership were boom years for Spain, seeing the highest levels of economic growth in the EC, with GDP rising at over 4 per cent per annum. This boom was financed mainly from an inflow of foreign direct investment which accounted for 35 per cent of total investment in the manufacturing sector.

Investment was attracted by improved market access to the EC, by the size and increasing strength of Spain's domestic market, and by skilled surplus labour and low wages. The behaviour of Spain's trade in manufactured goods was consistent with the transitional arrangements. Exports to the EC rose slightly whilst imports, mainly of capital equipment, rose considerably, as did imports from non-EC countries as Spain aligned its tariffs with the CET. The trade deficit was largely financed by capital inflows, supported by a tight monetary policy to put Spain into the ERM.[24]

Agricultural trade with the EC intensified after accession, though imports to Spain rose by 245 per cent between 1984–85 and 1988. Tsoukalis argues that trade creation and trade diversion mainly benefited EC exporters to Spain. This is consistent with the removal of Spain's relatively high trade barriers. Yet the size and diversity of Spain's economy has allowed the country to experience both intra- and inter-industry trade effects, a reflection of the more developed state of Spain's economy compared with Ireland, Greece or Portugal.

Empirical studies suggest that economic integration will lead to an increase in intra-industry trade where countries have similar factor endowments.[25] Manufacturers look to export to markets with similar consumer preference and income patterns, leading to increasing horizontal trade and the exploitation of economies of scale. Where factor endowments diverge, inter-industry specialisation is more likely to occur, as economies tend to exploit their factor endowments, for example access to raw materials. The two processes are not mutually exclusive, though the extent to which they might affect the overall economy of a new EC member depends on that country's industrial structure. Small countries with economies concentrated particularly in primary sectors are unlikely to benefit as much from intra-industry trade, as larger, more diversified economies.

Overall, economists have tended to judge the Spanish adjustment to membership a success.[26] A number of factors account for this. Spain embarked on the domestic reform process well in advance of accession, though it has paid a heavy price in terms of unemployment. The size and diversity of its economy have allowed Spain to absorb the overall adjustment shocks, though the adjustment in some sectors, such as steel, has been painful. Regional imbalances have also been exacerbated with the more prosperous Catalonian and Madrid regions benefiting more than the agricultural North West (where the fishing industry is concentrated) and the South. Spain has been a net beneficiary of Structural Fund resources though, given the size of its economy, it has been a relatively smaller beneficiary than Ireland,

Greece or Portugal. Most importantly, there has been a broad-based consensus in both elite and public opinion that adjustment is necessary. Spain sees herself as a first-division EC member state and has been willing to make economic sacrifices accordingly. The consistent commitment to full economic and monetary union has imposed tight constraints on macroeconomic policy.

Within the EC, Spanish foreign policy, priorities have concentrated on strengthening the EC's relations with Latin America and, most importantly, with the Mediterranean region and the Middle East. After decades, Spain finally recognised the State of Israel immediately on joining the EC in 1986. This opened the way to more active participation in EC initiatives in the region, co-ordinated through EPC. More recently, during its 1995 Presidency, Spain sponsored a new Euro-Mediterranean initiative to improve trade relations with the Mahgreb and Mashreq countries, as a counterbalance to moves towards Eastern EU enlargement.

PORTUGAL

Portugal entered the EC in a more vulnerable economic and political condition than Spain. The political transition to democracy was turbulent, whilst the small size and peripheral location of its economy, heavily biased towards agricultural and traditional industrial sectors such as textiles and footwear, gave cause for concern. The Portuguese experience of membership, therefore, exhibits many of the same patterns of development as Ireland and Greece. Portugal has been a considerable beneficiary of the Structural Funds, amounting to 2.3 per cent of GDP in 1991, though less than the 5 per cent of GDP in the cases of Ireland and Greece, due to its lower receipts from the CAP's Guarantee Section.

For the five years following EC accession, Portugal experienced accelerated GDP growth and an influx of foreign investment, together with declining inflation rates. This was similar to Spain's experience, though with a lower average rate of unemployment. Despite these positive effects, however, structural problems have persisted, with a strong bias towards traditional industries.

In political terms, Portugal has not been a high-profile leader of new initiatives, usually preferring to support Spanish-led initiatives, for instance in Latin America and the Mediterranean. However, neither has it adopted 'difficult' positions, as has Greece, preferring to protect the benefits of cohesion spending through low profile diplomacy.

AUSTRIA, SWEDEN AND FINLAND

The recent accession of Austria, Sweden and Finland gives limited opportunities to assess the impact of membership on their economic and political systems. Nevertheless, some trends can be identified. Unlike previous new members, the EFTA countries were joining a more integrated Union, incorporating a Single European Market, a timetable for convergence towards EMU, and a commitment to develop a Common Foreign and Security Policy. However, although the acquis is more demanding than in previous enlargement rounds, the accession threshold has been lowered by the policy convergence achieved by the 1973 Free Trade Agreement and, most importantly, the EEA process. The extent of potential trade creation and diversion in manufacturing sectors is therefore very limited. A recent study[27] concluded that in Austria and Sweden, 'sensitive sectors', that is those vulnerable to the removal of non-tariff barriers, such as preferential public procurement and discriminatory technical standards, comprised 40 per cent of manufacturing employment and, in Finland, 30 per cent. The equivalent EC level was, on average 50 per cent, with a range from 40 per cent to 70 per cent, though the effects of deepening integration on former EFTA members may be considerable, particularly given the peripheral locations of Sweden and Finland. The degree of industry restructuring directly attributable to full membership is likely to be small. The effects on agriculture are more marked, given that EFTA countries maintained higher levels of price support than the CAP. Open borders are likely to lead to trade creation, though this is likely to benefit EC exporters and new members' consumers at the expense of their farmers. The export potential of EFTA's farmers is extremely limited.

As sophisticated democracies, the former EFTA countries have not experienced any major administrative difficulties in adjusting to EU membership. Adaptations to the machinery of government were already in place before accession. The deeply rooted conservative style of politics has meant that consultation processes with interest groups are well developed. However, strong groups, particularly farmers, still remain hostile to membership in all three new members. Whilst supportive of moves towards further integration and committed to meeting the Maastricht convergence criteria for EMU, the three are likely to be pragmatic rather than zealous promoters of further deepening.

CONCLUSION

Despite the diversity of the nine acceding members' experiences, certain general trends can be identified. Five principles are important. First, adjustment depends more on the domestic response to membership than on the provisions of the acquis itself. Whilst the mechanisms of the acquis trigger a restructuring process, their longer term effects depend on how far these are reinforced by a complementary internal reform programme. The more successful of these, for instance Spain's, usually start well in advance of accession, and recognise that European integration is linked to wider global trends which also require new responses. The deregulation process undertaken in the EFTA countries in the late 1980s and early 1990s in response to global competition, as well as the Single European Market, therefore helped prepare them for full membership. Delaying the reform process, as in Greece's case, is likely to be more problematic. The EC is likely to have moved to a new, deeper level of integration before adaptation to the previous level is complete. Constant requests for safeguards, derogations and compensatory payments are, in the long term, likely to reduce that member state's credibility.

Second, the CAP distorts the economies of new members, entrenches the farm lobby and makes the adaptation process more difficult. For the first, second and third enlargements, with the exception of the UK, CAP receipts were an attractive feature of full membership. Yet, by distorting prices and arbitrarily redistributing income, the CAP has often worked against the grain of the reform process in the new members. Each enlargement increases the range and complexity of producer interest groups who would be adversely affected by the prospects of further enlargement, though this process is now somewhat mitigated by the MacSharry reform of the CAP and the gradual reduction of price support to closer to world-market levels.

Third, the size of a new member's economy is important as well as its wealth level. Larger countries with diversified economies are better able to restructure and absorb shocks and to trade off losses in one sector against gains in another. The UK, despite the long-running dispute over budget contributions has made a marked trade reorientation towards the EU, and, despite concerns about its competitiveness in some sectors, has been able to exploit the larger market in areas where it has a strong comparative advantage, such as financial services. Larger economies are likely to have more scope for exploiting intra-industry trade; the growth of the Spanish car industry after accession is one example. Should further integration lead to more inter industry specialisation, then larger countries are more likely to be able to exploit economies of scale and scope in their stronger sectors.

Small economies are more vulnerable, though there are several qualifying factors. Wealthier small countries may have strong sectors that can still exploit integrating markets despite their small domestic base and peripheral locations – the Danish food, Finnish pulp and paper, and Swedish pharmaceutical industries, for instance. Their national economies are therefore dependent on the capabilities of a small number of firms. Poorer states have fewer options. With limited scope for developing intra-industry trade, Greece, Ireland and Portugal are vulnerable to developing a 'dual' economy, where inter-industry specialisation is in low-value manufacturing such as textiles, with competition coming from Third World countries.

Fourth, EC structural spending has only limited effects and may create dependency. Whilst Structural Fund receipts may have a significant impact on net budget balances, they have been unable to close the development gap, even though particular localities and sectoral groups may have benefited. The dependence on these receipts, particularly for Ireland, Greece and Portugal, is likely to make their reform more difficult.[28]

Fifth, a new member's self perception as a 'follower' or 'leader' in the EC is important. Much of the success of Spanish integration into the EC can be attributed to its determination to act, and be seen to act in the first division. EC membership has, therefore, provided Spain with a new framework to manage its reintegration into the mainstream of European political developments. This involves leading major initiatives where extending or upgrading Community action is both in the national interest and commands wider support, whilst not complaining too much about the budget. The need for a more active Mediterranean policy to counterbalance the pull to the North and East is such an example. Small states can have this capability, though usually in more limited policy areas. It is likely, for instance, that Austria, Sweden and Finland will make environmental, employment and social policy a priority.

Given these considerations, the UK's position has been more ambiguous. As a large member state with wide-ranging political, economic and security interests, it has been expected to play a leading role, and, as was the case with the development of the Single European Market, has proved capable of doing so. However, the lack of a widely shared and deeply rooted belief that the UK's major interests should be managed within an EU framework has often reduced, if not marginalised, its influence.

For smaller, poorer member states, there are fewer options, though they can gain credibility by brokering deals, usually during their Council Presidency, and by not over-exploiting their veto power to hold back EC initiatives. Greece's behaviour in EPC during the 1980s, for instance, significantly reduced its credibility.

Drawing up a balance sheet of the political and economic net benefits of membership is fraught with difficulties. Yet these calculations, though often imprecise and subjective, are integral to the Community process and political debate. Most importantly, they shape the perception of new member states about how EC internal and external policies should be reformed and where the emphasis should be placed on the overall development of the EC.

7   The impact of enlargement on the EU's internal policy agenda

INTRODUCTION

The political and economic adaptations made by new members, set out in Chapter 6, also require adaptations by the Community itself. Whilst the classical method of enlargement places the onus of adaptation on the new member, it also transfers some of the responsibility for adaptation from the national to the European level by developing new policy instruments or reforming existing ones. Enlargement therefore changes the relationship between the national and EU policy domains, and alters the focal point of policy development, leading to complex, and often overlapping patterns of competence. This chapter therefore examines how enlargement has affected the scope of the EC's internal policies. It examines first the policy agenda established by the Rome Treaty and the processes by which these policies were expected to develop. It then examines the key 'cohesion' policies, regional and social, developed to cope with the increased diversity of an enlarged EC, before looking at the impact of enlargement on the Single European Market and the prospects for EMU. The chapter concludes with an examination of how the EC's budget has been developed to facilitate these policies.

THE EC'S INTERNAL POLICY DOMAIN

The scope of the EU's internal policy domain is derived from the allocation of competences in the Rome Treaty, and by the initial policy 'mix' chosen by the founder members to pursue further integration. This initial policy mix was set out clearly in Article 3 of the Rome Treaty which called for:

> The elimination of intra-Community customs duties and quantitative restrictions over a twelve year period, the establishment of a

Common Custom Tariff, the abolition of intra Community obstacles to the free movement of people, services and capital, the adoption of common policies for agriculture and transport, a common competition policy regime, the co-ordination of economic and monetary policies, legal approximation, the creation of a European Social Fund and a European Investment Bank, and a European Development Fund for the assistance of associated overseas territories.

The agenda reflected the preferences of the six founder members, meeting at the Messina Conference to focus on progressive internal liberalisation, complemented with some active common policies, agriculture in particular, in order to meet the general objectives of the EEC, as set out in Article 2 of the Treaty, to establish

a Common Market and progressively approximating the economic policies of Member States to promote throughout the Community a harmonious development of economic activities, a continuous and balanced expansion, an increase in stability, an accelerated raising of the standard of living and closer relations between the States belonging to it.

THE COMMUNITY METHOD

The 'Community method' developed by Monnet and Schumann, encapsulated in the above Articles, envisaged the incremental involvement of the Community in policy areas, previously reserved for nation states. This was closely linked with the neo-functionalist theory of integration, developed by Lindberg[1] and Haas,[2] who argued that, as the activities of regional institutions expanded, so they increasingly became the focus of demands and expectations from interest groups, political parties and politicians. The process of functional spillover, whereby action taken in pursuit of a given (EC) goal creates a situation in which the goal can only be achieved by expanding the range of actions taken, underpin neo-functionalist theory. This process is complemented by political spillover in which the groups affected gradually increase pressure for further integration. As Harrison has written:

The integrative step itself should be inherently expansive. That is, the joint activity will be larger than the sum of the original independent activities if possible. It should involve some sacrifice and some disruption of existing activities. Strains and distortions may well be felt in other sectors. These effects will give rise to a need, and consequently a demand for remedies. The remedies could well be measures of further integration which extend the scope of central decision making.[3]

Thus neo-functionalism envisages, for instance, that the removal of internal tariff barriers would lead to demands for the removal of non-tariff barriers and other distorting measures and that monetary union would lead to full economic union and the harmonisation of tax policies. Neo-functionalism has been much criticised for being over-deterministic and for its technocratic bias.[4] Yet, in describing the 'expansive logic' of integration, it draws attention to the developing patterns of issues linkage in the integration process and has been used by the European Institutions, particularly by the Commission and Parliament, to justify the expansion of their policy competences.

SPILLOVER AND ENLARGEMENT

The concept of spillover is important in understanding the enlargement of the EC. Whilst the neo-functionalists concentrated on the behaviour of internal Community actors, many of the effects of integration spill over to the Community's near neighbours. Thus, spillover has a geographical, as well as a purely functional dimension. Changes in internal trade regimes create demands from external interests for active involvement in policy development. For the Community, enlarging its policy domain increases the possibility that 'the joint activity will be larger than the sum of the parts' and that demands for further integration will follow.

The links between widening and deepening are complex. The progress of the EC from a customs union, through the Single European Market, and possibly to full EMU, cannot all be attributed to the enlargement process. However, the predicted effects of enlargement and the actual consequences of absorbing new members, has usually stimulated policy reform. Both applicants and existing member states make widening to some degree conditional on deepening.

The effects of enlargement on the EC's internal policy agenda fall into three categories. First, at the pre-accession stage, the debate in the applicant state concerning the consequences of adjusting to the acquis is mirrored by an internal EC debate about how far internal policies need to be reformed for enlargement. The spillover effects for agricultural, regional, social and environmental policies are potentially very wide. This internal EC debate has a number of dimensions. For member states, cost benefit considerations, particularly relating to the budget, are critical. Whilst a member state might be willing to accept a reduction in its net budgetary position, it is likely to demand some other form of benefit in kind. For the Commission this debate is usually seen as an opportunity to extend existing policy instruments and, if possible, to make a 'great leap forward' to a new level of integration.

Second, during the transition period, as the new member is making the necessary domestic adjustments, so the acquis itself goes through a period of transition as new policy instruments are phased in, and costs and benefits are reallocated among existing members. The long transition period for agriculture during the Iberian enlargement was due less to the needs of Spanish and Portuguese farmers, than to the need to bed down the new Mediterranean agricultural acquis within the EC's policy process.

Third, once fully integrated into the Community, the new member state is positioned to press its own policy priorities and to participate fully in the reform of the acquis. Whilst this participation may lead to a positive sum game and an upgrading of the EC's policy competencies, particularly if the Commission can identify a winning coalition amongst the member states, it need not necessarily do so. Enlargement may lead to stagnation, or even retrenchment, if the new member's interests are too diverse or idiosyncratic to be accommodated comfortably.

DEVELOPMENT OF EC REGIONAL POLICY

Critical to explaining the links between enlargement and internal policy development, has been the need to manage the spatial effects of economic integration. These effects did not become an EC policy issue until the first enlargement of the Community. The prospects of integrating Ireland, which was predominantly agricultural, and the UK, which had declining industrial regions with concentrations of sectors such as steel and shipbuilding as well as peripheral agricultural regions, raised the political salience of regional issues.

During the 1960s, most European countries maintained extensive regional policies, designed to attract capital to peripheral regions, to support employment and to restrict growth in congested, metropolitan regions. Governments pushed these policies for a variety of economic and political motives and financed them through national budgets. By removing national tariff and non-tariff barriers, European integration potentially exacerbated these problems, but without any countervailing redistributive mechanisms. The economic rationale for a Community-level regional policy is based on the need to prevent member states and their regions outbidding each other, to deal with cross-border 'spillover' effects and to counterbalance agricultural spending, which has tended to favour richer regions.[5]

The origins of the EC's regional policy can be traced to the creation in 1967 of the Commission's Directorate General for Regional Policy, though it was only after the 1969 agreement to develop a plan to achieve economic and monetary union by 1980, and the opening of the enlargement negotiations that the possibility of an active Community regional policy was taken seriously.

The Paris Summit of October 1972 agreed to establish a Regional Development Fund by the end of 1973 with the aim of correcting the structural and regional imbalances within the Community, which might affect the realisation of EMU. The Commission's initial ambitions, set out in the Thomson Report of May 1973,[6] were modest, and concentrated on complementing national measures. However, the Report rejected the principle of '*juste retour*' and argued for the allocation of resources on objective Community-wide criteria of regional disparities, with an initial Fund of 2250 MUA allocated over three years.

The objective Community dimension was soon submerged in the political horse trading between member states over the size and method of fund allocation.[7] Because of their net contributions to the EC budget arising from the Common Agricultural Policy, the UK saw the proposed ERDF as a way of offsetting their contributions and argued for all of their Assisted Areas to be eligible, thereby ensuring that control of ERDF allocations remained in Whitehall. National control was further reinforced by an eventual compromise on national quota allocations. The size of the Fund at 1300 Mua for three years, less than half the Commission's original proposal, reflected the reluctance of the Germans to make open-ended commitments. This was reinforced by the reluctance of the British to pool oil reserves following the Yom Kippur War and the subsequent oil crisis.

Although the creation of the ERDF is directly attributable to the first enlargement of the EC, the increase in the scope of the EC's policy domain was, at least initially, marginal. The classical method ensured that regional spending provided side payments to applicants, specifically the UK and Ireland and to some existing member states, in particular France and Italy, to ensure their agreement to enlargement.

As the member state with the strongest commitment to enlargement, Germany paid the bill. The intergovernmental bargains underpinning its establishment and its small size in relation to national expenditures ensured that national, rather than regional, interests predominated. Control of allocations by the Council of Ministers, and the limited means of the Commission to monitor projects led to questions of 'additionality', that is whether ERDF receipts 'topped up' national funds or substituted for them.[8] The introduction of a 5 per cent non-quota section in 1979 marginally increased the discretion of the Commission though eligible projects still had to be part of national plans.

MEDITERRANEAN ENLARGEMENT AND REGIONAL POLICY

The impact of the impending Greek and Iberian enlargements on regional policy was addressed in the Commission's paper, admitting that 'in the absence of suitable corrective policies, trade liberalisation might even go so far as to jeopardise the continued development of a number of weak regions in the enlarged Community'.[9] The overall impact of Greek accession, however, was small. The side payments implicit in the classical method could be made without major policy reform. No specific new initiatives were proposed and the accession of Greece led to a reallocation of national quotas.

The 1984 reforms expanded the non-quota section and converted national quotas to indicative ranges, and moved to programme rather than project-based financing, using common Community criteria in co-ordination with the ESF and FEOGA. These were undertaken in anticipation of Iberian enlargement and led to the Integrated Mediterranean Programmes (IMPs) for Italy and Greece, as their price for accepting Spain's and Portugal's accession. It is questionable whether these programmes were any more than lists of planned capital expenditure projects.[10]

Although the second and third enlargements had only a slight direct impact on the ERDF, they led indirectly to a much more fundamental shift in the EC's spending priorities. The Single European Act, agreed in 1987, had added a Title V 'Economic and Social Cohesion' to the Treaty of Rome with the new Articles 130(a) and 130(e), linking the 'harmonious development' of the Community to the co-ordination and expansion of the Structural Funds. The focus on 'cohesion' was part of the grand bargain underpinning the development of the Single European Market and it was the price exacted by the poorer, mainly southern, EC members for their consent to further internal deregulation. The outline of this bargain was already clear before Spain and Portugal acceded. However, immediately on taking up membership, they used their new positions as insiders to extract specific financial benefits, as all previous new members had done.

The 1988 reform of the Structural Funds agreed to double the resources of the three Funds between 1987 and 1993, as part of the Delors package on budget reform. The reforms led to the designation of five priority objectives and a greater concentration of aid in Greece, Ireland, Northern Ireland, Portugal, Spain and the Mezzogiorno. The reforms also involved five-year programmes, requiring close co-operation between the Commission and the implementing local and regional authorities, and led to a considerable increase in overall structural spending; by 1992, up to 27 per cent of overall EC expenditure. The concentration of resources meant that Structural Fund transfers represented 3.5, 2.9 and 2.3 per cent of GDP for Portugal, Greece and Ireland respectively.

POLICY LINKAGE WITH EMU

During the run-up to the Maastricht Treaty, the debate on structural spending was linked to the plans for EMU. In 1993, a Cohesion Fund was established, mainly as a concession to Spain for its agreement to the EMU timetable. In this way, Spain had learnt to use its membership card, as Greece had done in 1981 over Iberian enlargement, to extract specific benefits. The Fund is limited to Ireland, Greece, Portugal and Spain and is explicitly linked to programmes for economic convergence.[11]

The fourth, EFTA, enlargement also led to the adaptation of EC regional policy though no overall increase in spending. All the applicant states maintained extensive policies to prevent rural depopulation and to preserve farming in extreme climatic conditions. Their accession led to the creation of an Objective 6 criterion based on their population density, to allow arctic and subarctic regions to benefit from the Structural Funds, as if they were Objective 1 regions. However, the relatively small scale of problems involved meant that the fourth enlargement did not become entangled in a major debate on cohesion.

NATIONAL OR COMMUNITY REGIONAL POLICY?

Over the twenty years of the ERDF's existence there has been a notice-able shift in the EC's spending priorities away from agricultural price support and towards structural spending. This has been driven by the demands of enlargement and has been increasingly linked to the costs of other policy areas, in particular the Single European Market and EMU. The concentration of resources in a small number of member states has increased, in part because the UK's net budgetary position has improved following the 1984 Fontainbleau Settlement, reducing dependence on Structural Fund receipts. Arguably, there has been an incremental increase in the EC's policy domain in this sector. Local and regional authorities in eligible areas increasingly look to Brussels for developing and funding initiatives and many of them maintain representative offices there.[12] Community-funded programmes facilitate cross-border and pan-European links of regional development bodies. The Commission has been active in developing pan-European criteria of regional disparities, and has facilitated the exchange of ideas.

Yet the extent to which the expansion of the EC's policy domain has superseded the national policy domain is questionable. More than 90 per cent of funds are allocated through the Community Support Frameworks (CSFs) which are either sectoral or regional, but in which the map of eligible areas and the overall share of funds are determined by member states with the Commission acting as a 'partner'. As Hooghe and Keating have written:

> In the CSF's partnership is the chief vehicle for widening the circle of power and thus for increased regional participation. Member states, however reserved for themselves the right to decide who would be part of the partnership. ... Regional interests are drawn into the European arena within a strongly protected national niche.[13]

This pattern of policy development is largely attributable to the EC's classical method of enlargement. The original intergovernmental bargain that created the ERDF has been further entrenched by the need to buy off recalcitrant interest groups in member states at each enlargement round. Acceding member states expect a 'right of access' to the Fund even when, as in the case with the fourth enlargement, they may have GDP per capita well above average EC levels. All applicants bid to have as much of their land area designated as eligible regions to retain the maximum degree of central government control.

In the case of Ireland and Greece, these covered the entire country. Although the concentration of resources in the poorer states may have increased the effectiveness of regional spending, paradoxically it has further increased national control of Structural Funds. Ireland, Greece, Spain and Portugal have a major national interest in the Funds which will affect their views of further reforms.

SOCIAL POLICY

The basic commitments of the Treaty of Rome in the social policy area related to the free movement of workers (Articles 48–51) and the freedom of establishment (Articles 52–58) can be seen as an integral part of the customs union. Articles 117–28 covered wider objectives of social policy, including the principle of equal pay for equal work (119) and the facilitation of the improvement in living and working conditions through collaboration between member states (117–18). A European Social Fund (ESF) was established (Article 123) to promote employment opportunities and geographical and occupational mobility for workers within the EC. All of these policies were seen as necessary to complement the removal of trade barriers and to deal with their possible social consequences.

Despite the high-minded objectives of the Treaty's articles, the achievements of the early years remained limited. Attention was focused on removing the large range of national restrictions to the free movement of labour, achieved by 1968, as part of the customs union timetable. It was based on the principle of 'national treatment' for workers from other EC countries for occupational and social benefits. High levels of growth reduced pressure for intervention at EC level, although, as was the case with regional policy, national governments experimented with a wide range of national policy instruments during this period. The ESF was largely directed towards employment initiatives in the Italian south, though its resources remained limited.

In the early 1970s, there was a shift of opinion in the Community towards a more active social policy. It became clear that removing national barriers to free movement had not solved problems of social exclusion and discrimination, whilst economic growth had very uneven social and geographical effects. Social policy therefore complemented the debate taking place at this time concerning regional policy. The effects of integration on labour markets can work both ways. The growth effects in central core regions can pull surplus labour from high-unemployment peripheral regions, acting as a safety valve. This was largely the experience for Southern Europe in the 1960s. However, this leads to peripheral regions falling further behind because they lack skilled labour to exploit new opportunities. The objective of EC labour market policy, therefore, is to improve the quality of human capital in disadvantaged regions whilst reducing structural barriers to labour mobility.[14]

SOCIAL POLICY AND THE FIRST ENLARGEMENT

The prospects of enlargement also influenced this debate. Both Ireland and parts of the UK had major social and employment problems which might increase on accession. Given the net migration from Ireland to the UK, it was argued that that might easily 'spill over' into the enlarged Community. Structural employment issues became a legitimate area of EC concern. The 1972 Paris Summit called for a programme of social policy measures which led to the 1974 Social Action Programme designed to achieve upward harmonisation of working conditions and of the active involvement of workers in their firms. In 1972, the ESF had also been reformed, with all its resources being targeted on the alleviation of labour market imbalances due to EC policies and the reduction of structural unemployment in declining regions.[15] The first enlargement, therefore, gave the Commission the opportunity to develop a more active role in this policy area.

The 1974 Social Action Programme was the first attempt by the European Commission to develop a social dimension to this integration process. However, a number of the measures, particularly those relating to worker participation, were resisted by employers and some national governments, presaging more divisive arguments in years to come. Despite the activism of the Commission, social policy was still perceived as being largely within the national policy domain.

SOCIAL POLICY AND MEDITERRANEAN ENLARGEMENT

The prospects of Southern enlargement in the early 1980s increased the range of structural labour market issues which the Community would have to internalise. The Commission's Paper on enlargement noted that:

> Industrial and agricultural restructuring and the trend towards capital intensive production systems will release manpower and seriously worsen unemployment in the Community. The number of

jobless in the Twelve countries combined now totals over 7.5m. The arrival on the labour market of considerable numbers of young people in view of the high rate of unemployment among these age groups will aggravate the problem and make this phenomenon one of the main challenges and policy constraints in the 1980s.[16]

The Commission therefore called for a bold employment policy focused on vocational training, mobilising financial resources at European level. Despite the Commission's hopes, the Mediterranean enlargement did not lead to a noticeable strengthening of European social policy. The accession debates mainly focused on migrant labour fears in the existing member states and on the transition periods before full free movement could be granted.

Indirectly, however, enlargement led to the 1984 reform of the ESF, which focused resources on young people, and disadvantaged regions, as part of the co-ordinated programme approach with the ERDF. However, the ESF has been subjected to the same criticisms as the ERDF: that its resources are small in relation to the tasks undertaken, that its implementation remains largely under the control of national governments, and that additionality is not proven.

The major attempt to increase the EC's social policy domain came in 1989 with the presentation of the Community Charter of the Fundamental Rights of Workers. The Social Charter, which constituted an attempt to create a minimum set of employment rights across the Community, was strongly supported by France and Germany, as well as by other countries with Socialist governments such as Spain and Greece, and led to the development of a social action programme covering the regulation of 'atypical' (i.e. part-time) work, maximum duration of work, and consultation and participation of workers in enterprises. The upgrading of the Community's social dimension was seen by the Commission and the key member states as a necessary counterbalance to the deregulatory supply side reforms of the Single European Market Programme in order to ensure widespread social support for the predicted industry restructuring.[17]

Successive enlargements facilitated the Commission's search for a consensus on social policy. With the exception of the British Government, all the other EC member states were willing to support an extension of EC social policy.

The Charter and the work programme were vigorously rejected by the British Government, which argued that the philosophy was interventionist and ran counter to its own economic liberalism. Moreover, despite the rhetorical support for the initiative from the newly integrated Mediterranean member states, various concerns were raised about aspects of the Commission's proposals.[18]

Support for the Charter was strong from German trade unions, who feared 'social dumping' – that in a deregulated Single European Market, their social benefits might be undercut by enterprises moving to Community regions with lower wages and social charges. The possibility of pan-European minimum wage legislation was therefore removed from the work programme, in view of concerns that this might remove the competitive advantage enjoyed by the poorer, mainly Southern member states in attracting and retaining mobile capital.

The social policy acquis proved relatively unproblematic during the fourth enlargement. The EFTA applicants all had high levels of social protection which could easily be reconciled both with their underpinning philosophy and with the detailed provisions of the directives. However, they also had pockets of persistent structural problems, giving them access to the ESF. Thus, the fourth enlargement has strengthened the consensus that social policy is an appropriate area for Community action, and has further isolated the UK.

Although the Community has increasingly identified social cohesion as vital to underpinning the development of further integration, specific extensions of the Community's social policy domain have been more limited. Progress has been most notable and uncontroversial in areas where there are clear Treaty provisions, such as health and safety and equal pay. Similarly, the role of the ESF has been upgraded as part of the EC's structural spending, though the total sums involved remain small. The Commission has made several major attempts to upgrade the status of social policy, most notably in the late 1980s, and has justified these on the grounds of complementarity with other policy initiatives. The prospects of enlargement or the consequences of absorbing new members have influenced the debates surrounding reforms, though the classical enlargement method has ensured that these reforms have been limited.

Leaving aside the specific ideological objections of the UK Conservative Government, the Commission has encountered other obstacles to extending its competencies. Different national traditions of labour market organisation have proved difficult to integrate within a common legal framework.[19] National governments have resisted microeconomic intervention, except, in the carefully defined areas where Community Funds are attached. Successive enlargements, even when they involve countries broadly sympathetic to the Commission's basic philosophy, have reinforced this trend, again making radical reform more difficult.

ENLARGEMENT AND THE SINGLE EUROPEAN MARKET

From the mid-1980s to the early 1990s, the internal policy debate in the EC was dominated by the plan to create a Single European Market (SEM). Despite the implementation of the customs union by 1968, it was clear by the early 1980s that the European economy was far from integrated. Numerous non-tariff barriers remained, and national governments retained significant controls in sectors such as public procurement, transport, telecommunications and other utilities.

During the late 1970s and early 1980s, the Community became increasingly concerned about its competitiveness in relation particularly to the US and Japan, of which the latter was starting to make significant inroads into sensitive European industries such as motor cars and electronics. This Euro-sclerosis was attributed partly to market fragmentation in Europe, which was preventing European companies from restructuring to exploit economies of scale on a pan-European basis.[20]

In terms of the stages of economic integration originally developed by Balassa,[21] the SEM is the logical development of a customs union, in that it removes the remaining barriers to the free movement of labour, capital, goods and services. It is also an intermediate step towards full economic union in that the harmonisation process is likely to create new demands for economic policy co-ordination. The Commission's plans for the SEM were encapsulated in the 1985 White Paper,[22] which identified nearly 300 measures which needed to be taken at European level in order to remove physical, technical and fiscal barriers to intra-EC trade. Although there was a coherent theoretical rationale to the White Paper, it was not an exhaustive list and recognised the political sensitivity of its proposals by excluding some sectors, such as utilities, from its 1992 implementation deadline.

Although this rationale drew on the idea of 'spillover', a conjunction of political factors linked to enlargement led to the presentation of proposals at that particular time. Lobbying by European industrialists reinforced an emerging consensus among European political leaders that supply side reform, through deregulation, was necessary for wealth creation. Following the resolution of the British budget issue in 1984, the British Government was more favourably disposed to new initiatives, particularly since the White Paper's philosophy was compatible with its domestic reform programme.

The impending Iberian enlargement was critical. In economic terms, the addition of two new markets, one of which, Spain, was large by European standards, would substantially increase the potential for trade creation in the enlarged domestic market. Improved access to the Spanish market was important in convincing some member states, particularly Britain, that some measure of deepening was compatible with further widening. Determined to benefit from the enlarged market, and particularly from inward investment, the Spanish initiated a major domestic reform programme well in advance of the SEM deadline. The economic objectives of the SEM were tied up in a package deal contained in the Single European Act (SEA), presented to the Milan Summit in June 1985, which modified the EC's decision-making rules in order to facilitate the market-building process. The initiative can be seen as an attempt by the Commission, in particular the new President, Jacques Delors, to assemble a winning coalition that would ensure simultaneous widening and deepening and increase the Commission's competencies.[23]

The development of a major new initiative in parallel with the enlargement process, provided an additional convergence discipline during a period when the new members aspired to be 'good Europeans'. The White Paper initiative and the SEA appeared during the final stages of the Iberian accession negotiations, by which time the accession terms had been largely settled and Spain and Portugal were informally participating in Community decision making. The SEM's implementation deadline, therefore, became an integral part of the acquis that they adopted.

Although the SEM programme had a strong deregulatory bias, facilitated by the use of the mutual recognition principle, rather than complete harmonisation,[24] it nevertheless considerably extended the EC's policy domain. The Commission sought to extend the scope and sectoral coverage of framework directives, particularly into product markets, such as food and pharmaceuticals, where the complexity of national regulations acted as a *de facto* trade barrier. Although the EC's institutions were not, and could not, be responsible for the detailed regulation of every product and service market in the EC, they are responsible for the establishment of general principles governing sectoral regulatory regimes, and for ensuring coherence and consistency in the way these regimes evolve. Greater diversity in regulations, practices, institutions and market organisation, brought about by successive enlargements, necessitated this new approach.[25] The expansion of the EC's policy domain was therefore achieved in ways consistent with further widening.

COHESION AND THE SINGLE EUROPEAN MARKET

Although the Community's new members participated actively in the Internal Market building process, they also raised concerns about the likely distribution of costs and benefits from the programme. The Commission's study of the economic impact of the programme, the Cecchini Report, had focused on the static cost savings and dynamic trade effects of eliminating the remaining trade barriers, and had placed considerable emphasis on the scope for the creation of further scale economies in key industries.[26] Further detailed studies undertaken by the Commission of 'sensitive sectors' (i.e. those most vulnerable to damage, following the removal of barriers) showed that their share of employment was highest in Greece and Portugal, the economically weakest EC economies. The studies also concluded that successive enlargements of the Community had increased the heterogeneity of the Community, leading to greater inter-industry trade. Liberalisation would therefore have a marked impact on those countries specialising in more labour intensive industries. Moreover, the emphasis on price reduction meant that protected sectors, such as Southern Europe's financial services industry, might be adversely affected by extensive market opening measures.

These fears were articulated by the poorer, peripheral members of the EC and led to the introduction, through the SEA, of Title V of the Rome Treaty, dealing with economic and social cohesion. These changes underpinned the Delors package involving a large increase in Structural Funds and the reform of the CAP, agreed in 1988 as part of a 'global deal', to ensure the political acceptance of the Internal Market programme.

MONETARY INTEGRATION

The debate about the role of monetary policy in furthering European integration has a long history. Whilst the Rome Treaty recognised that macroeconomic policy and balance of payments were legitimate matters of common concern, they remained firmly in the national policy domain. During the 1960s, economic theory focused on exploring the 'optimum currency area' in order to identify whether capital and labour mobility and prices would be flexible enough to substitute for exchange rate movements in absorbing external shocks and trade effects. Although the original Six were relatively homogeneous (with the exception of southern Italy), they were still far from being an optimum currency area, implying that any plans for a common monetary policy would have to overcome the objections of weaker member states to their being denied the devaluation option.

The completion of the customs union in 1968 led to the first serious attempt to achieve EMU. In 1969, the Hague Summit committed the Community to achieving EMU and set up the Werner Committee to investigate its feasibility. The Hague Summit was the first example of a Community package deal designed to achieve deepening and widening. The Six were confronted with applications from the UK, Ireland, Denmark and Norway and were determined to ensure that the increased diversity of the enlarging Community would not undermine economic policy convergence. The role of sterling as a reserve currency was potentially destabilising in this respect. The Werner Report of October 1970 envisaged full EMU by 1980, to be achieved in three stages with the ultimate objective of irrevocably fixed exchange rates and centrally managed economic policies.[27] The plan was debated during a period of considerable international monetary instability, caused by the dollar's fluctuation. Although the Paris Summit of October 1972, immediately before enlargement, reiterated the political commitment to achieving EMU by 1980, attempts at narrowing exchange-rate fluctuations through the 'snake in the tunnel' failed. The external shocks from the 1973 oil crisis further compounded the difficulties of gaining agreement on joint monetary arrangements and by the mid-1970s it was clear that the EMU deadline could not be met.

Enlargement was not the primary cause of the collapse of the EMU plan. There was, in fact, considerable disagreement between France and Germany about the method, if not the end, of EMU. Nevertheless, the first enlargement contributed to its postponement. The UK was sceptical about the political implications of EMU and indeed has remained so ever since. Furthermore, the increased economic diversity following from enlargement reduced the likelihood that a larger EC would be an 'optimal currency area',[28] in which capital and labour mobility would substitute for exchange-rate movements.

Plans for EMU reappeared in the late 1970s when a proposal by Commission President Roy Jenkins led to the creation of the European Monetary System (EMS) in 1979. During the 1980s membership of the EMS grew. At the outset, all EC members, apart from the UK, joined in either the narrow 2.5 per cent or wider 6 per cent fluctuation margins. Greece, Portugal and Spain remained outside following their accession. Nevertheless, EMS membership became an important test of their Community commitment. In June 1989, close to the conclusion of its Presidency, Spain joined.

The attraction of EMS membership was linked to the renewed plans for full EMU, which had been given considerable momentum by the Single European Market Programme. The Commission sought to capitalise on the apparent consensus amongst member states for further integration and to extend its winning coalition into plans for EMU. The Commission explicitly linked its proposals for EMU to the Single European Market process and drew heavily on functional spillover arguments. Increasing trade interdependence and cross-border business linkages would highlight the transaction costs carried by businesses and the distortions caused by exchange rate fluctuations. Free capital movements would strengthen the calls for the centralisation of monetary policy at European level.

The June 1988 Hanover Summit established a committee for the study of EMU under Jacques Delors' chairmanship and submitted its Report in April 1989. The Delors Report advocated a three-stage move to full EMU.[29] The first stage, which began in 1990, envisaged the strengthening of economic policy co-ordination and the inclusion of all currencies in the Exchange Rate Mechanism (ERM). Following the Rome Council (October 1990) it was agreed that Stage 2 should start in 1994, with the establishment of a European System of Central Banks and a European Monetary Institute to prepare the ground for full EMU, three years later. This third stage would involve the creation of an independent European Central Bank which would be charged with maintaining price stability. Progress to this third, irrevocable, stage would be based on member states meeting a set of 'convergence criteria' specifying targets for inflation rates, public deficits and borrowing.

Whilst the EC, following Mediterranean enlargement, was even less of an optimal currency area than it had been following the first enlargement, this did not necessarily impede progress towards EMU. Spain's determination to be positioned in the EC's first division overrode economic misgivings. The Delors Report was explicit about the political dimension of EMU in arguing that jointly managing a currency area necessarily involved common institutions. Though these might be subject to democratic controls, national governments would clearly lose their independent control of monetary and exchange rate policy. This would constitute a major increase in the EC's policy domain at the expense of the national domain.

The Delors Report led quickly to the convening of an intergovernmental conference (IGC) which would prepare the Treaty revisions necessary for full EMU. The IGC, meeting in Maastricht in December 1991, agreed a timetable and specific convergence criteria for membership. The EMU proposals agreed at Maastricht implied a commitment from nearly all the EC's member states to a substantial increase in the EC's policy domain.[30] In addition to the specific powers over monetary policy, the commitment implied a willingness to adopt common complementary economic and fiscal policies in order to achieve the convergence criteria.

The economic diversity in the EC meant that compensating mechanisms had to be developed at a European level to ensure continued political support among the economically weaker member states. The Community, therefore, established a Cohesion Fund in order to help Greece, Portugal, Ireland and Spain meet the convergence criteria.

Although the ERM experienced extreme turbulence during 1992, the momentum behind EMU is strong, and some form of monetary union is likely to be implemented around the year 2000. The 1995 enlargement round also strengthened the prospects for EMU. Although Sweden and Finland experienced considerable difficulties in shadowing the DM in the ERM in the early 1990s because of inflation and public debt constraints, as full members, they have fully committed themselves to the Maastricht convergence criteria. Austria's currency has, for a number of years, been closely linked to the DM and would be likely to join the first group of EMU participants.

The plans for EMU represent a clear example of how the Community expands its internal policy domain. Ambitious targets are set for a deadline which is far enough ahead to provide some flexibility for political and economic circumstances, but is close enough to concentrate the minds of decision makers. Some variable geometry is incorporated in the plan. Enlargement reinforces this process. Though not all member states are expected to meet all the criteria at the same time, the ambitions of the plan are such that new member states are anxious not to be left too far behind and are, therefore, willing to make sacrifices (in the case of EMU, largely through high unemployment rates) to meet the convergence criteria. Side payments are made to the economically weaker members to ensure their support.

EC BUDGET

The expansion of the EC's policy domain into regional and social policy, the SEM and EMU has brought to the foreground issues of financial redistribution. As the focus of policy development has shifted from national to European level, so the EC has also been expected to deal with the negative consequences of further integration, largely through the mechanism of budgetary transfers. The developing role of the EC's budget is, therefore, an integral part of the EC's expanding policy domain. Given the package deals created to facilitate enlargement, the budget is also an important component of the classical method, linked to the capacity of the EC to make side payments and to add new policy instruments.

During the early years of the Community, the EC budget was merely an aggregation of the expenditure decisions taken by different EC Councils of Ministers, financed by national contributions. However, the completion of the customs union opened the possibility that customs levies on imports from outside the EC could legitimately be regarded as the Community's 'own resources', and could be used to underpin the development of independent institutions and policies. At the Hague Summit of December 1969, the Community endorsed a plan, agreed in 1970, to fund EC expenditure on the basis of agricultural levies, customs duties and a share, set initially at 1 per cent of member states' receipts from VAT.

This was agreed as part of the package deal on linking widening to deepening, before the first enlargement negotiations commenced and was, therefore, part of the acquis which the applicants were expected to accept. The British view, that the budget structure unfairly penalised the UK was met by the reiteration of Community orthodoxy that the problem would be much diminished by giving Community preference to agricultural and industrial imports. Whilst the British position was understood, there was a reluctance to concede the principle of *juste retour*, the idea that member states should receive back approximately what they contribute, for fear of undermining one of the cornerstones of Community solidarity. Although the 1975 agreement on the UK renegotiation referred to the need to avoid 'unacceptable situations' during a period of convergence, the mechanism recognised the net position of member states as a factor to be considered and, therefore, introduced an element of equity, if not full *juste retour* into the EC budget.[31]

The 1975 agreement was a temporary measure and, in the early 1980s, pressure grew for a more comprehensive budget restructuring. The UK Government, under Mrs Thatcher, was determined to achieve a more permanent solution to the British budget problem. The Community was getting close to the ceiling of its own resources, a constraint which was made more pressing by the impending enlargement to include Spain and Portugal. In its 1982 paper on enlargement, requested by the Council, the Commission argued that, without an increase in own resources, it would be necessary to abandon the ambition of implementing the new policies which the Community needs to strengthen its capacity, notably in the industrial and technological field, and to combat the aggravation of regional disparities.[32]

The package deal agreed at the Fontainbleau Summit of 1984, raised the ceiling on the VAT contribution to own resources to 1.4 per cent, introduced new measures to control agricultural surplus and introduced a permanent mechanism for partially compensating the UK for its net shortfall on the difference between its VAT contribution and overall budget receipts.[33] The rebate can also be seen as a side payment to the UK to allow enlargement to proceed.

The pressures created by enlargement and the need to finance the cohesion commitments of the SEA led to a further agreement at the Brussels Summit in February 1988. This agreement created the 'fourth resource', based on GNP calculations, which introduced 'the ability to pay principle' as part of the political bargain securing the support of the poorer member states for the SEM.[34]

A similar agreement was concluded at the Edinburgh Summit in December 1992 as part of the package securing agreement to the EMU plan.

Whilst the EC budget has grown steadily since its own resources were created in 1970, its levels of expenditure remain small in comparison with those of national governments. Although total EU expenditure has risen from 3.6 billion ecu in 1970 to 72.3 billion ecu in 1994, expenditure as a proportion of member states' own public expenditure has risen in the same period from 1.9 per cent to 2.4 per cent. Both the total volume of own resources, and their proportion of EC receipts has not been enough to give the EC institutions a strong independent financial base. Although it has run counter to Community orthodoxy, an increasing proportion of EU expenditure is financed by the 'fourth resource' directly from member states' exchequers. Thus, while the principle of *juste retour* has been resisted, a large measure of equity has been introduced into the system in order to ensure sufficiently widespread political support for the expansion of common policies.

Despite these limitations, however, the expanding EC budget has been an important component of the classical method of enlargement. It has facilitated side payments and has allowed the costs of enlargement to be dispersed across a wider range of member states. The Commission, particularly under Jacques Delors, was skilful in constructing the packages necessary to allow enlargement to proceed. However, these budgetary mechanisms have become progressively more complex. Some reform is necessary before further enlargement can take place.

CONCLUSION

The development of the EC's internal policy domain over the past 30 years has been extensive. The gradual process of building on the foundations of the customs union to create a Single European Market, and to set specific target dates for EMU, suggests that the deepening process is well rooted and is underpinned by a strong economic rationale and political consensus. Detailed examination of the development of the key policy areas suggests that EC policy has become critical for an increasing range of public and private actors, at both national and subnational level. Even in areas where EC institutions and policy makers do not have authoritative powers, for instance, in macroeconomic management issues, national policy is increasingly made in a framework at European level, negotiated between EC institutions and other member states. Although the national policy domain remains robust, it has been increasingly penetrated by the EC; in some areas, such as regimes governing trade in goods and services, decisively so.

This process is closely linked to the widening of the EC. A strong underlying theme, usually articulated most clearly by the Commission, is that successfully integrating increasingly diverse new members into the EC required an extension of EC policy competence to oversee the convergence process, to remove structural impediments and other distortions to integration, and to deal with the negative spillover effects. The Commission has argued these points forcefully when it has been asked to review the consequences of enlargement. These arguments have been most effectively deployed in relation to the Structural Funds and cohesion issues in general.

It can also be seen that major deepening initiatives are usually clustered around enlargements. This was the case with the establishment of the ERDF at the first enlargement and with the Structural Fund reforms in 1984 in anticipation of the third enlargement, with the 1988 reforms linked to the absorption of the Iberians. The SEM White Paper was similarly a way of preventing the dilution and fragmentation of the enlarging Community. In addition to the economic rationale of the spillover theory, this 'clustering' has a strong political rationale. Deepening can be presented to applicants as part of a total accession package. So long as suitable 'sweeteners' are provided, overall agreement can be obtained, probably more easily than once the new member is fully absorbed, when the price of agreement to further deepening is usually increased.

Yet the relationship between deepening and widening also creates tensions. The Commission's search for an economically rational, optimal policy domain is rarely accepted uncritically by all the member states. They may accept the incremental extension of EC policy competences while still retaining significant control over implementation. Regional policy is a clear example of this trend. Whilst enlargement has increased the significance of the EC's cohesion policies, national governments still view them as part of a larger intergovernmental bargain.

In some policy areas, widening does not help deepening. In monetary policy, for instance, economic diversity has made the search for an optimal currency area more protracted, despite the fact that the fourth enlargement probably helped consolidate the EMU timetable. The acceptance that not all member states will be able to meet the Maastricht convergence criteria at the same time is an implicit admission that enlargement may increase the need for policy differentiation, or variable geometry.

Although the extension of the EC's policy domain into the national domain has often been challenged, considerable effort has been put into making the EC's internal policies more coherent. As the enlargement process has developed, so the linkage between policy areas, in particular cohesion policy, the SEM and EMU have been strengthened. This, itself, is part of the deepening process since it makes it more likely that future initiatives will involve more complex policy packages extending the EU's policy domain still further.

8 The impact of enlargement on the EC's external policy agenda

INTRODUCTION

Whilst much attention has been focused on the EC's internal policies, the integration process takes place within a wider global economic and political context. As a major regional group with an expanding policy agenda, the EC both shapes and is shaped by the dynamics of the international system. This has been so since the origins of the EC. External forces, in particular the influence of the US in supporting early integration initiatives and the threat from the USSR, were powerful forces underpinning the establishment of the EC. Since that establishment, the EC has built up a range of policy instruments to manage its external economic and political relations.

Many of these are a direct consequence of the EC's four enlargements, which have greatly expanded the range and complexity of political and economic interests that have to be aggregated. This chapter therefore sets out, first, the basic principles underpinning the EC's external policies, before examining the four key effects of enlargement on external policies. These four effects are that new members' interests have to be internalised into the EC system; that the priorities of the EC's external relations are thereby reordered; that the importance of the EC in the international trading system is increased; and that the need to strengthen linkages between economic and political relations is intensified. The chapter then examines the impact of each enlargement on the EC's external policies and concludes with a review of how the EU's foreign policy identity is being developed.

THE EC'S EXTERNAL POLICY FRAMEWORK

The external policy framework of the EC was constructed around the basic commitment to the customs union and the common internal policies set out in the Rome Treaty. The choice of a customs union rather than a free trade area, by introducing a common external tariff, implied a common commercial policy. The new institutional arrangements of the GATT, OECD, UN and the Council of Europe, the possibility of enlargement and the need to negotiate agreements with third parties also required specific responses. The core commitment to this common commercial policy was contained in Article 113, which stated that

> after the transitional period has ended, the common commercial policy should be based on uniform principles, particularly in regard to changes in tariff rates, the conclusion of tariff and trade agreements, an achievement of uniformity in measures of internalisation, export policy and measures to protect trade, such as those to be taken in case of dumping or subsidies.

Further articles defined other specific relationships. Article 131 established Association with the former overseas dependencies of the member states; Article 228 vested the power of concluding international agreements in the Commission; and Articles 229–231 established co-operation with the UN, GATT, Council of Europe and the OECD. Article 237 established that 'any European state may apply to become a member of the Community' whilst Article 238 provides for the conclusion of agreements with third parties for 'association involving reciprocal rights and obligations, common action and special procedures'.

'EXPRESS' AND 'IMPLIED' COMPETENCE

The external competences of the Community can be divided into two categories: 'express' and 'implied'. The Community has express powers under Articles 113 and 238 to negotiate trade agreements with third parties and association agreements. These express powers are exclusive and a member state cannot conclude a bilateral trade agreement with a third state. Member states are also under an obligation to advance the EC's interests and to proceed in international economic organisations by common action. This express competence does not depend on the Community having agreed a precisely formulated internal policy on the relevant policy area. The case law of the Community has also established over the years that, where the Community has regulated a matter internally, it also has the 'implied' competence to regulate it externally, though member states still retain residual rights until the Community's competence is actually exercised.[1]

DEEPENING OF EXTERNAL POLICY

The implication of this is that the Community is capable of expanding and, in effect, deepening its external policy domain in response to the internal integration process which is itself shaped by the enlargement process. Thus, the legal processes of the Community reinforce the spillover mechanism noted by neo-functionalist theorists. This deepening process has essentially three dimensions.

First, the Treaty provisions and case law of external competence form part of the acquis that new members accept. All bilateral trade agreements must be revoked, or integrated into existing Community agreements, and the new member must comply with Community trade policy instruments, such as anti-dumping duties. This may involve considerable adaptation, both from the new member state and the Community, if the new member previously had extensive and exclusive bilateral trade arrangements.

Second, the original commitments of the Rome Treaty implied that much of the substance of Article 113 would be concerned with trade in goods. But as the Internal Market has developed, and as global liberalisation has progressed, so the scope of the Community's external competence has extended into trade in services, again increased by the enlargement process. This has increased the complexity of the EC's external relations and the range of factors affected by Community actions.

Third, as Community competence has expanded into new policy areas, so the boundaries between external economic and political relations have become increasingly blurred. The use of trade sanctions and aid as foreign policy instruments has grown steadily. This has necessitated a convergence in member states' external policy perspectives and an acceptance, as part of the Maastricht Treaty that the EU should develop its own Common Foreign and Security Policy (CFSP).

THE IMPACT OF ENLARGEMENT ON EXTERNAL POLICY

New networks of external relations

Enlargement affects the external relations of the EC in four dimensions. First, new members bring their own networks of external relations, which need to be internalised into the Community system and reoriented towards Community goals. It thereby adds the interests of new members to the overall external policy mix. Here, as Pedersen has noted, enlargement debates are usually conducted on two levels.[2] The first 'adaptive' level is an explicit debate about the prospective member's capacity to absorb the acquis, whilst the second 'systemic' level concerns the overall external reorientation of the enlarged Community. For the first enlargement, the adaptive debate focused on Commonwealth and EFTA trade issues and how this would affect the EC's Common Commercial Policy, particularly in relation to agricultural trade. However, the systemic debate focused on how far UK membership would alter the EC's relations with the US and the EC's policy towards the developing countries. Enlargement did lead to the Lomé Convention promising trade and aid with the ACP countries, and to the upgrading of EC–EFTA relations through the 1973 Free Trade Agreement.

During the second and third enlargements, the adaptive debate concentrated on trade in Mediterranean agricultural produce, whilst the systemic debate focused on the EC's global Mediterranean policy. This encompassed the politico-strategic debate about security in the Eastern Mediterranean, about the possibilities of further enlargement (i.e. Malta, Cyprus and Turkey), and policy towards the Mahgreb and Mashreq countries. The need to upgrade EC relations with Latin America was also considered necessary.

During the fourth enlargement, the adaptive debate again concerned specific policy areas, such as agriculture and fisheries, whilst the systemic debate concerned the effect of integrating previously neutral states into the Union's developing CFSP. This was, in turn, linked to wider geopolitical concerns about stability in Central and Eastern Europe and the Baltic region.

Hierarchy of trade relations

The second effect of enlargement has been to reorder the EC's external relations into an informal hierarchy of preferential trading relations. Hine argues that within the EC's 'pyramid of privilege' preference is given to EFTA, which had the first comprehensive regional free trade agreement with the EC, subsequently upgraded into the European Economic Area.[3] The second position is occupied by potential EC members associated under Article 238. The scope of Article 238 is very wide and has been used as the framework for managing relations with diverse countries at different stages of economic development and with widely differing prospects of EC membership. The agreements usually involve a timetable for the reciprocal removal of trade barriers, though the EC usually reserves the right to determine the scope and pace of this timetable. In recent years, Association Agreements, such as the Europe Agreements with the

CEECs, have become more comprehensive, linking trade with political developments.

The next position in the hierarchy is occupied by agreements with near neighbours who are ineligible for full EU membership. The most significant of these are the North African and Middle Eastern countries of the Maghreb and Mashreq. The Mediterranean enlargement of the EC effectively reduced the value of the trade preferences that the EC had granted them. These agreements were renegotiated following enlargement. Similar considerations apply to the former states of the CIS, in particular Russia, Moldavia and the Ukraine, whose economic and political stability is critical to further Eastern enlargement of the EC.

Links with the developing states of the ACP, mainly the former colonies of France, Belgium, Holland and the UK, form the next step in the hierarchy which, through the Lomé convention, have guaranteed access to the EC market with no reciprocal tariff concession for EC imports. This hierarchy is a rough reflection of the economic importance of these different groups of countries to the EC and has developed in a piecemeal, incremental fashion through four enlargement rounds. Whilst the impact of preferential tariffs has been gradually reduced through successive rounds of GATT liberalisation, other trade measures, such as quotas and aid programmes, still confer variable levels of preference.

The EC in the international trading system

The third effect of enlargement is to increase the importance of the EC as an actor in the international trading system. Successive enlargements have increased the volume of intra-European trade as a proportion of world trade. This has had three major effects. First, the 'expansive logic' of enlargement suggests that, as the size of the trade group increases, so an increasing number of external actors are likely to seek preferential trade deals with it in order to reduce the trade diversion effects. Second, this may, even if unintentionally, push the world trading system into regional trading blocs. The growth of regional trade groups in the 1990s in North and South America and South East Asia suggests that this is a powerful force. Third, this growth in size has sensitised the EC's major trading partners to the EC's internal trade policy debate and to whether enlargement is likely, overall, to lead to a more liberal or protectionist external trade policy. In the late 1980s, these concerns shaped the EC's relations with the US and Japan, both of which were concerned that the internal liberalisation of the Single European Market could lead to an external 'fortress Europe' policy. The overall trade philosophy of new members, and the reshaping of internal coalitions resulting from enlargement, are significant factors for external trade partners.

Linkage between economic and political relations

The fourth effect of enlargement has been to increase the pressure for linkage between economic and political relations and to strengthen the diplomatic profile of the EU. For many years, the imbalance between the EC's trade weight and its political profile was a major feature of the debate on European integration. Yet the development of European Political Cooperation has been increasingly linked to trade issues, for instance, through the use of trade sanctions. The desire for a CFSP has emerged from the recognition that, in areas of major strategic interest to the EU, such as Eastern Europe, economic, political and security considerations overlap.

EXTERNAL POLICY AND THE FIRST ENLARGEMENT

The adaptation of the EC's external trade policies to take account of new members' interests is most clearly visible in the development policy field. At the founding of the EC in 1957, France and Belgium still had extensive colonies in Africa, imports from which France was unwilling to submit to the common external tariff. Since preferential trade with one EC member state was incompatible with the customs union, the founding members agreed to extend special treatment to imports from French colonies for a limited period. As colonies then became independent, they pressed the EC to continue their preferential access. These were aggregated into the Yaoundé Convention, signed in 1963. This was extended in 1970 until 1975. The British application for membership raised the issue of Commonwealth preference. The British accepted that the continuation of tariff-free import into the UK market was incompatible with full membership. Nevertheless, they insisted, using the French precedent, on special arrangements for Commonwealth developing countries.

The British Government offered three options to the African, Caribbean and Pacific Commonwealth countries. They could associate under a renewed Yaoundé Convention, under the Arusha Convention (similar to Yaoundé, but covering a more limited range of goods) or under a more limited trade and commercial agreement. The Asian Commonwealth countries of Bangladesh, India, Malaysia, Pakistan,

Singapore and Sri Lanka were not offered association, ostensibly because of their different economic structures. However, Hine argues that their inclusion would have diluted the association system too much.[4] In the event, they associated under an extended Yaoundé Convention and the enlarged EC then negotiated a new agreement.

THE LOMÉ CONVENTION

In 1973, the EC negotiated a new agreement with the twenty Commonwealth ACP countries and the existing Yaoundé Convention countries. The Lomé Convention ran from 1976 to 1980 when a second convention was negotiated until 1985. The second and third Lomé Conventions extend the agreements until the year 2000 and now cover sixty-four countries.

The main provisions of the Lomé Convention cover tariff preferences for nearly all ACP exports to the EC with no reciprocal tariff preferences demanded from them. Reduced levies on ACP export of Common Agricultural Policy products, export earnings stabilisation measures (STABEX and SYSMIN) and investment aid through the European Development Fund underpin the whole Convention. The package of measures was designed to integrate member states' responsibilities towards their former colonies within an overall Community framework. It was therefore an important component in the classical method in reviewing a policy area of particular importance to a new member state once accession had taken place.

Lomé has been much debated and often criticised for providing few tangible benefits to the ACP countries. Hine argues that the scope for trade creation under the Lomé Convention is now due to the complementary, rather than competitive, structure of EC–ACP economies. Where economies are competitive, for instance, in sugar production and trade, ACP exports earnings are constrained by the depression of world-market prices caused by the EC's subsidised exports of its own sugar-beet production.

The shape of the Lomé Convention reflected French and British post-colonial interests. These, however, have tended to reduce over time. Mediterranean enlargement eroded ACP preferential access, by giving Greece, Spain and Portugal unrestricted access for some competitive products, such as textiles and tobacco. The desire to upgrade links with Latin America, following Iberian accession, has also diluted the special status of the Lomé countries. Multilateral liberalisation through the GATT has also tended to reduce the value of the Lomé preferences and EC member states, such as Germany, have tended to argue in favour of a global approach to international trade. The fourth enlargement is likely to reinforce this trend, given the strong liberal trade stance of the former EFTA countries.

TRADE RELATIONS WITH NEAR NEIGHBOURS

Despite the importance of development policy raised by the first enlargement, greater emphasis has been placed on the EC's trade relations with its near neighbours. Here the distinction between potential full members and ineligible countries is critical, since it shapes the trade preferences granted and the extent of the economic adjustments expected from each partner. These issues are most clearly illustrated in the Mediterranean. The region has always been of economic and strategic importance, particularly to the EC's Southern members, and from the start of the EC a range of trade agreements were concluded. In 1958, Greece and Turkey applied for membership and, in 1961 and 1963 respectively, negotiated Association Agreements under Article 238, which envisaged a customs union and eventual, though undated, full membership. Other Association Agreements, with Morocco and Tunisia, reflected France's desire to retain its post-colonial links. Hine argues that, by the early 1970s, this 'mosaic' of trade agreements was in need of rationalisation.[5]

In 1972, the Commission proposed a global approach to the Mediterranean. The package eventually agreed and implemented in 1978, following strong opposition from EC agricultural interests, involved improved access for agricultural exports and tariff-free industrial access to the EC, with no reciprocity demand for the Mahgreb and Mashreq countries. Although the agreements improved access, they were far from uniform in terms of size and timing of tariff cuts and product coverage. They also make a clear distinction between potential EC members, of whom reciprocal concessions were expected, and the ineligible states.[6]

MEDITERRANEAN ENLARGEMENT AND EXTERNAL POLICY

These issues were brought into sharper relief by the two Mediterranean enlargements. It was widely acknowledged that Community preferences in agriculture would erode the benefits of the concessions granted to the Mahgreb and Mashreq countries. The free movements of workers within the enlarged Community was also recognised as affecting outsiders who had traditionally received remittances from immigrant workers. The Commission's Paper on enlargement noted:

There is no avoiding the fact that, as matters stand, the Community market's capacity to absorb its agricultural and industrial consumer goods, trade in which is important to the economies of some non-member countries, particularly in the Mediterranean region, will be limited. The agreements with these countries, however, are designed to promote trade for the benefit of both sides, and this objective will have to be pursued after enlargement.

It concluded that:

> The Community will, therefore, have to seek with these countries, parallel to the process of enlargement, a new equilibrium, based on active co-operation to permit orderly trade and to enable them to pursue their development with the support of the Community.[7]

Despite these intentions, enlargement did not lead to an improvement in the trade position of the Mediterranean non-members. The agreements with the Mahgreb and Mashreq were revised in 1986–87. Yet the share of these Mediterranean countries in the EC's external trade has not increased over the last twenty years. Tsoukalis notes the fundamental economic and political inequality of the relationship, exacerbated by the fact that the Mediterranean countries do not negotiate as a coherent group.

The EC has provided aid for restructuring to the region. Between 1973 and 1991, the Maghreb and Mashreq countries received 1,337 million ecu in budget funds. Mediterranean policy was overshadowed in the late 1980s and early 1990s by the shifting of the Community's focus to Northern and Eastern Europe. As the Mediterranean enlargement brought into the Community a group of states with specific regional interests, so EFTA enlargement brought to the fore trade and political issues with the liberalising economies of central Europe.

REVIVAL OF MEDITERRANEAN POLICY

However, renewed concern at instability in Northern Africa led Spain, France and Italy to push Mediterranean issues further up the EU's agenda in 1994 and 1995, and the Corfu Summit of June 1994 called on the Commission to re-evaluate the EU's global Mediterranean policy. The Commission proposed the creation of a Euro-Mediterranean Economic Area by the year 2010, encompassing reciprocal free trade in all manufactured products, preferential and reciprocal access for agricultural products, and free trade between the Mediterranean countries themselves. Given that none of the Mahgreb and Mashreq countries are possible candidates for EU membership (although Morocco applied and was rejected in 1987), EU policy has sought to upgrade the relationship but without eroding the benefits conferred on its own Mediterranean members.

The EC's Mediterranean policy demonstrates a key principle of the classical method: that there is a substantial difference in being an insider, which overrides the specific accession terms and the transition periods.

EC–EFTA RELATIONS

The development of the EC's policy towards EFTA reflects its position as the EC's major trading partner, its geographical contiguity and its position as the major provider of the EC's new members. EFTA has, therefore, been more intimately linked with the enlargement process. This has led to experimentation with new forms of partnership and more differentiated models of integration than has been the case with any other regional trading group. The accession of the UK and Denmark to the EC led to the conclusion of bilateral free trade agreements between the remaining EFTA countries and the EC. Thus, the adaptive debate focused on how to minimise trade diversion.

Trade between the two groups expanded considerably and for the following ten years no major systemic debate took place concerning the EC's relation with EFTA. The Greek accession raised the need for closer co-operation on transit arrangements with the Alpine countries in order to improve Greece's land links with the EC. The Iberian enlargement led to the extension of the free trade agreements to Spain and Portugal, though the effect of these was largely discounted by EFTA's 1980 preferential trade agreement with Spain.[8]

THE TWIN-PILLAR APPROACH AND THE STRUCTURAL DIALOGUE

This pragmatic approach was strengthened by the multilateral dialogue established under the 1984 Luxembourg process, though the European Commission's Single European Market White Paper considerably raised the stakes for EFTA. The Delors proposal in January 1989 to create a 'structured partnership' with EFTA based on the 'twin-pillar' approach was an attempt to reconcile different EC and EFTA objectives. Pedersen argues that, during this period, the Commission, supported by France and Germany, was developing a strategy of 'concentric circles' which would allow the EC to combine deepening and widening, with, at least in the short term, priority being given to the former.[9, 10]

The Commission was well aware that the 'spillover' effects of further integration would be felt most acutely in the EFTA countries. The complexity of the Internal Market-building process necessitated a more comprehensive regime than the Luxembourg process allowed if EFTA- and EC-based companies were not to be confronted by over-lapping regulatory regimes in the same *de facto* market area. However, the Commission was also aware that over-generous treatment of the EFTA countries would meet opposition from the Spanish who felt that their own accession negotiations had been very tough.

The EC's twin-pillar proposals, by expecting EFTA to replicate its own institutional structures, confirmed the extent to which the EC was the dominant regional power. It also reflected a general toughening of the EC external trade stance, pushing EFTA towards more explicit reciprocal concessions in return for Single Market access.

THE FAILURE OF THE EEA MODEL

The failure of the EEA (European Economic Area) to satisfy the longer term aspirations of most of the EFTA countries reflected the fundamental ambiguities in the twin-pillar model. It also reflects the growing rigidity, particularly as regards institutional and legal questions, of the EC during the negotiations. Pedersen argues that this was due to the internal pluralism of the EC leading to rigidity in external negotiations. He argues that requests for quasi-membership are more threatening to an organisation when some of its own members are less committed to integration. The perception of some member states, in particular France, that the strong support of the UK and Denmark for a more flexible relationship with EFTA reflected their own desire to loosen the membership rules, arguably pushed the EC into adopting a more uncompromising negotiating position. He states:

> An actor with a weak cohesion like the Union as we know it, will be forced to maintain a sharp demarcation line between members and non members of the unit. Otherwise new privileged partial membership arrangements risk reopening sensitive debates inside the regional unit.[11]

Whilst the EEA may have appeared as the pinnacle of the EC 'pyramid' of preference, particularly to those further from it, the outcome suggests that the gap between associates and full members is still real. The experiment in blurring the boundaries between the EC's internal and external policy domain is important in reinforcing the classical method. Full membership is still seen as a worthwhile goal, even if accession terms involve painful compromises.

THE EC IN THE WORLD TRADING SYSTEM

The third major effect of enlargement has been to increase the importance of the EC as an actor in the world trading system. The spillover effects of internal integration have therefore been more keenly felt by the EC's global trading partners as the EC's size has increased. Its partners have also become more acutely aware that new members are likely to push the enlarged EC towards a more liberal or protectionist trade stance. The following section, therefore, examines the impact of the enlarging EC on the GATT, protectionism and the regionalisation of trade.

THE EC AND THE GATT

The original Community of Six was established within the context of the GATT. Article XXIV of the GATT stated that a customs union could be considered compatible with the GATT so long as the CET was not to be 'on the whole higher or more restrictive than the general incidence of duties and regulations of commerce' than had been applied by the member states before the formation of the customs union. Thus the EC's external trade policies, including the potentially discriminatory preferential agreements, have been acceptable so long as they are, overall, more trade creating than diverting. The EC Six contributed actively to the early rounds of GATT tariff liberalisation. The Kennedy Round (1964–67) was stimulated largely by the desire of the US to prevent the EC's CET, due to be introduced at the end of the transitional period in 1969, from increasing overall levels of protection. Agriculture was left outside the scope of the GATT, thereby insulating the most protectionist of the EC's internal policy areas from external pressures for liberalisation.

The first enlargement brought in three new member states committed to liberal trading policies, and the Tokyo Round (1973–79) succeeded in further reducing tariff barriers. Despite its reservations about the CAP, however, the UK was in no position during the 1970s to fundamentally shift the EC's external trade policy.

The second and third enlargements brought in three states dependent on agricultural trade. Their integration was partially managed by externalising some of the effects on to third countries, in particular the Mediterranean and ACP associates. However, the Mediterranean enlargements did not lead to any overall increase in EC protectionism, in part because of the expanding global economy of the mid-1980s reducing the incentives of protectionism. Whilst the fourth enlargement increases the liberal trading coalition with the EU, the Union still retains some of the specific trade barriers, particularly against imports from Eastern Europe.

Whilst successive enlargements have, overall, strengthened the world's trading system, and not led to the erection of new trade barriers, by internalising a greater percentage of world trade, it may lower the cost of maintaining protectionism in specific, sensitive sectors, particularly during recessions.[12] Agriculture is the best example of this. Until the early 1990s, the agricultural lobby, strengthened by the Mediterranean enlargement, resisted both internal and external pressure for reform. However, pressure from the EU's trading partners, particularly the US, during the GATT Uruguay Round, has brought more fundamental changes to the CAP, which the prospects of further enlargement are likely to accelerate.

ENLARGEMENT AND PROTECTIONISM

Enlargement has also led the EC into the temptations of protectionism in other sectors, such as steel and textiles, where EC producers have, for a number of years, seen declining competitiveness against Third World producers. The EC steel regime involved imposing compulsory protection quotas on EC producers and voluntary export restraints on importers. The Spanish accession considerably increased the oversupply of steel within the EC during the sensitive period in the development of the EC's crisis regime. Although Spain accepted the EC's production quotas, the Spanish requested the maintenance of restrictions on special steel imports beyond the general tariff reduction period.

The Mediterranean enlargement also increased the Community's textile production, a sector where trade has been managed according to the Multifibre Agreement. All three countries had to accept the Community's bilateral agreements under the MFA, restricting access to the European market. The MFA, however, by retaining national market quotas, both fragments the European market, and makes it more difficult to agree a liberalisation policy at European level.

REGIONALISATION OF TRADE

Enlargement has also increased the trend towards the regionalisation of trade and towards the consolidation of American, European and Asian trade blocs. Whilst opinions differ as to how strong this trend is, moves in the EC towards widening and deepening have often caused the EC's major trading partners to respond.[13] Given that a large part of the economic rationale underpinning the initiative was to counter the threat from Japanese and US business, their response was to increase their investment within the EC, to ensure that they were treated as European companies. In sectors where protectionist pressures have always been high, such as the car industry, disputes have arisen over the minimum local content rules for the subsidiaries of Japanese car companies. Whilst these disputes have usually been resolved, they have heightened suspicions that the EC can only agree to new internal initiatives by discriminating against outsiders. This is linked to the classical enlargement principle that present members will use enlargement as a way of externalising their own disputes.

In 1991, the GATT reviewed the EC's external trade policies and concluded that, whilst the SEM had not, overall, raised new protectionist barriers, the EC still had a tendency to pursue sector specific initiatives, in areas such as coal, steel and cars.[14] GATT noted that the EC's decision-making system, in which the Council gives a mandate to the Commission, exacerbated this by tending towards lowest common denominator positions sustained by the more protectionist member states. The EC's negotiating position on agriculture, during the final stages of the GATT Uruguay Round, was largely derived from the protectionist policy of the French. Although the fourth enlargement increased the weight of the free trade lobby within the EU, increasing the size of the EU multiplies the range and complexity of special interests that have to be accommodated.

Similar dynamics can be seen in the Association Agreements negotiated with the Central and Eastern European countries. Whilst the Europe Agreements set out a framework for the achievement of bilateral free trade, they also maintained substantial protection for sensitive sectors, including textiles, coal, steel and agriculture. Even after the removal of tariffs, contingent protection measures such as voluntary export restraints could still be used.[15]

LINKS BETWEEN ECONOMIC AND POLITICAL RELATIONS

The fourth effect of enlargement has been to increase the pressure for more explicit linkage between the Community's external economic and political relations. As the EC's size has grown, so it has engaged in a wider and more complex set of global issues. However, whilst enlargement has increased the need for common action, the enlargement process has, at times, made this more difficult to achieve.

Since its earliest days, the EC has acknowledged that its economic power gave it political responsibilities. However, given the EC's specific external competences, these responsibilities were exercised outside the Rome Treaty framework. The first major initiative was linked to the EC's first enlargement. As part of the package deal on completion, further development and enlargement agreed at the 1969 Hague Summit, the Council asked its Foreign Ministers 'to study the best way of achieving progress in the matter of political unification, within the context of enlargement'. The resulting Luxembourg Report of 1970 set up the framework for European Political Co-operation, by establishing consultation mechanisms between EC foreign ministries.[16]

THE DEVELOPMENT OF EUROPEAN POLITICAL CO-OPERATION

European Political Co-operation (EPC) was a purely intergovernmental process designed to achieve better co-ordination of foreign policy positions. The structure reflected Pompidou's concern to retain his Gaullist credibility whilst supporting a European initiative. However the gradualism also found favour with the three applicant states who would not have supported a more integrationist framework.

The 1972 Paris Summit called for a second Report on this operation of EPC. The 1973 Copenhagen Report consolidated the gradualist, pragmatic, working methods of EPC.

Although the EPC framework was developed primarily to deal with 'high politics', such as the establishment of the CSCE and the war in the Middle East, member states were soon confronted with the need to link political and economic responses. The EC's response to the collapse of the Spanish and Portuguese dictatorships was handled primarily through the Community framework, given the trade and economic aid issues involved. There, EPC simply supported the overall direction of Community action. Further afield, particularly in Africa, the member states had more difficulty in finding common positions, given their widely differing historical experience on that continent.[17]

By 1978, the prospects of the Mediterranean enlargement led the EC to examine how EPC would need to be modified. Greek accession complicated EPC's discussion of Eastern Mediterranean issues, given Turkey's possible entitlement to ultimate EC membership. A compromise was eventually reached whereby Turkey would be informally consulted by the Presidency, accompanied by representatives of the past and future Presidencies. This troika formula was designed to deal with the problems created by a Greek Presidency.

The Greek accession also led the EC into incorporating EPC into the acquis, which the Greeks would be expected to adopt on accession. Whilst the collected texts of EPC did not have the legal force of the acquis derived from the Treaties, they became part of what, in the future, new members would be expected to accept.[18]

During the early 1980s, EPC sought to reconcile two tendencies. Some member states, in particular Germany and Italy, argued that the weaknesses of EPC, demonstrated in the weak reactions to the Soviet invasion of Afghanistan, necessitated a new Treaty on European Union, extending political co-operation into security policy. The British argued for modest procedural improvements incorporated in the 1981 London Report, in particular for an extension of the role of the troika. The German and Italian initiative led to the more ambitious Genscher–Colombo proposal for a European Act with a 'common foreign policy' as its ultimate aim. Yet, despite the high-mindedness of the Genscher–Colombo proposals, the reality of the enlarged EC's experience of EPC was very different. The Greek PASOK Government which took power in October 1981 was reluctant to adopt common positions. Under its first Presidency, in September 1983, Greece refused to condemn the USSR for the shooting down of the Korean airliner. In 1982, Greece had refused to support EC sanctions against Poland following the imposition of martial law. During successive initiatives on the Middle East, Greece refused to support EC initiatives. These idiosyncratic Greek positions were indicative of deeper flaws in EPC which further enlargement risked exacerbating.

The next major initiative to improve the integration of foreign policy was undertaken as part of the negotiations leading to the Single European Act. These negotiations were themselves linked to the need to improve the decision-making capability of the EC in the process of enlarging from ten to twelve member states. The possibility of bringing EPC within a single EC Treaty framework was key to the negotiations. The 1985 Milan European Council set up a Conference to examine

EC Treaty revisions, and called on the Political Committee of EPC to draft a Treaty concerning political co-operation with a view to a common foreign and security policy. The text eventually agreed did not markedly upgrade the commonality of EPC's decisions which were to remain strongly intergovernmental. Article 30, 3, for instance, provided that 'the High Contracting Parties shall, as far as possible, refrain from impeding the formation of a consensus in keeping with the majority opinion'.[19] Article 31 ensured that the jurisdiction of the European Court of Justice was not extended to EPC, thus avoiding the possibility that Community competence in external political relations might be extended, as in economic relations. Yet, by integrating EPC into the EC's legal framework, the member states opened the way for the further strengthening of the legal basis for a CFSP.

The 1991 intergovernmental conference (IGC) made further efforts towards integrating the foreign policies of member states by establishing a CFSP as one of the two non-Community pillars of the European Union. Articles J 1–10 of the Maastricht Treaty, defined the CFSP to 'include all questions relating to the security of the Union, including the eventual framing of a common defence policy, which might, in time, lead to a common defence'.

Between 1991 and 1993, Austria, Sweden and Finland all reviewed their neutrality policies in order to make them compatible with the objectives of the CFSP. Yet the effects of enlargement on the EU's external identity are more difficult to evaluate. Whilst it increases the profile of the EU in the international arena, the effectiveness of its actions depends on a real convergence in underlying perspectives on the issues affecting Europe. The complexity of the issue linkage and institutional overlaps between foreign, security and defence policies is formidable, and is unlikely to yield simple solutions for the near future.

CONCLUSION

As with the EC's internal policies, successive enlargements have expanded and strengthened the EC's external policy domain. The functional and geographical spillover effect, reinforced by the demands of Internal Market integration have pushed the Community to upgrade its common policy capability, particularly in trade. Here the powers conferred on the Commission under Article 113 have been given greater weight by the increasing number of member states on behalf of which the Commission negotiates. Again, as with internal policy, much effort has been made to improve horizontal linkages between policy areas to ensure greater consistency and co-ordination.

Links between trade policy and EPC leading to the CFSP have expanded the scope of Community activity, the salience of which is further increased as the EU enlarges.

Yet, beyond trade policy and its direct political implications, more traditional models of foreign policy endure. Member states have been reluctant to incorporate all their external relations with third parties into a Community framework. The creation of new pillars in the Maastricht TEU confirms this. Here enlargement has more ambiguous effects. The need to incorporate an increasing number of national perspectives into common positions risks rendering them ineffective. Fundamental dilemmas arise about the intergovernmental nature of the EU and how enlargement affects its capacity to act decisively. The role of institutional structures and processes is critical in implementing the EU's internal and external policies.

9   The impact of enlargement on the structure and processes of the EU

INTRODUCTION

The expansion of the EC from a membership of six to a Union of fifteen, with a queue of further applicants, is strong proof of the attractiveness of the EC/EU. Whilst the difficulties of reaching the accession threshold and the demands of adjusting to membership have often proved politically and economically challenging, most new members have been strongly committed to the further development of European integration. The investment of economic, diplomatic and human resources in the EC's institutions and decision-making processes, together with the internalisation of the EU's behavioural norms, has helped to create a durable regime whose basic institutional and legal structure has changed little since 1957. Despite concerns voiced at each enlargement that widening would be at the expense of deepening, momentum has been sustained, though at a variable pace, depending on the contextual factors outlined in earlier chapters.

This chapter therefore examines the effect that enlargement has had on the institutional structure and decision-making processes of the EC/EU. It argues that the adaptation of these structures and processes has been driven by the need to manage the more complex patterns of policy interdependence, outlined in the previous two chapters. The classical enlargement method ensures that the outcome of these adaptations is a compromise between maximalist and minimalist views of European integration. It further leads to different sets of reform priorities: those concerned with accountability and those concerned with effectiveness. The chapter then reviews the impact of each enlargement round on these issues and looks at the outcome of the reforms, concluding that the durability of the classical method limits the scope for radical reform.

INCREMENTAL CHANGE

The continuity in the basic legal framework of the EC partly conceals the extent of the incremental change in the EC's structures and processes that enlargement has caused. As the two previous chapters have shown, the EC has seen a steady expansion in both its internal and external policy domain, as areas of previously exclusive domestic responsibility have been penetrated by the EC policy, legislation and decision-making processes. This has led to more complex patterns of interdependence across policy areas and between member states. Horizontal linkages between policy areas, both internal and external, have increased. The process of moving from a customs union to a Single European Market and, possibly, to full European and Monetary Union, sensitises an increasing number of policy areas, as does linking external trade policy to the development of a common foreign policy. Vertical linkages between regional, national and European levels of decision making have also increased. EU structures and processes have become increasingly multidimensional.

Enlargement has necessarily increased the number of variables that impact on each other within this framework. Accepting new members with different policy priorities involves some degree of mutual adjustment in order to redefine the Community interest. Those national policy positions are, themselves, the outcome of complex bargaining with domestic groups who may themselves have transnational linkages. Managing this diversity within a coherent framework has become increasingly challenging for the EU.

For these reasons, the prospect of enlargement always stimulates a debate within the EU on institutional and decision-making reform. Much of this debate is not linked to the specific implications of a particular applicant or group of applicants acceding, but to more general concerns about the shape of the EU and its capacity to meet new demands. Moreover, this debate exposes a spectrum of different models of how the EU should adapt to increasing diversity.

MODELS OF DEVELOPMENT: 'MAXIMALISTS' AND 'MINIMALISTS'

At one extreme the maximalists argue that enlargement necessitates a qualitative shift in decision-making power from the national to the European level to ensure that the larger Union retains and enhances its cohesion. Its proponents argue for an increase in the powers of the European institutions, specifically the European Parliament and the Commission at the expense of those of the member states, and for bringing more policy areas within the scope of Community competence and decision-making systems.

This view has been most strongly supported in the Benelux states, Italy and Germany, though it has also been popular in the Mediterranean states. This position is linked to the concept of federalism which seeks to allocate powers to institutions and levels of government according to clearly stated constitutional principles.[1] Reform proposals have, therefore, tended to be radical and inclusive in terms of their effect on member states and their participation in European structures.

At the other extreme, minimalists argue that enlargement necessitates limited, incremental adaptation in order that the new and existing member states can make mutual adjustments in terms of new policy priorities and working methods. This 'intergovernmental' view argues that nation states are still the key actors in the EU and that any reforms resulting from enlargement should be pragmatic and specifically task related. This position has been most forcefully argued by the UK and has been supported by Denmark and occasionally by France.

EFFICIENCY AND EFFECTIVENESS

The institutional debate is also characterised by a conflict between principles which leads to different reform priorities. Two sets of issues are important here. The first concern the efficiency and effectiveness of the EU decision-making processes. The ever-expanding internal and external policy domains have raised concerns that the EU risks overload and that the complexity of its decision making and, increasingly important, implementation procedures, makes policy evaluation very difficult, thereby undermining the credibility of the whole integration process.[2] Enlargement exacerbates the problem by compounding the number of actors and interests involved. Reform proposals have therefore tended to focus on the internal working methods of the European Institutions and their inter-institutional linkages. The relationship with national governments and their officials (for instance in Council working groups), and external consultations with interested groups are considered critical. The debate over subsidiarity which emerged in the late 1980s, concerned with establishing principles for the assignment of task responsibilities to different governmental levels, is in large part a response to efficiency and effectiveness concerns.

REPRESENTATION AND ACCOUNTABILITY

The second set of issues concern representation and accountability. Here concern is focused on whose interests are being represented and whether the EU decision-making process is transparent enough to allow public and private interests to be balanced. This leads to a debate about how democratic accountability should be exercised. Federalists have tended to argue in favour of more direct supranational control, particularly through the European Parliament, with intergovernmentalists focusing on strengthening national Parliaments and their scrutiny of the Council of Ministers. The developing debate on how to close the democratic deficit is closely linked to these concerns. Again, enlargement complicates this debate, particularly since new members bring their own traditions of consultation and doctrines of accountability which have to be integrated into the EC/EU framework.

ENLARGEMENT AND INSTITUTIONAL REFORM

The reform debate stimulated by the prospects of enlargement incorporates elements of all the above factors. However, the outcome of the reform proposals varies considerably, depending on the contextual factors surrounding each enlargement round. The first enlargement saw only a limited debate on decision-making reform. However, the October 1972 Summit, which linked widening with deepening and called for European Union by 1980, stimulated a series of institutional reform proposals to underpin the commitment to political and economic union. The debate became more active in the late 1970s when the likelihood of Mediterranean enlargement presented the EC with the prospect of greatly increased diversity. Models of differentiated integration and integration became more openly discussed during this period. The debate in the mid-1980s, leading to the signing of the Single European Act, linked the effective implementation of the Single European Market to the enlarged Community.

The radically transformed geopolitical situation in the late 1980s, in opening up the EU to potentially much wider and more diverse groups of applicants, led to a renewed debate on institutional structures and processes, particularly following on from the Commission's Paper on enlargement to the Lisbon Council in June 1992. Though the EFTA enlargement sustained the institutional conservatism of the classical Community method, the EU has accepted, at least in principle, that it will have to tackle institutional reforms in order to facilitate further Mediterranean and East European enlargement.

Although the reforms actually implemented as a result of enlargement have been incremental and, from the maximalists' perspective, modest, they have, nevertheless, changed the character of the EU. The overall outcome has been that, whilst enlargement has decreased the power of individual member states, whatever their size, it has entrenched the power of member states acting collectively. The following sections explore how this has taken place.

THE INSTITUTIONAL FRAMEWORK OF THE EC/EU

The institutional and decision-making framework of the EU is set out in Part Five of the Treaties, which describes both the internal structures of the key Community institutions and the principles of inter-institutional relationships. The provisions of the Treaties themselves were a compromise between maximalist and minimalist models of how the Community should bring about the basic objectives outlined in Article 2, and the common tasks and policy areas set out in Article 3.

The central role of initiating and implementing policy within the areas of Community competence was given to the Commission. The Commission was given five main areas in which to exercise its authority.[3] First, as the proposer and initiator of new policies, given that the objectives of the Treaties are only broadly sketched out. Second, as the executive power to implement Treaty provisions, for instance, over external trade and CAP. Third, to act as guardian of the Treaties, to investigate possible infringements and refer cases to the Court of Justice if necessary. Fourth, to promote its policies by attending meetings of the Council of Ministers and, fifth, to represent the Community to non-member countries.

The Treaties also created a European Assembly. Composed at the outset by nominated members of national Parliaments, the Assembly had only limited powers to scrutinise, debate, give its opinion and vote on Commission proposals before they were forwarded to the Council. The Assembly also has the right, under Article 144, to dismiss the entire Commission, though it has never used this power.

Decision-making power was vested in the Council of Ministers, the Presidency of which was held by each member state for a period of six months (Article 146). The Treaties allowed for three types of voting arrangement in the Council, unanimity, simple or qualified majority. There is a presumption in favour of majoritarian procedures, since Article 148(1) states that 'save as otherwise provided in this Treaty, the Council shall act by a majority of its members'. Where qualified majority voting applied, a decision required twelve out of the total seventeen votes in the Council (see Appendix 1).

The Messina negotiators, building on the decision procedures of the ECSC, had to find a generalised voting system for the EC which satisfied two principles.[4] The first was that no single member state would be able to block a proposal, thereby moving away from the classical intergovernmentalism of bodies such as the OEEC. The second was that only certain combinations of states would be able to form a blocking minority. Under a single 50 per cent + 1 majority system, the three Benelux states, comprising less than half the population of any other state, could have formed a permanent blocking minority, which would have been quite unacceptable to the larger countries. The system eventually agreed was a hybrid with votes allocated degressively according to population size. Thus, the three large member states received twice as many votes as the smaller ones. Setting the voting threshold at twelve out of seventeen votes (71 per cent) avoided the danger of 'non-majorities' which did not constitute a majority of both member states and the Community's population. Minority and small-state interests were to be protected by the Commission acting independently. The strict QMV rule would apply only to proposals made by the Commission. Acting on its own initiative, the Council would have to achieve a QMV of weighted votes and a two-thirds majority of member states.

The original political bargaining underpinning the Treaty's institutional provisions incorporated both federal and intergovernmental concepts. The Assembly and, most importantly, the Commission, were established as supranational institutions. As well as giving them explicit legal powers, neo-functionalists also assumed that the Commission would become an increasing focus of elite loyalty, as the spillover process enhanced its credibility in the management of new joint tasks. Yet the power vested in the Council of Ministers was an indication of the central role that the founding governments continued to play. The QMV system was designed to ensure that the three largest member states retained effective control, though an alliance of two large and one smaller member state was enough to take a decision through the Council. This hybrid system also contributed to the development of the classical enlargement method. It ensured that only limited incremental adaptation would be acceptable during accession negotiations.

During the early years of the Community, the creative tension of this institutional process worked well. An active Commission, led by its President, Walter Halstein, supported by the member governments, extended the work of the Commission. However, in 1965, the Commission announced a package deal of measures which would have increased the powers of the Assembly and the Commission. The French Government considered that the Commission had overreached itself and boycotted the Community for seven months.

LUXEMBOURG COMPROMISE

The crisis led to the Luxembourg Compromise, which stated that, where decisions were taken by majority voting, the Council would endeavour to reach solutions acceptable to all where 'very important interests of one or more partners are at stake'.

The Compromise reinforced the intergovernmentalism of the Community's decision-making system, since the Commission's proposals had threatened to extend QMV across the whole of the Community's competences. Though a source of frustration to federal-ists, it, nevertheless, became an important part of the acquis. Paradoxically, it also later came to facilitate the enlargement process. By explicitly appealing to the right to defend the national interest in the Council, potential applicants such as the UK and Denmark were able to square full membership with their domestic political concerns about sovereignty more easily.

FIRST ENLARGEMENT

The Community's first enlargement did not activate a major debate about institutional questions consistent with the classical method. It was agreed early in the negotiations that the UK should be represented in the institutions in the same proportion as France, Germany and Italy. Thus the Commission was expanded to fourteen members, with the UK having two Commissioners and thirty-six members of the European Parliament.

In the Council, with the UK having ten votes, and Ireland and Denmark three each, the principles of preventing a single member state, or Benelux bloc, veto, were retained. Two large states could still form a blocking minority, though a single large state needed both Belgium and the Netherlands for such a block. The negotiations also sought to introduce two further principles into Council voting. First, that the four applicants (including Norway) should have a collective veto over the other six, in order to reduce the possibility of their being isolated in the Council and, second, that the five smaller states (excluding Luxembourg) should also be capable of forming a blocking minority. However, these last two principles were never implemented after the rejigging of voting weights following Norway's withdrawal. In the event, the original six had their voting weight multiplied by 2.5 (with the exception of Luxembourg whose weight only doubled). Though the threshold was maintained at 71 per cent, the increase in the Council's size strengthened the tendency to maintain the status quo since more member states would be needed to form a blocking minority.

The first enlargement had been part of a package deal that also included a commitment to deepening. So, whilst enlargement had been negotiated according to classical principles, it opened up the need for more extensive decision-making reforms. The October 1972 Summit had committed the member states to an ambitious plan to create a European Union by 1980. These plans were reaffirmed at Copenhagen (December 1973) and Paris (December 1974), which called for reports from the institutions on how these objectives could be achieved. The Council also called on Leo Tindemans, the Belgian Prime Minister, to prepare a separate Report on European Union.

THE TINDEMANS REPORT

Published in 1976, Leo Tindemans' Report was an unequivocal statement of the maximalist position. It argued for a comprehensive reform of both common policies and institutional structures since 'in this vast scheme everything goes together and it is the sum of the progress achieved in parallel which constitutes the qualitative change which is European Union'.[5] The Report called for a 'single decision-making centre' for external relations with an end to the distinction between discussions of Political Co-operation and Treaty matters, and to the development of a common foreign policy. The Report also identified the need to strengthen the institutions according to the criteria of authority, efficiency, legitimacy and coherence. It proposed that the Parliament, following direct elections, should have a legal right of initiative, that the Commission should 'reassert its freedom of action' and make greater use of Article 155, and that the Council should normally use majority voting, even on common foreign policy matters.

The uncompromisingly federalist tone of the Tindemans Report did not find favour with enough member states and, although it appeared on European Council agendas for several years, it was never discussed by heads of government. The accession of the UK and Denmark, both concerned about the sovereignty issue, further reinforced this.

MEDITERRANEAN ENLARGEMENT AND INSTITUTIONAL REFORM

Institutional reform, however, was never far from the surface, and it was once again raised in the 1977 Papers prepared by the Commission in preparation for Mediterranean enlargement.[6] In the Paper the Commission recognised that the greater heterogeneity of the enlarged Community would impose strains on the institutional structure designed for only six members. However, as was the case with its analysis of economic and sectoral issues, its institutional proposals also attempted to combine increasing operational flexibility with the maintenance of political cohesion within the existing Treaty framework.

The Commission argued for a broader interpretation of Article 237 (concerning Treaty adjustments on enlargement) than had been the case in 1973. In terms of numerical representation, the Commission reaffirmed the basic principle that all member states must be represented in all the institutions. For the Parliament, though its numbers would increase to 516, the Commission argued against altering the distribution of seats among the existing nine member states.

For the Council, assuming Spain was allocated eight votes, Greece and Portugal five, the Commission proposed setting the QMV threshold at fifty-one, out of seventy-six votes. The Commission argued that this would maintain the existing power balance between large and small states, since the four large countries and Spain would still not form a qualified majority. Conversely, two large member states would still need the support of at least one smaller member state to form a blocking minority.

Rather than reopen the dispute over the Luxembourg Compromise, the Commission proposed the pragmatic extension of majority voting into areas where no vital national interests were at stake. The Commission identified the approximation of laws and technical standards under Article 100 as the key area for such voting, though it recognised that tax legislation, under Articles 99 and 100, would still need to be subject to unanimity. These proposals, therefore, identified some of the procedural reforms that were later linked to the implementation of the Single European Market.

SECOND ENLARGEMENT

The global approach outlined in the Commission paper was pre-empted by the Council's decision to open accession negotiations with Greece before those with Spain and Portugal. The 'fast track' negotiations effectively bypassed the emerging internal Community reform debate. As with other aspects of the acquis, the Greeks were helped by their relatively small size, yielding them five votes in the Council and twenty-four seats in the European Parliament (directly elected since June 1979). The classical method prevailed. The institutional adjustments necessary for a Community of ten had already been identified for Norway during the first enlargement negotiations, and therefore raised no major issues of principle.[7] By setting the QMV threshold at forty-five out of sixty-three votes, it did, however, revive the two 1973 principles of a veto for the five small states and for the four new members.[8]

THE REVIVAL OF REFORM PLANS

The late 1970s and early 1980s were a period of gridlock in the EC's development. The problems in redefining the agricultural acquis to cope with Spanish and Portuguese accession, together with the long-running UK budget dispute, made radical reform improbable. Yet there was a continuing awareness that reform was unavoidable if Mediterranean enlargement was not to prevent the Community from taking on new collective tasks.

THE GENSCHER–COLOMBO INITIATIVE

In November 1981, the German and Italian Governments presented a Report to the EC heads of government, drafted by their Foreign Ministers. The Genscher–Colombo initiative called for a 'solemn declaration', referred to as the European Act, to closely co-ordinate foreign and security policies. It also sought to formalise the role of the European Council which had grown up outside the Treaty framework, to strengthen the role of this European Parliament in policy review and decision making, and to make more use of majority voting in the Council.

The Genscher–Colombo initiative led to the June 1983 Stuttgart 'solemn declaration on European Union', which, while calling for increased co-ordination and development between the European institutions, was unspecific as to how and when these could be achieved. At the same time, the European Parliament, under the leadership of the

Italian former Communist MEP, Altiero Spinelli, put forward a comprehensive plan for a federal European Union. The powers of the Commission and the Parliament would be enhanced, with the Commission having the power to implement and prepare the budget, and to oversee the implementation of the proposed Union Treaty. The Parliament would have joint legislative powers with the Council of the Union (formerly the Council of Ministers) which would make more extensive use of majority voting. The plan formed the basis of the Draft European Union Treaty which was adopted in February 1984 by the European Parliament.

Despite the scepticism of many of the member states about the more overtly federalist proposals, by 1984, it was clear that real momentum for reform was building up. French President Mitterrand, (in his capacity as President of the European Council) had indicated his willingness to the European Parliament to consider its Draft Treaty on European Union. Accession negotiations with Spain and Portugal were reaching their most critical stage, and agreement on institutional reform could be included as part of the package. Following the breakthrough on the UK budget issue at the Fontainbleau Summit in June 1984, the Council agreed to establish the Committees to explore how the renewed commitment to deepening could be reconciled with the impending accession of Spain and Portugal.

The Committee on a People's Europe (the Adonino Committee) explored ways to promote a common European identity. More importantly, the Ad Hoc Committee on Institutional Affairs, under the chairmanship of the Irish Senator Jim Dooge, was established to explore ways of ensuring that the more ambitious goals of the EC were supported by an appropriate institutional framework.

The Dooge Committee, which reported in March 1985,[9] proposed that the Council should use majority voting in all areas, except new areas or new accessions, that the Commission should have only one member from each country, that its power of initiative and implementation should be enhanced, and that the Parliament should be given joint decision-making power with the Council. The Committee also called for the convening of an intergovernmental conference (IGC) to consider the reform package and the Treaty amendments it would necessitate.

All of these reform proposals were taken in the light of impending Iberian enlargement. Although the classical method insulated the accession negotiations from these wider reform debates, applicants and member states were fully aware of their longer term implications.

MILAN SUMMIT

The June 1985 Milan Summit was critical in taking forward both the development of the acquis and institutional reform. The heads of government unanimously endorsed the White Paper on the liberalisation of the Internal Market, presented by the new UK Commissioner, Lord Cockfield. There was little agreement, however, on how far decision-making reform was necessary. The French, German and Italian governments were looking for a bold initiative which would build on the Dooge Committee's recommendations. The UK Government, though aware that Internal Market liberalisation and enlargement required some procedural reforms, was sceptical as to how far this necessitated Treaty amendments.[10]

In the event, the Italian Presidency forced a vote in the European Council in which it was agreed to set up an IGC to consider the tabled reform packages. Though Denmark, Greece and the UK opposed the vote, they agreed to participate in the proposed conference in order to avoid isolation. Prime Minister Thatcher, in particular, was sensitive to the possibility of being left in the second tier of the two-speed Europe to which Mitterrand had alluded to in his speech to the European Parliament in May 1984.[11] Despite the maximalist rhetoric of the Milan Summit, the actual negotiations over the SEA favoured a minimalist strategy. Moravscik argues that this happened in three stages. First, the negotiations blocked significant reform in areas not directly connected to the Internal Market. Second, they obstructed the extension of majority voting to contentious Internal Market issues, social and fiscal regulation for instance, and third, they offset limitations on the use of the national veto with exemptions and safeguard provisions.[12]

Most of the serious negotiations were undertaken in the autumn of 1985 and focused on voting procedures under Article 100 in relation to Internal Market liberalisation. All the member states sought safeguards against the possibility of being outvoted. Whilst Article 100A states that measures relating to the Internal Market should normally be considered using QMV, Article 100(4) allows states outvoted in the Council to invoke a safeguard clause to retain national regulations 'on grounds of major needs' under Article 36, so long as the Commission has first verified that the national measure is not a 'disguised restriction' to trade. At the Luxembourg Summit in December 1985, the heads of government resolved the final details of the package which also included a 'co-operation' procedure with the Parliament, giving the European Parliament limited additional powers of decision making. Following a delay for a Danish referendum on the Treaty amendments in February 1986, the Single European Act was implemented on 1 January 1987.

The outcome of the SEA was an intergovernmental bargain on how to achieve deepening and widening together. Spain and Portugal were party to the negotiations even before they were full members and argued strongly for cohesion measures as the price of their support. Despite the acrimony of the accession negotiations, they wished to appear as 'good Europeans' and therefore strongly supported the Single European Act. Although the maximalists were disappointed that the reforms were incremental and linked to Internal Market issues only, the package was seen as a success, given the chequered history of Community reform. The key factor was the 'preference convergence'[13] of the major EC actors. The British Government's agreement to Treaty amendments was critical. Mrs Thatcher was persuaded that majority voting was necessary to overcome the resistance of protectionist states, Greece in particular, to measures which favoured UK economic interests and which were consistent with her programme of domestic deregulation. The failure of the French Socialist Government's experiment of pursuing protectionist economic policies in the early 1980s led Mitterrand to take a more positive view of pan-European economic initiatives. The German Government strongly favoured improved market access. This convergence was exploited by the new Commission led by Jacques Delors, who created a package of measures which would be acceptable to the key member states.

IMPLICATIONS OF THE SEA

Despite the limited incremental nature of the SEA, its implications for EC decision making and 'inter'-institutional relations have been far reaching. When acting under QMV, the Council most closely resembles a 'supranational entity in the sense of being an authoritative decision maker above the nation-state'.[14] The elimination of the single member state veto allows the Council to move beyond lowest common denominator bargains. Budden and Monroe argue that this affects the role of both the Commission and Parliament.[15] The Commission is able to play a more constructive role in the bargaining process when it does not need to cater for a hard core of minority views in the Council. The QMV rule has also allowed the European Parliament, through the co-operation procedure, to integrate itself into the decision-making system. If the European Parliament can persuade the

Commission to accept its amendments to Commission proposals, then only a qualified majority of Council members is needed to accept the revisions. The European Parliament can, therefore, promote a 'maximalist' agenda pitched at only the minimum winning coalition in the Council.

THE SINGLE EUROPEAN MARKET AND QMV

The enormous volume of legislation necessitated by the 1992 deadline for implementing the Internal Market led to a considerable increase in the use of the QMV procedure. Wessels notes that already in 1986, in anticipation of the SEA, the Council used QMV on ninety-three occasions, ninety-six in 1987, seventy-eight in 1988 and sixty-one in 1989. Wessels explains the decline over that three-year period as part of the 'learning process by which member governments in minority positions, realise that they might gain at least some minor points if they agree to the total package'.[16]

This suggests that the most far-reaching effect of the SEA has been the way in which the QMV rule has been 'internalised' by member states' officials in the Council's working groups. The possibility of a proposal being put to a vote leads to a more active search for compromise at an earlier stage. This suggests that widening is not necessarily at the expense of deepening, so long as appropriate decision-making reforms are implemented.

Despite the conventional wisdom that enlargement slows down the decision-making system, the evidence, at least from the late 1980s, suggests that this is not always the case. Sloot and Verschuren[17] concluded that, from 1975 to 1986, there was a decrease in the time lag of decision making of over 30 per cent, with the adoption rate increasing from 75 per cent to 90 per cent over the same period, though this may be due to the increased sophistication of officials in working an increasingly complex machine.

However, the preference convergence underpinning the Internal Market programme could not be sustained indefinitely. By the early 1990s, decision-making and institutional issues were again being discussed within the EC. The SEA called for a further IGC to review the prospects of monetary and political union. However, by the time the Conference convened in Maastricht in December 1991, the geopolitical situation in Europe had already changed dramatically. Whilst there was a realisation that the structures and processes of the EC would have to respond, there was no consensus as to what that response should be. The IGC therefore focused on the timetable for

EMU, and for institutional issues, some minor incremental developments of the provisions of the SEA.

By this time Malta, Cyprus, Austria and Sweden had already applied for full EC membership, with the expectation that further EEA members would apply soon. As well as the commitment to open enlargement negotiations as soon as the EC had completed its own resources negotiations in 1992, the Council asked the Commission to present a paper to the Lisbon Council in June 1992, on the implications of enlargement.

COMMISSION PAPER: THE CHALLENGE OF ENLARGEMENT

By 1992, the possibility of a twenty- or even thirty-member Community was stimulating a more active debate on possible institutional reforms. The Commission's Lisbon paper[18] identified safeguarding the Community's effectiveness as a key priority and called for a less comprehensive and detailed programme of legislation for the Parliament and Council, a more 'balanced attribution of tasks' to regional, national and Community levels, and a clearer distinction between responsibility for decision and implementation. The Commission also raised three sets of questions, in relation to improving the preparation of decisions, ensuring that the number of actors (in particular the number of MEPs and Commissioners) is appropriate to the tasks, and that decisions are taken in an equitable manner, in particular relating to voting weights and the QMV threshold in the Council. The Commission reaffirmed the classical principle that enlargement to a limited number of new members could proceed on the basis of the limited institutional adaptations necessary under Article O (accession procedure of Maastricht Treaty). However, there was no political will amongst member states to put enlargement on hold whilst further deepening took place.

THE FOURTH ENLARGEMENT AND INSTITUTIONAL REFORM

Despite the agreement to negotiate the four-state EFTA enlargement on the basis of the existing institutional system, political tensions threatened to impinge on the classical method of accession negotiations. The March 1994 crisis over the QMV threshold exposed deep underlying disagreements in the Council, particularly concerning the balance of power between large and small states. Giving Council voting weights of four to Sweden and Austria and three to Finland

and Norway, and maintaining the QMV threshold at 71 per cent, would have set the QMV threshold at sixty-four out of ninety votes. However, this threshold would have increased the conservatism of the voting system, requiring more member states to form a blocking minority. The UK position, supported, at least initially by Spain, was that the threshold should remain at sixty votes, thereby decreasing the threshold to sixty-six per cent and retaining a closer fit between voting weight and population size. The Ioannina Compromise, invoking a 'reasonable delay' whilst the Council Presidency seeks compromise if a veto block of between twenty-three and twenty-seven is achieved, was simply a short-term move to meet UK concerns, mainly shaped by internal political considerations. The compromise reinforced the classical method by refusing to undertake major institutional reforms during enlargement negotiations.

The eventual non-accession of Norway and the re-casting of the QMV threshold at sixty-one votes, retained the existing 71 per cent threshold. However, this still left a bias in favour of small states, made more pronounced by the unification of Germany in 1990, adding sixteen million to its population with no increase in its weighted Council vote. Furthermore, on procedural issues where a simple unweighted majority is adequate, for instance, on calling an IGC, the eight smallest states could carry a vote while representing a minority of the EU's population.

In practice, there are far fewer coalitions in the Council than the range of theoretically possible combinations would suggest. Though member states may divide up into different subgroups depending on the issues at stake, most of the coalitions are usually quite predictable.[19] For instance, they include the Mediterranean states and Ireland over Structural Funds and cohesion issues; and the Benelux states, Germany and the UK, reinforced now by the three former EFTA states, over free trade issues. Proposals are therefore shaped accordingly at an early stage in the decision-making process in order to avoid provoking a Council vote on a politically contentious issue, though the occasional isolation of a single member state, for instance as happened to the UK over social policy, is an unavoidable consequence of using the weighted voting system to promote Community action in new areas.

CONCLUSION

Enlargement and systemic conservatism

Although enlargement has not, so far, paralysed the Council, the increase in systemic conservatism resulting from four enlargements could, itself, make institutional reform more difficult. The incrementalism of the classical method, though useful in strictly delineating accession negotiations, impedes strategic thinking. Creating a coalition in favour of reform which, in pursuit of greater efficiency, would almost certainly necessitate greater use of majoritarian procedures, would involve some of those coalition members accepting the possibility of being outvoted. Whilst the ten member states (supported by the two applicants) were able to achieve this with the SEA, the larger EU makes this more difficult to achieve again. The problem is compounded when institutional reform is linked to substantial reform of the acquis, particularly in sensitive areas such as structural spending where net recipients presently have enough votes to block major reforms.

Enlargement has, therefore, heightened the tension between the 'majoritarian demand for efficiency and the minoritarian claim for conservatism'[20] in the Council. This tension has brought into sharper focus the widening democratic deficit in the Community, brought about by the increasingly complex and opaque decision-making procedures in the Council, and the lack of effective scrutiny from national parliaments and the EP. Enlargement also brings into the EU process different styles and traditions of democratic accountability. Yet, despite the accession of EFTA states with a strong reputation for open government, there is increasing concern that the EU policy process risks losing legitimacy. Member states' governments mostly focus their concern on how voting weights and thresholds in the Council might affect their domestically based democratic mandate. The European Parliament's concern focuses on using its own direct mandate to improve democratic control by increasing its own powers of scrutiny over legislation and budget matters. These two sources of legitimacy are, to a large degree, in conflict, a situation which four enlargement rounds have compounded.

Part III

Future enlargements

10 Further Enlargements: Eastern Europe

INTRODUCTION

The EC's classical method of enlargement, the adaptation of its internal and external policies, and its institutional structures and decision-making processes, have all been thrown into sharp relief by the geopolitical changes in Eastern Europe. The collapse of the Soviet Union and its power over the former COMECON and Warsaw Pact states has profoundly altered the dynamics of European integration and the possible future shape of the EU. From being an exclusively Western European organisation, based on the core economies of West Germany and France, with an institutional framework and set of policy priorities reflecting their preferences, the EC is now confronted with the possibility of more profound changes and a rediscovered role to consolidate political and economic stability throughout the region. The response of the EU, initially offering aid and some trade liberalisation leading to Associate status and, more recently, the possibility of eventual full EU membership, means that the size of the EU could expand dramatically. By December 1995, the EU had concluded or initialled ten Europe Agreements which explicitly acknowledge the possibility of accession. However, the implications for both the EU and potential applicants have only begun to be considered.

This chapter therefore examines these changes, their implications for the EU and particularly the classical enlargement method. It examines, first, the initial response of the EU to the changes in Eastern Europe in the late 1980s. Second, the creation of Europe Agreements in the early 1990s is analysed, arguing that they are asymmetric. Third, following the acceptance that some countries in Eastern Europe will become full EU members, the EU's 'pre-accession strategy' is examined. It concludes with a review of the implications for the EU and its classical enlargement method, and argues that extensive policy adaptation is necessary if further enlargement is to take place.

1986–91: INCREMENTAL RESPONSE TO CHANGE IN EASTERN EUROPE

Until the mid 1980s, relations between the Communists and Eastern Europe were cool. The USSR under Brezhnev refused to recognise the EC officially and, with several exceptions, notably Romania, who concluded a general trade agreement with the EC in 1980, the East European countries complied with Soviet policy. During the 1970s the USSR had started to adopt a slightly more constructive attitude to the EC and wished to develop trade links through COMECON. The EC was reluctant, since doing so would effectively recognise Soviet hegemony over Eastern Europe. Talks failed to make progress, since neither side had strong enough real economic interests at stake. Soviet exports to the EC averaged 1 to 2 per cent of Soviet GDP and comprised mainly oil, gas and other primary products, most of which were outside the scope of the EC's commercial policy.[1] EC trade with COMECON was at about the same level. The East European countries, themselves, were more dependent on trade with the EC, imports from which averaged 5–10 per cent of their GDP. About half their manufacturing exports to the EC, in particular textiles, footwear and steel, met Community tariffs and quotas. Although the EC negotiated some modest trade liberalisation with Yugoslavia, leading to a co-operation agreement in 1980, overall EC–East Europe relations were blocked by larger geopolitical concerns, such as the Soviet invasion of Afghanistan and the imposition of martial law in Poland in 1981.

The first major change occurred when Gorbachev accepted that COMECON members should be able to negotiate their own trade agreements with the EC. In 1986, negotiations between the EC and COMECON were opened, though they proceeded slowly, in parallel with bilateral trade negotiations with the East European countries themselves. However, by June 1988 the EC and COMECON recognised each other's diplomatic status and, by December 1988, the EC's first trade and co-operation agreement with Hungary came into force. This was followed by similar agreements with Poland (December 1989), the USSR (April 1990), Czechoslovakia and Bulgaria (November 1990), and Romania (March 1991). The GDR opened negotiations but these were overtaken by unification and, hence, in effect, full integration into the EC.

TRADE AND CO-OPERATION AGREEMENTS

The trade and co-operation agreements were an important stage in the development of EC assistance towards the transformation process. For trade, the agreements negotiated for ten years (except for Poland's which was for five years) covered all goods except those coming under the ECSC Treaty. This, as Pinder notes, was a device to keep steel and Polish coal out of the agreements.[2] The EC also maintained its textile quotas under the MFA and only granted limited tariff reductions for agricultural products. The real significance of the negotiations was the agreement to a timetable for the removal, in phases up to 1995, of EC quotas on imports from Eastern Europe. The process started with the least sensitive and moved to the most sensitive products. This process was buttressed by 'safeguard clauses', designed to protect EC producers in sensitive product markets.

The 'co-operation' element in the agreements was less precise and included lists of areas such as health and the environment, education and vocational training with which the East Europeans needed support. However, though the member states provided substantial bilateral aid to the East Europeans, they were reluctant to grant the EC exclusive competence in this field. The agreements were therefore concluded under both Article 113 and Article 235, which allow the Council, voting unanimously, to take specific measures to achieve Community objectives where the Treaty does not provide the necessary powers. The agreements, though useful, were piecemeal and were seen as barely adequate for the scale of the economic and political issues they confronted.[3]

The rapid pace of change in Central Europe in 1989 and 1990, in particular the liberalisation process in Poland, Hungary and Czechoslovakia, and the fall of the Honeker regime in the GDR, called for a more active EC policy towards the region. The prospect of unification led Germany to give a high priority to securing regional stability. In 1989, the G24 countries invited the European Commission to co-ordinate aid to the countries of Eastern Europe. At the same time the EC established the PHARE programme, designed to support the reform process in the recipient states. The programme was initially targeted at Hungary and Poland and was allocated 500 million ecu from the EC's 1990 budget. The programme's coverage was quickly extended to Romania, Bulgaria and Yugoslavia in mid-1990, to Albania and the Baltic States in December 1991, and to Slovenia in summer 1992. The overall budget allocation was raised to 785 million ecu in 1991 and to one billion ecu in 1992. The PHARE programme was further supported by G24 aid for balance of payments stabilisation measures, debt relief and the establishment of the European Bank for Reconstruction and Development. By July 1992, the total amount of aid to the region added up to 46.9 billion ecu.[4]

1991–1993: ECONOMIC AND POLITICAL ENGAGEMENT AND THE NEGOTIATION OF 'EUROPE AGREEMENTS'

As early as 1990, it was becoming clearer that the scale of the transformation process required a more broadly based response from the EC. In August 1990, the Commission had proposed to the Council that 'second generation' association agreements should be negotiated with Czechoslovakia, Hungary and Poland, and eventually with other countries.[5] The proposal of these new upgraded agreements reflected the development of Commission thinking concerning the architecture of the new Europe. The objective of the phased economic and political integration of the states of Eastern Europe fitted with the emerging debate of a Europe of concentric circles, which underpinned the development of the EEA concept for the EFTA states.

The Europe Agreements, negotiated first with Poland and Hungary, extended beyond the scope of traditional association agreements in making provision for political and cultural dialogue, and co-operation. They introduced an element of economic and political conditionality by linking implementation to the 'actual accomplishment of political, economic and legal reforms' in the partner country.

CONTENT OF THE EUROPE AGREEMENTS

The core of the Europe Agreements (EAs) is the commitment to create a free trade area over a ten-year period, divided into two periods. The EU is committed to removing its trade barriers faster than the partner countries remove theirs, though the actual timetables and the sectors to which they apply vary with each agreement, largely depending on the sensitivity of the products involved. The EU agreed to abolish all tariffs by the beginning of 1995, with the exception of the 'sensitive' products. The agreements are, therefore, to some degree asymmetric. Duties on coal and steel were to be phased out by the beginning of 1996, and duties on textiles by the end of 1996. Remaining quantitative restrictions on textiles should be eliminated by the end of 1997. Thus far, the EAs consolidated the objectives of the earlier trade and co-operation agreements though extending the liberalisation process.

The agreements mostly exclude agricultural trade from liberalisation, since their provisions state explicitly that the EAs should 'not restrict in any way' the agricultural policies of either the EU or the CEECs.

The agreements also look forward to the gradual realisation of the further three freedoms of services, capital and people. However, the provisions reflect the desire of the CEECs to protect their infant service industries and of EU members to keep their labour markets closed. The right of establishment for EU firms was initially restricted to the industrial sector, whereas the free movement of workers from the associated countries is proscribed in the first five-year period. Some free movement of capital is permitted, in particular payments arising from the movement of goods, services and people, and capital transfers concerning direct investments. CEEC companies are able to bid for EU public procurement contracts.

The EAs make provision for the alignment of and approximation of laws in the CEECs to EU norms. Priority was given to competition and state aid rules and the CEECs agreed to introduce provisions similar to those in the Treaty of Rome within three years of enforcing the interim agreements. Protection of intellectual, industrial and commercial property is provided for within five years. The agreements also provide for extensive economic co-operation in promoting structural industrial change, participation in Community research programmes, and support for the energy, environmental and telecommunications sectors. The agreements institutionalise a political dialogue on more broad-ranging European issues, including CSCE matters. A ministerial level Association Council, Committee and Parliamentary Association Committees were created. This dialogue began under the interim agreements, before the full agreements took effect.

LIMITATIONS OF THE EUROPE AGREEMENTS

Although the Europe Agreements upgraded relations between the EU and the CEECs, they have fallen short of expectations, in terms of their content, the manner of their negotiation and in aspects of their implementation. First, many of the key provisions of the agreements are protectionist. The limitations imposed on 'sensitive' agricultural products, steel, coal and textiles are precisely those in which the CEECs have a comparative advantage, and on which international trade theory suggests export-led growth should be based. Second, EAs are bilateral agreements, rather than being part of a larger multilateral regional trade framework. Whilst this allows the diversity of the CEECs to be reflected in the specific content and timetables of their agreements, it reinforces the tendency towards 'hub and spoke' bilateralism.[6] Individual CEECs are encouraged to trade only with the EU rather than with each other, given the persistence of intra-regional trade barriers, which can lead to problems for rules of origin and cumulation, and therefore possible trade diversion. The attempts to create a Central European Free Trade Area (CEFTA) and a Baltic Free Trade Area recognise the dangers of this bilateralism, though the trade weight of the EU reduces incentives for enhanced intra-regional co-operation.[7]

The negotiation of Association Agreements by the Commission and concluded by the Council voting unanimously under the Article 238 procedure, leaves the Commission with limited room for manoeuvre with potential associates.[8] The national veto over such an agreement also makes negotiations vulnerable to special interest groups in EU member states.[9] The associates' lack of diplomatic resources makes this kind of lobbying difficult to resist. Furthermore, the use of 'mixed' agreements incorporating elements of both Community and national competence, has meant that the agreements have also had to be ratified by each of the member states' parliaments, further increasing the strength of domestic lobbying groups. Though the trade provisions of the agreements were implemented more speedily, using Interim Agreements negotiated under the Article 113 procedures (allowing the use of QMV in the Council), the formal ratification procedures for the full agreements were very slow. Hungary's and Poland's agreements were only implemented in February 1994, more than two years after they had been signed. The slow development of the political dialogue has also created problems. Though informal meetings took place before the full agreements were implemented, these were confined to exchanges of information with little opportunity for the CEECs to negotiate seriously.

The limitations imposed on the EAs by member states' concerns about imports from the CEECs, together with their limited capacity to cope with full integration, were well recognised by the Commission. In its paper on enlargement to the Lisbon Council, the Commission acknowledged that:

> the countries which are not yet in a position to accept the obligations of membership have political needs that go beyond the possibilities of existing agreements. They desire the reassurance that they will be treated as equal partners in the dialogue concerning Europe's future.[10]

The Commission pushed for building on the existing architecture in order to create a 'European political area'.

Already by 1993, the EU was under increasing pressure to set out its policy on the further enlargement to the East even before the enlargement negotiations were completed. The limitations implicit in the EAs were already starting to frustrate some of the CEECs, in particular the Visegrad Group, of the Czech and Slovak Republics, Hungary and Poland, who in the Copenhagen Declaration of April 1993 outlined their aspirations to become full Union members. Acting on the Commission's Report 'Towards a Closer Association with the Countries of Central and Eastern Europe', the Copenhagen European Council in June 1993 set down the basis for developing future relations.

The EU heads of government agreed that the associated countries in Central and Eastern Europe that so desired should become members of the European Union. Accession would take place as soon as an associated country was able to assume the obligations of membership by satisfying the economic and political conditions required. Initially EU member states were reluctant to admit the possibility of full membership, and only grudgingly allowed the EAs at least to mention the 'desire' of these associates to join.

The explicit acknowledgement that the EU *will* rather than *might* enlarge was a major policy shift and reflected the higher priority given to pan-European stability issues, particularly by Germany. However, the Copenhagen Council restated the principles of the classical Community method of enlargement. It stated that:

> membership requires that the candidate country has achieved stability of institutions guaranteeing democracy, the rule of law, human rights and respect for and protection of minorities, the existence of a functioning market economy as well as the capacity to cope with competitive pressures and market forces within the Union. Membership presupposes the candidate's ability to take on the obligations of membership including adherence to the aims of political, economic and monetary union.[11]

Reaffirming the classical method for such a diverse group of countries presented the EU with some difficult dilemmas. Whilst providing the associates with a clear goal to aim at, and providing a set of externally imposed disciplines during the transition process, it also imposed additional obligations on the EU. Member states undertook to engage with the CEECs in a more active and structured way.

In order to facilitate this process, the Council proposed that the associated countries should enter into a 'structured relationship with the Institutions of the Union within the framework of a reinforced and extended multilateral dialogue and concentration on matters of common interest'.[12] This could cover matters coming under any of the three pillars of EU activity. The Council also recognised the centrality of trade liberalisation to the transition process and agreed to speed up the removal of EU trade barriers in advance of the timetable agreed in the Interim Agreements.

In June 1994, the Corfu European Council called on the Commission to prepare a strategy paper on how these commitments could be implemented. The Commission's paper[13] proposed practical steps for integrating the associates into the EU's policy process, in particular holding joint Council meetings on matters of mutual interest under all three pillars, such as policy on drugs and organised crime under the third pillar, and security issues under the second pillar. First-pillar issues were focused on developing a programme for integrating the associates into the Internal Market.

ESSEN COUNCIL PRE-ACCESSION STRATEGY

At the Essen European Council in December 1994, the member states adopted a broad pre-accession strategy based on the Commission's proposals. The Council recognised that negotiations on the future enlargement of the Union would go beyond those states already associated but would encompass other CEECs. It called for EAs to be concluded with the Baltic States and Slovenia. Institutional change would be necessary before enlargement could proceed.

INTERNAL MARKET WHITE PAPER

The centrepiece of the pre-accession strategy was the phased adoption of the Internal Market acquis by the associated states. Consequently the Commission prepared a White Paper, presented to the Cannes European Council in June 1995.[14] The White Paper provided both a conceptual framework for the definition and delineation of the internal acquis and a detailed list of all the relevant legislation and policies in different sectors.

The White Paper dealt with three elements of the Internal Market adaptation process. It identified the key areas of legislation and indicated which measures needed to be tackled first. It described the administrative and technical structures which are needed to ensure that the legislation is effectively implemented and enforced and, finally, it outlined how technical assistance from the EU can be focused to best effect. It also defined the delimitation of Internal Market legislation as the 'Treaty articles and secondary legislation which directly affect the free movement of goods, services, persons or capital. It is legislation without which obstacles to free movement would continue to exist or would reappear'.[15] It therefore includes some social and environmental legislation which could result in unequal costs for economic operators and consequently threaten to distort competition. This delimitation was itself the result of internal debates within the Commission about priority areas of the acquis for extension to the associates. The outcome reflected the importance given to the market mechanism in the transition process in order to bring the associates to the accession threshold.

The White Paper further identifies which measures address fundamental principles, and provides the overall framework for more detailed measures, and the pre-conditions for implementing and enforcing legislation. The Paper noted that 'this is a complex process requiring the creation or adaptation of the necessary institutions and structures, involving fundamental changes in the responsibilities of both the national administrative and judicial systems and the emerging private sector'.[16]

The Commission has stressed that alignment with the Internal Market is distinguished from accession to the Union which will involve acceptance of the *acquis communautaire* as a whole. The White Paper is not part of the accession negotiations, has no legal effect and does not create any new conditions. It is indicative rather than prescriptive and can, therefore, be seen as an incremental modification of the classical method of enlargement, rather than as a fundamental revision.

Although providing more information on the acquis than has been the case for previous applicants, the White Paper has limitations. First, as has been the case in previous enlargements, it follows the classical method in placing the onus of responsibility for adjustment firmly on the applicants. Though the EU has pledged technical assistance for the adaptation process, the principle of the acquis remains inviolable. Second, it contains no timetable for achievement of the alignment process or specific quantifiable targets against which to judge progress. The associates have argued that it is difficult to mobilise opinion to undertake the necessary reforms without a commitment from the EU on when full accession negotiations might start. It is a road map without kilometre marks.

The Commission's view is that the transition process cannot be precisely defined in a way which would be helpful to either side. Over-precise targets, for instance, for market reforms such as privatisation, might lead to over-reliance on the indicators, rather than the under-lying changes. The stress in the White Paper on supporting organisational structures and processes requires qualitative, rather than quantitative measures. The transition process is also iterative; new obstacles may be encountered at a later date which require further mutual adjustments.

Despite the need for flexibility, the Commission's approach is largely determined by the lack of consensus among member states about the internal reforms necessary before enlargement. The Community method has always involved using the prospect of enlarge-ment as a catalyst for reform, though the hard bargaining is usually delayed until the pressures for enlargement are urgent. The pre-accession strategy can therefore be seen as a way of delaying enlargement while the EU builds its own internal consensus on reform.

The associated countries face the prospect of having to adjust more quickly to a much more extensive acquis, now encompassing the Maastricht commitments to EMU and a CFSP, from a lower base than has been the case with previous enlargements. In the past, coun-tries wishing to join were given Association Agreements with long time-scales for the achievement of free trade in industrial goods. Greece spent twenty years at the association agreement stage before full membership; Spain spent sixteen years. Even the wealthier EFTA countries, as a result of their 1972 Free Trade Agreement with the EC and their participation in the Internal Market through the EEA, had twenty years of tariff-free trade in industrial goods before moving to the next level of integration. Any CEEC hoping to join the EU around the year 2000 would, therefore, be squeezing this process into eight to ten years. All the CEECs are substantially poorer than EU member states. In the Visigrad Four (and Slovenia), in 1991, incomes ranged from 22 per cent (Slovakia) of EU average GDP per capita to 64 per cent (Slovenia). It is likely that at least some of the CEECs could make their adaptation more quickly than has been the case in the past, given their more enthusiastic adoption of reform than was evident with many poorer applicants previously, though the obstacles are still formidable. However, there is evidence that at least some of the CEECs are making a rapid transition and are likely to meet the Copenhagen criteria around the year 2000.

HUNGARY: A CASE STUDY OF TRANSITION

The formal application for EU membership was presented to the EU on 1 April 1994. It suggested confidence on the part of the Hungarian Government that they will meet the following Copenhagen criteria.

Stability of democratic institutions

Hungary's transition to liberal democracy was gradual. By the end of 1988, the Hungarian Communist system had started to disintegrate. In the spring of 1990 the first free elections took place and led to the establishment of a coalition government dominated by the conservative Democratic Forum under Josef Antall. Though the economic dislocation caused by the reform process led to the return to power of a leftist Government, led by the former Communist Hungarian Socialist Party, with personnel from the former regime in key positions, the reform process was not reversed. The goal of eventual EU membership has become the cornerstone of democratic credibility.

Existence of a functioning market economy

Johnson and Miles[17] identify four variables: macroeconomic stabilisation; price and trade liberalisation; a legal framework suitable for a market economy; and the transfer of ownership from the public to private sectors, as critical to meeting this Copenhagen criterion.

Macroeconomic stability was initially undermined by the collapse of the COMECON trading system. The supply side reforms undertaken led to a collapse in real GDP, an eight-fold increase in unemployment between 1990 and 1992, an increase in inflation to 35 per cent in 1991, and a collapse in industrial and agricultural output, all leading to current account deterioration and worsening deficits. Although the external deficits have persisted, industrial production stopped falling in 1993 and by mid-1994 was 8 per cent higher than in the same period in the previous year. The reform programme was put into question by the economic policy drift that followed the Socialist Government's election in May 1994. However, in March 1995, the Government announced a package of spending cuts and a 9 per cent devaluation in order to restore confidence in its reform plans.

The COMECON economies protected themselves from the allocative effects of the price mechanism by retaining extensive controls and subsidies. These have mainly been removed, though the shift in domestic utility prices has been politically, very unpopular. The trade liberalisation brought about by the implementation of Hungary's Europe Agreement in February 1994, exposed Hungarian enterprises to increased competition, though strict conditional protection of infant industries and those undergoing restructuring is allowed. Reform of the legal system has been undertaken to ensure consistency with EU legislation, with priority being given to competition, company, property and bankruptcy law, to reassure inward investors.

Privatisation and foreign investment are also necessary pre-conditions for a functioning market economy. The EBRD estimated that, by mid-1994, 55 per cent of Hungary's GDP was generated by the private sector with the intention to extend that further to about 75 per cent by restructuring and sale of large scale enterprises and utilities.[18] Hungary has also been very successful in attracting foreign investment totalling $6.07 billion from 1990–94 (compared with $4.75 billion to Poland and $2.05 billion to the Czech Republic).[19]

The Copenhagen criteria also identify the capacity to cope with competitive pressures and market forces within the EU as critical for full membership. Given the extensive industrial restructuring, trade re-orientation and economic globalisation presently under way, predictions of competitiveness are necessarily uncertain. However, recent work suggests that Hungary's industrial structure is diverse and less dominated by heavy industry, relative to that of other CEECs. Skill levels are high. The role of foreign investment in upgrading the indus-trial infrastructure in order to develop the Hungarian economy's export potential is critical. FDI patterns suggest that some sectors of the food-processing industry could achieve international competitiveness.[20]

The Hungarian case demonstrates the determination of the more economically advanced CEECs to meet the Copenhagen criteria rapidly. By mid-1995, already 48 per cent of Czech exports were to the EU, with the Klaus government arguing that it needed EU aid programmes less than some existing EU member states.[21] By mid-1995, the Polish government was arguing that 60 per cent of the Internal Market legislation outlined in the White Paper was already in place, though there are concerns about the institutional framework for implementation.[22] Other CEECs, notably Estonia and Slovenia, have also stabilised their economies rapidly and have identified themselves as wishing to be in the first wave of new entrants. The rapid transition process, therefore, challenges the incrementalism of the classical method of enlargement more than previous sets of applicants have been able to.

The keenness of the CEECs to pursue full membership of the EU presents the EU with a series of uncomfortable challenges. The likelihood that it will have to respond to nine or ten applications during the same period as critical decisions are being made concerning the feasibility of EMU, raises in acute form the dilemma of widening and deepening. The pre-accession strategy deliberately avoids the most contentious issues concerned with the reform of its own internal policies, specifically the CAP and the Structural Funds.

EU POLICY REFORM

The CAP

The CAP has been a contentious issue at each enlargement, either because of the burdens it places on new members (in the case of the UK) or on the EC as a whole. In the latter case, the burden can be both to the EC budget and to specific producer groups who may face new sources of competition. In the previous four enlargements, these problems were managed by the use of long transition periods for sensitive product categories, in parallel with CAP reform packages designed to limit the overall level of price support to farmers. Successive budget reform packages linked to the liberalisation of world agricultural trade have succeeded in shifting the balance of EU spending away from the CAP price support towards structural spending. The 1992 MacShary reforms, linked to the Uruguay Round, were intended to bring EU producer prices down to world prices by around the year 2000.

However, the incremental reform of the CAP could be undermined by extending price support to the CEECs using existing criteria. In the ten associated states, agriculture accounts for 25 per cent of the workforce and 8 per cent of GDP, compared with 6 per cent of the workforce and 2.5 per cent of GDP in the EU.[23] Agricultural production and exports in the CEECs collapsed as a result of the economic restructuring of the early 1990s. With the exception of Hungary, Bulgaria and Estonia, the CEECs have become net importers of food products. Whilst this suggests that the EU is unlikely to be flooded with cheap imports, the fear of which delayed the Spanish accession negotiations, the low producer prices in the CEECs mean that extending EU price support to them would put enormous strains on the budget. Many of the CEECs have fertile land and climatic conditions well suited to products most heavily protected by the CAP, in particular grain, and dairy and livestock produce. Baldwin argues that extending price support and production to the Visigrad Four alone would increase their output of farm produce by almost $10 billion, mainly concentrated in the livestock sectors.[24] To maintain European prices, surplus production would be exported to third countries requiring further subsidies, and the depression of world prices, leading to a further increase in export subsidies. In a recent study, Anderson and Tyers[25] estimate that the total extra cost to the EU budget would be $476 million per annum. This is higher than the total cost of the CAP in any of the last four years.

The Structural Funds

Extending the present eligibility criteria to the CEECs would result in further budgeting consequences since all of the associates have average GDP per capita below the 75 per cent of EU average, which is the threshold for Objective 1 eligibility. Recent studies undertaken for the European Commission[26] estimated that Greece, the poorest EU member, receives 400 ecu per person from the Structural Funds, amounting to 5 to 6 per cent of GDP. Using this criterion, EU aid would amount to 13 per cent of GNP in the Czech Republic and 34 per cent of GNP in Bulgaria and Romania. Aside from doubts as to whether these countries could absorb such aid levels, the strain on the EU budget would be intense. Baldwin calculates that, on the above assumptions, the Visigrad Four would receive 26 billion ecu from the Structural Funds. In 1993, Greece, Spain, Ireland and Portugal received 16 billion ecu. Assuming growth rates at three times the EU average (2 per cent), he argues that it will still take twenty years for the Visigrad Four to pass the 75 per cent cut-off point.[27]

These figures, though open to debate, still suggest that the budgetary costs of enlargement before well into the next century, on the basis of the present acquis, are enormous. Two sets of internal EU interests are at stake. First, the major net contributors, Germany and the UK would be unwilling to underwrite the expansion in EU revenue necessary to pay for such spending. For the first three enlargement rounds, Germany was willing to sanction budget increases, though, since unification, this willingness has declined markedly. Second, the present net beneficiaries of the EU budget would be unlikely to allow a significant shift of resources away from their own regional programmes to fund programmes in the CEECs. Given that a decision to enlarge requires unanimity, even one net recipient could, in theory, block enlargement. However, given that the classical method involves making side payments to existing member states, this is less likely to happen. However, assuming the accession of some CEECs, there might be increased competition for scarce resources between the CEECs and the present net beneficiaries.

Alternatively, this group of net recipients could form a new enlarged coalition. Assuming the extension of existing Council voting weights and QMV thresholds, Baldwin calculates that the addition of only Hungary and the Czech Republic would be enough to achieve a blocking minority. He concludes that 'if ever the political power of the new poor-four were added to that of the old poor four, the tone of the debate in the Council of Ministers would change considerably'.[28] Whichever scenario prevails, patterns of issue linkage and coalition building are likely to become increasingly complex. This linkage between budgetary and voting issues, though far from predictable, is of major concern to all present member states, and of particularly acute concern for the larger net contributors. Institutional and policy reform will be a pre-condition of agreeing to open accession negotiations with any of the CEECs.

CONCLUSION

So far, the EU has endeavoured to retain the elements of the classical method of enlargement in its approach to the CEECs. Once geopolitical factors allowed, the CEECs were granted limited forms of association leading to freer trade, though with major exceptions for sensitive products. This suggests that the asymmetry characteristic of previous association agreements has not changed significantly. Under intense pressure from the CEECs, these were eventually upgraded into more broad-ranging Europe Agreements as part of the architecture of the new Europe. However, there is little evidence that the 'structured dialogue' has changed this basic imbalance. Arguably, the limitations of the EAs have speeded up the rate of applications for full membership, as the limitations of the EEA did for EFTA members. Despite the EU's commitment to a pre-accession strategy, decisions on how and when to move to accession negotiations have been carefully reserved. The Copenhagen criteria are an orthodox restatement of the inviolability of the acquis, whilst the Internal Market White Paper, though a useful handbook, does not provide the associates with the timetable that they seek above all else. So far the pre-accession strategy has been focused on preserving the essential principles of the classical method, rather than speeding up the accession process.

11 Further Mediterranean enlargement

INTRODUCTION

In 1989, Jacques Delors characterised Malta and Cyprus as the 'Mediterranean orphans'. Though potential EC members for many years through their associate status, they, together with Turkey, had tended to be left behind whenever the momentum of integration brought the enlargement debate to the fore. The needs of other groups of states always appeared more pressing to the EC. Were Malta, Cyprus and Turkey to accede to the EU, the Mediterranean enlargement of the EU would be complete. It would close a chapter in the EU's external relations which, opening with the Greek application for association in 1959, and continuing through two rounds of enlargement, has been characterised by ambivalence on both sides as to how far full membership was desirable. Whilst this ambivalence is evident to some degree with all groups of applicants, it is particularly acute in the Mediterranean case.

This chapter, therefore, examines the membership applications of Malta, Cyprus and Turkey, and the challenges they pose to the classical method of enlargement. The development of the EC's relations with each is examined in turn. The chapter concludes that Turkey's membership application is unlikely to be pursued, though equally unlikely to be publicly and formally rejected. Cyprus' and Malta's applications depend on internal EU reforms, and a settlement of the internal Cypriot political situation.

TURKEY, MALTA AND CYPRUS, AND THE EC'S EXTERNAL RELATIONS

All three states have tended to be marginalised in the EC's hierarchy of external relations, though for very different reasons. Cyprus and Malta have been considered too small to wield much influence amongst EC member states and have been easily relegated in favour of other states with more powerful patrons or urgent needs. When they have pressed their case, internal political problems in the case of Cyprus and concerns about the role of small states in the EC's decision-making system have blocked their progress. Turkey presents opposite problems. With a population of fifty-seven million, and with 50 per cent of the working population engaged in agriculture, with an average GDP per capita approximately 10 per cent of the EC(12) average, in a position between Europe and Asia, Turkey raises too many economic and political issues to be an EU priority. However, in the last five years, all three states have succeeded in engaging the EU's attention and significantly upgrading their relations, to the point at which Malta and Cyprus at least have been promised full accession negotiations after the completion of the 1996 IGC.

NEW POLITICAL AND ECONOMIC CONTEXT

The possibility of further Mediterranean enlargement is driven by a new set of Mediterranean stability issues, incorporating new political and economic considerations. The end of the Cold War has shifted concern in the Eastern Mediterranean from traditional security issues to issues of regime instability and religious fundamentalism in North Africa, leading to northward migratory pressures. In the case of Turkey, these extend to concerns about the Middle East, the Trans-Caucasus and even Central Asia. Malta, Cyprus and Turkey are therefore 'front line states' for Europe in new and complex zones of instability, and both these countries and the EU have therefore been looking for mutual reassurance. The countries' applications for membership reflect a desire not to be isolated by any further shifts in the balance of power on Europe's southeastern flank. The following section gives an overview of these issues before examining each country in more depth.

EC POLICY IN THE EASTERN MEDITERRANEAN

EC policy towards all three states has been ambivalent since the late 1950s. Turkey has been the most problematic, in large part due to the linkage with Greece, most acutely felt in the division of Cyprus, but extending over wider political and economic issues. The EC tried to pursue a strategy of even-handedness between Greece and Turkey. Greece's 1959 application for associate status was followed shortly by a similar request from Turkey. By granting both requests the EC was implicitly accepting that both might, in time, become full EC members, a promise to Turkey which the EC subsequently regretted. This even-handedness became less credible following Greece's accession to the EC in 1981. Though it was a condition of accession that Greece would not block the development of EC relations with Turkey, once she became a full member, she did. Turkey's last application for membership was an embarrassment for the EC. The Commission's Opinion, issued in 1989, took thirty months to prepare and, by indefinitely postponing the opening of accession negotiations, fudged the issue. Whilst the subsequent upgrading of relations led to the implementation of a customs union in 1996, the EC has never clarified the position on Turkish accession. Economic concerns, compounded by demographic and labour fears, concern about human rights and Turkey's European 'status' have all left Turkey in limbo.

EC policy towards Cyprus has been linked to both Greek and Turkish problems. Though associated to the EC since 1972, the partition of the island in 1974 created a political impasse which has proved difficult to overcome. Differences between member states made a co-ordinated EC response to the Cyprus problem more difficult. Though trade expanded within the framework of the association agreement, the physical division of the island hampered its development. The EC's Internal Market initiative highlighted this internal border issue and led to the (Greek) Cypriot Republic applying for membership in 1991. The generally favourable Opinion on the economic consequences of membership led the EU to use the possibility of membership to try and break the internal deadlock. The 1995 agreement on the customs union with Turkey was part of a package deal to broker a political settlement.

EU policy towards Malta has largely been shaped by the polarised attitudes of Malta's two main political parties towards the EC. Though Malta has had an association agreement since 1970, under periods of Labour government, Malta was strongly anti EC, adopting a policy of non-alignment. The EC has, therefore, proceeded very cautiously in developing relations with Malta lest it internalise this dissent. However, in the 1990s this internal polarisation declined and a new consensus emerged which was more favourable to the possibility of EC membership. This led to an application in 1991 and a broadly favourable Opinion being produced in 1993, arguing for accession subject to some internal Maltese reforms, and some progress at the 1996 IGC on institutional issues. The following sections now consider the development of the EC's relations with all three states in more detail.

TURKEY

Discussion of Turkey's suitability for full EU membership has always centred on whether Turkey fulfils the basic eligibility criterion of being a European state. Since the formation of the EC, Turkish politicians have been at pains to prove Turkey's 'European vocation', basing their arguments on the strong secular and Westernising policies of successive governments since the founding of the Republic in 1923 by Kemal Ataturk. Yet, whilst this 'vocation' is deeply felt, at least amongst political elites, the issue of identity is more ambiguous and presents more difficult issues for both sides.

Although some re-orientation towards Europe was evident in the nineteenth century (for instance in Turkey's siding with France and Britain during the Crimean War), the change was most marked in the 1920s following the collapse of the Ottoman Empire in the First World War. From 1924 the caliphate and religious courts were abolished and a Western-style constitution was adopted.[1] Though this secularisation was resisted in rural areas, it developed and strengthened from the 1930s onwards. Turkey joined the OEEC in 1948, the Council of Europe in 1949 and NATO in 1952.

This choice of foreign policy orientation was confirmed by Turkey's application for associate membership of the EC in 1959. The application was made for political reasons, largely as a response to the Greek application made two months earlier. No studies of the impact of association on the Turkish economy were undertaken. The EC's initially positive response reflected a desire for a diplomatic success in its external relations, following the proposal to establish EFTA. The US was also concerned that the EC should maintain a balance in its dealings with both NATO members in the Eastern Mediterranean. Though this search for balance has characterised EC relations with Greece and Turkey, since this period, equilibrium has proved elusive.

EC ASSOCIATION AGREEMENT WITH TURKEY

Negotiations with Turkey were delayed, following an anti-Government coup. When signed in September 1963, the agreement was less generous than that with Greece, reflecting alarm, particularly in France and Italy, about both economic and political identity issues. The agreement, effective from December 1964, consisted of three stages. The first involved a preparatory stage of between five and nine years during which tariff quotas would be reduced for Turkey's main exports of tobacco, raisins, dried figs and hazelnuts. During the second stage of between twelve and twenty-two years, the EC and Turkey would move to a customs union, with Turkey adopting the EC's CET and some sector-specific integration. The agreement also envisaged the possibility of a third final stage which could involve full EC membership, though no timetable was given for this. The Turks took this to mean that they would, ultimately, achieve full EC membership, but the EC was more guarded, accession being dependent on the achievement of concrete measures (at that stage unspecified). The Turkish Association Agreement therefore typifies such agreements in that it raised the associate's expectations without adequately clarifying how these might be met.

Implementation of the first stage of the agreement had only a very limited impact and was treated only very generally in Turkey's Development Plans to 1972. Again, no studies were undertaken, reflecting the political nature of the request to move to the transitional stage. Following negotiations over improving market access to the EC for Turkish goods, the position of immigrant labour in the EC, and EC financial assistance to Turkey, the additional provisions were agreed in 1970 and implemented in 1973. The main provisions were that the EC would abolish all duties on industrial imports from Turkey, whilst Turkey would divide its imports into two lists and reduce tariffs over twelve and twenty-two years. Eighty per cent of EC agricultural imports from Turkey would receive preferential access whilst Turkey would adapt to the CAP, the CET, and the free movement of labour and capital over twenty-two years. Neither side fully appreciated the implications of the agreement. Turkey's third Five Year Development Plan incorporated import substitution proposals incompatible with the Association Agreement, whilst the EC's commercial concessions were vulnerable to special pleading from domestic producers' interests. As was the case with other Association Agreements, access to the EC market was most restricted for goods, such as textiles, for which Turkey enjoyed the strongest competitive advantage. The value of these trade concessions was further eroded by the adoption of the EC's Generalised System of Preferences in 1971, the development of the EC's Global Mediterranean Policy, and the impending second enlargement.

Enthusiasm for the agreement on the EC's side was tempered by a growing realisation of what accession might involve, particularly regarding the free movement of labour in the post-1973 recession. This was a particular concern for Germany, the EC member state with the greatest number of Turkish immigrant workers. The Turkish invasion of Cyprus also created new obstacles, particularly when it became clear that Greece was likely to join the EC. By 1976 the Association Agreement was in trouble, and in 1978 Turkey formally requested a five-year freeze in its commitments. The agreement, however, was effectively finished off by the 1980 military coup. Even after the restoration of democracy in 1983, it proved difficult to reactivate. Redmond cites the Cyprus issue in the Council of Ministers and human rights issues in the European Parliament as the major obstacles, particularly once Greece became a full EC member.[2]

1987 APPLICATION FOR EC MEMBERSHIP

The Turkish Government attempted to break the deadlock by submitting an application for full EC membership in 1987. Preoccupied with its Internal Market plans and the Single European Act, the EC found the application an unwelcome embarrassment. The Commission's Opinion, which took thirty months to prepare, gave a strongly negative response to the application.[3] Whilst reaffirming the principle that no enlargement could take place before 1993, following completion of the Single European Market, the Opinion, in any case, listed a number of formidable economic obstacles to Turkish membership, all of which posed fundamental challenges to the classical enlargement method.

Beyond general concerns about the capacity of the Turkish economy to adapt to the acquis, the Opinion noted major structural disparities leading to a GNP per capita one-third of the EC average, with 50 per cent of the labour force still employed in agriculture, high levels of inflation, unemployment and industrial protection, and low levels of social protection. In terms of the political dimension, the Opinion conceded that there had been progress towards parliamentary democracy but considered that human rights provisions were still inadequate and that conflicts with 'one Member State of the Community' (i.e. Greece) still impeded relations. The Opinion adopted by the Council in February 1990 instead proposed the intensification of co-operation within the framework of the association agreement, leading to the completion of the customs union, with full membership postponed indefinitely. In public, the Turks expressed frustration at the Opinion and the implied double standards in comparison with Greece, Spain and Portugal, though privately they were not surprised.

The Opinion crystallised many of the concerns that the EC had had about Turkey on economic, political, strategic and cultural grounds.

Economic concerns centred on three major areas; the capacity of Turkish industry to withstand the competitive pressures of the Internal Market, the implications for both Turkey and the EC of extending the CAP, and the free movement of workers.

Several major studies of Turkey's industrial competitiveness were undertaken in support of its membership application. According to Turkey's Foundation for Economic Development, 75 per cent of Turkish industry would be capable of withstanding international competition. It argued that, of the fifty-three industrial sectors studied, only fifteen, representing about 22 per cent of industrial output, would be in a weak financial position.[4] However, this overview conceals substantial competitiveness differences within sectors. Textiles, leather goods and steel all have competitive and uncompetitive subsectors which, the Commission conceded, were difficult to assess accurately given the degree to which they had been supported by the state.

The size of Turkey's agricultural sector would also pose enormous challenges to the CAP. Full integration would increase the EC's agricultural land area by 22 per cent and nearly double the agricultural workforce. Turkey's output covers both Mediterranean and temperate products and has received only limited subsidies. Given stronger price support, the productive potential is high, particularly in some sectors such as cereals where Turkey is already one of the world's largest producers. All of these would have directly confronted EC domestic producer interest groups. The side payments implicit in any classical accession package deal would have been very large. As well as the impact on the EC's budget which would involve substantial payments from the Structural Funds, extending the CAP to Turkey would also lead to higher Turkish consumer prices, exacerbating internal inflationary pressures. Although more recent reforms of the CAP are likely to have mitigated some of these effects, they are still formidable obstacles, proportionately greater than those for Eastern Europe, and therefore likely to keep Turkey at the back of the accession queue.

The free movement of labour provisions of the acquis also work against Turkey. During the 1960s, substantial numbers of Turkish workers migrated to West Germany, thereby reducing unemployment levels and increasing remittances of migrants' earnings, which helped Turkey's balance of payments. However, as a result of the post-1973 recession, these opportunities declined, leading to concerns, most acutely felt in Germany, about the assimilation of Turkish workers, particularly given the high Turkish birth rate. The Association Agreement, which entered into force in 1964, should have provided for free movement of labour by 1986, though the impracticality of this was recognised on both sides and was not pressed actively. As with agriculture, new migratory pressures from Eastern Europe in the 1990s have further reduced Turkey's attractiveness as a full EU member.

Turkish relations with Greece also reduced the likelihood of accession. Greece voted against asking the Commission to prepare an Opinion on the Turkish application and blocked the financial protocols in Turkey's Association Agreement, in an attempt to exert pressure on Turkey over Cyprus and territorial disputes in the Aegean Sea. During the 1980s, the EC itself did not intervene in these disputes, though the diplomatic language of the Commission's Opinion indicated the concern felt by member states at the possibility of these disputes becoming internalised in the EC.

Concerns about the strength of Turkish democracy and human rights have also hampered Turkish ambitions. Measures taken against Kurdish separatists, including banning of political parties, written into the Penal Code, have regularly been criticised in the European Parliament. Military interventions in 1960, 1970 and 1980 have all given cause for concern, though, as Redmond points out, the total period of non-parliamentary rule since 1945 is shorter than those of Spain, Portugal or Greece.[5]

Until the 1990s, Turkey regarded its strategically important position in the Eastern Mediterranean and NATO membership as enhancing its credibility with the EC. However, the collapse of the USSR has altered the nature of the regional threat and, therefore, Turkey's utility to the EC. Though Turkey played a valuable role during the Gulf Crisis of 1991, and has since been seen as a buttress against instability in the Trans-Caucasus and Central Asia, this has not been enough to overcome wider EC anxieties about Turkish membership of the EC.

EC–TURKEY CUSTOMS UNION

Although the Commission's Opinion effectively removed the full membership option, the proposal for an enhanced Association Agreement, leading to a customs union was pushed actively, in order to avoid the risk of Turkey turning away from Europe completely. In June 1990, the Commission proposed the completion of the customs union by 1995. Initially progress was slow, given the complexity of the outstanding issues. However, by 1992, there was an emerging consensus that EC–Turkish relations needed to be upgraded, particularly since Malta and Cyprus had applied for EC membership in 1991.

The Commission's paper on enlargement, to the Lisbon Council in June 1992, had noted that:

> Events have highlighted Turkey's geopolitical importance and the role which it can play as an ally and as a pole of stability in its region; the Community should take all appropriate steps to anchor it firmly within the future architecture of Europe.[6]

Achieving this required a breakthrough over Greco–Turkish relations and the Cyprus impasse. This did not arrive until the French Presidency of the Council in 1995. France, which traditionally enjoyed close relations with Greece, put together a package deal which linked a promise to open accession negotiations with Cyprus six months after the conclusion of the 1996 IGC, with Greek agreement to lift its veto on the EC financial protocol with Turkey, and the completion of the customs union scheduled for the end of 1995. The deal, agreed in March 1995, was also designed to facilitate a political settlement in Cyprus. The customs union involves improved market access to the EC and a 1 billion ecu aid package in return for Turkey lifting its high import barriers to EC goods. Whilst this is likely to result in increased competition in many industrial sectors, it is also expected to increase inward investment from the EC which provides about two-thirds of Turkey's inward investment of $1 billion a year.[7]

Under the Maastricht TEU the agreement with Turkey required ratification by the European Parliament. Given the Parliament's position on Turkey's human rights record, particularly in relation to army activity in Kurdistan, its ratification could not be taken for granted. However, following intense lobbying from a wide range of interests concerned at the possibility of Turkey becoming disillusioned with the EU and reorienting her foreign policy eastwards, the Parliament approved the agreement in December 1995.

The completion of the customs union consolidates EU relations with Turkey but without raising all the contentious issues involved in accession. In this respect, the classical enlargement method raises insurmountable obstacles for Turkey. However, Turkey is unlikely ever to surrender its aspiration to full membership. It has become the touchstone of credibility for Turkey's political elite and the clearest indication of its differentiation from its Islamic Middle Eastern neighbours. Given the high stakes involved, the EU is also unlikely to rule out publicly the possibility of eventual Turkish EU membership, however remote this may be. Whilst EU policy towards Turkey is now based on a clearer internal consensus among member states, particularly now that the Greek veto has been lifted, the fundamental ambiguity will remain.

CYPRUS

Some of the issues raised in the Turkish case are also linked to Cyprus. The division of the island since 1974 and the failure to date of international initiatives to reconcile the two communities have shaped the island's relations with the EC, and until 1995, blocked any serious consideration of membership. However, the completion of the customs union with Turkey was designed in part to break this deadlock.

Cyprus's early relations with the EC were determined by its position as a British colony until 1960 and its heavy trade dependence on the UK market. Following the UK's 1961 application for EC membership, Cyprus applied for association in 1962. Following the French veto in 1963, the Cypriot application lapsed but was reactivated in 1971, was agreed in 1972 and became effective in 1973, on the EC's first enlargement. As well as seeking to protect its existing trade position with the UK, the Cypriot government also saw association as a way of diversifying its economy and improving access to new European markets.

The agreement followed the classic association model and provided for the creation of a customs union after a two-stage, ten-year transition period involving internal tariff and quota reductions. The first stage which ran until June 1977, implemented a 70 per cent reduction in the EC's CET on Cypriot industrial products subject to EC rules of origin, and a 40 per cent reduction for Cypriot citrus fruits. In return Cyprus phased in tariff reductions of 15 per cent, rising to 35 per cent by the end of the first period. The UK and Ireland were also allowed to maintain the (more generous) Commonwealth system of preferences for Cypriot imports until the end of the first phase. The Cypriot association agreement was vulnerable to the same criticisms as other association agreements (in particular Mediterranean ones), namely that concessions were least generous in sectors such as textiles and citrus fruits where EC domestic interests were at stake.[8]

Whatever its specific shortcomings, the development of the agreement was, in any case, impeded by the de facto division of the island that followed the Turkish invasion of the summer of 1974. The EC attempted to maintain a neutral stance and, therefore, did not enhance the agreement for fear of being seen to favour the Greek Cypriots. The division of the island also had severe economic effects and led to the economic dualism which has subsequently characterised the Cypriot economy. Although the Cypriot Government wanted to move to the second stage of the agreement, the first stage was repeatedly extended for the next ten years. The first extension in 1977, implemented in 1980, involved an increased reduction in tariffs on Cypriot industrial exports from 70 per cent to 100 per cent, and the replacement of preferential access to the UK market with improved access to the whole EC. Though the Cypriot Government regarded many of the EC's proposals as inadequate, it was keen to avoid isolation given the likelihood of the EC's enlargement in the Mediterranean.

In November 1980, the Association Council agreed to move to the second stage of the agreement, with negotiations, to start in 1982, to be based on the principle that the expected benefits should extend to the whole population of the island. Disagreements in the Council between the UK, and France and Italy, over how extensive agricultural concessions should be, delayed negotiations. In the event, the agreement was not signed until October 1987, effective from the beginning of 1988. This second stage involved a further two-phase movement towards a full customs union. The first phase involved the abolition of all remaining duties on industrial goods, and of the quotas on some textiles, and the introduction by Cyprus of the EC CET over the ten years of the first phase. The second phase was to have lasted a further five years, and to lead to the free movement of industrial and agricultural products, and some approximation of EC competition and state aids law. The agreement also contained financial protocols giving soft loans and grants for upgrading the infrastructure of the whole island.

APPLICATION FOR FULL MEMBERSHIP

However, this second phase was overtaken by the decision of the Greek Cypriot Government to apply for full EC membership in July 1990. The timing of the application was largely a response to the Internal Market initiative and the fear of exclusion from EC decision making. However, other longer term trends underpinned the decision. The Mediterranean, particularly Greek, enlargement of the 1980s highlighted Cyprus' potential isolation in the Eastern Mediterranean, a situation exacerbated by the intractability of the internal political situation. The Greek Cypriot Government therefore also saw the application as a way of breaking this deadlock, particularly given the explicit linkage between the resolution of the Cypriot question and the Turkish application, noted in the Commission's 1989 Opinion on Turkey.[9] The Turkish Cypriots were not consulted about the application, arguing that the decision breached the 1960 Constitution, and that the internal issue had to be resolved before an application could be made. However, their response was more a sign of weakness and a recognition that they risked being further marginalised by the pace of events.

EC RESPONSE

The 1990 application for membership was made during a period of intense reconsideration of the EC's external relations following the end of the Cold War. The Cypriot (and Maltese) applications were a lesser priority than the EEA negotiations with EFTA and the negotiation of Europe Agreements with the East European Countries. No public positions were taken on the Cypriot application until the Commission's 1992 paper on enlargement. In this paper, the Commission was cautious about Cyprus, noting that 'there is inevitably a link between the question of accession and the problem which results from the de facto separation of the island into two entities, between which there is no movement of goods, persons and services'. The Commission argued that

> the Community must continue to encourage all efforts to find a solution, in particular through support for the resolutions of the United Nations and the initiative of its Secretary General. In the meantime the association agreement should be exploited so that Cyprus is enabled to pursue its economic integration.[10]

The Commission also noted that, although both Cyprus and Malta would not have any significant problems adapting to the acquis, the issue of small-state participation in the EC institutions would also have to be addressed before accession could be negotiated.

COMMISSION'S OPINION

Further consideration was deferred to the Commission's Opinion on Cypriot membership, published in 1993. The Opinion restated the EC's position that the Greek Cypriot Government had legitimacy and that, despite the objections of the Turkish Cypriots, the application was admissible. However, it argued that the de facto division of the island made the exercise of the basic freedoms of the acquis impossible, and that 'these freedoms and rights would have to be guaranteed as part of a comprehensive settlement restoring constitutional arrangements covering the whole of the Republic of Cyprus'.[11]

The Opinion took a positive view of the capacity of the Greek Cypriot economy, at least, to deal with the acquis, though it noted an over-dependence on tourism, as well as the need to diversify services and to consolidate industrial development, which, in some sectors, still hid behind high tariff barriers. The dualism of the economy, with the Turkish Republic heavily dependent on agriculture, tourism and budgetary support from Turkey, with lower levels of average incomes and a higher inflation rate, posed difficult transition problems. It further viewed the offer of possible membership as a catalyst for a possible political settlement, arguing that:

> the Commission feels that a positive signal should be sent to the authorities and the people of Cyprus confirming that the Community considers Cyprus is eligible for membership and that as soon as the prospect of settlement is surer, the Community is ready to start the process with Cyprus that should eventually lead to its accession ... [12]

Since the publication of the Opinion, and the quickening pace of the enlargement debate due to pressure from Eastern Europe, the Cypriot Government has been determined not to be left behind. Together with Malta, it has pressed member states with a strong interest in the Mediterranean, in particular France, Italy and Greece, to support early enlargement, in effect before the EU becomes embroiled in the complexities of Eastern enlargement.

In March 1995, under pressure from Greece, as part of the package deal brokered by the French Council Presidency to unlock the Turkish customs union, the EU agreed to open accession negotiations with Cyprus (and Malta) six months after the conclusion of the IGC. This commitment is intended to pressure both communities into finding a settlement. As the Opinion notes:

> While safeguarding the essential balance between the two communities and the right of each to preserve its fundamental interests, the institutional provisions contained in such a settlement should create the appropriate conditions for Cyprus to participate normally in the decision making process of the European Community, and in the correct application of Community law throughout the island. [13]

However, the Community has reserved its position in the event of a failure to agree. Given that it recognises the Greek Cypriot Government as legitimate, the EU has not ruled out the possibility of proceeding to negotiate solely with it. Nevertheless, this would be very much a second best approach and some form of federal political structure is the most feasible solution, though the obstacles to this are still formidable. [14] The hope is that pressure from Turkey will help to unblock policy in the government of the Turkish Republic of Northern Cyprus though political attitudes remain entrenched, as the crisis in the summer of 1996 showed.

MALTA

Malta's relationship with the EC has a number of important historical parallels with that of Cyprus. Like Cyprus, Malta was formerly a British colony and was heavily dependent on UK military bases, in particular its dockyards, and tourism. Malta's relations with the EC have, therefore, been shaped by a desire to find a new framework for external relations. However, the Maltese have also actively sought alternatives to the European option, and this has, to some extent, affected their relations with the EC. Malta was still a British Colony (until 1964) at the time of the first UK application for membership in 1961, though it negotiated a preferential trade deal directly with the EC. In 1967, Malta pressed for an Association Agreement, eventually signed in 1970. It followed the classic model in proposing the implementation of a customs union over a ten-year period, divided into two five-year phases. During the first phase, the EC granted a 70 per cent tariff reduction on all Maltese industrial exports (with some exceptions for textiles) whilst the Maltese introduced a three-step, 35 per cent reduction in tariffs on EC exports.

The agreement was negotiated in parallel with the EC's introduction of its generalised system of preferences (GSP) for less developed countries. This had the effect of reducing the value of the preferences given to the Maltese, an issue that was exploited by the incoming Maltese Labour Government, who were committed to renegotiating the agreement. Additional protocols were agreed in March 1976. However, the anti-EC stance adopted by the Labour Government did not play well in Brussels and in the late 1970s and early 1980s, EC–Malta relations deteriorated. The first stage of the Association Agreement was extended to 1980, but the Maltese Government indicated that it did not wish to move to the second stage.

The Maltese sought a more privileged status than other EC associates, reflecting their status as a former colony of a member state, involving better trade access and improved financial protocols. However, they overestimated their bargaining position with the EC, which had no reason to offer special concessions. In 1982, the Commission negotiated new financial protocols with Malta but even these were rejected by the Council of Ministers as too generous. Relations did not start to improve until 1985 when the Labour

Government realised that its policy was leading nowhere. EC/Maltese relations improved considerably after 1987 and the election of a Nationalist Government committed to applying for EC membership.

The application, made in July 1990, marked a decisive reorientation of Maltese foreign policy and an acceptance that the EC framework was the best option for a small state faced with a rapidly evolving geopolitical environment. This decision should be seen in the historical context of previous Maltese attempts to reconcile a desire for independence with military vulnerability. During the 1950s, the Maltese Labour Party had pushed a policy of 'integration' with the UK involving parliamentary representation at Westminster.[15] The policy led nowhere, particularly since British perceptions of its colonial relations changed after the Suez crisis of 1956. In the 1960s, Malta pushed a policy of independence (within the Commonwealth), though after the 1971 election of the Mintoff (Labour) Government, this evolved into a policy of neutrality and non-alignment. During the 1970s and 1980s, the strongly anti-Western stance, including the development of closer ties with the Libyan regime, created tensions in its relations with the EC. Government manipulation of domestic political institutions was also criticised by the European Parliament.[16]

The Maltese application was made on pragmatic, largely economic grounds, given the lack of a firm political consensus underpinning the EC question. The 1990 Department of Information Report[17] summarised the benefits as guaranteed access to the EC market, access to EC Structural Funds and an increase in foreign direct investment. The increase in competition from the EC was seen as necessary to restructure Malta's industrial base. Conversely, the Labour Party took the view that local industry would be unable to compete, that the CAP would push up food prices and that the local labour market would be swamped by foreign workers.[18]

As was the case with the Cypriot application, the Commission's Opinion on the Maltese application was delayed, pending further consideration of the whole enlargement issue. The Commission's Report on enlargement to the Lisbon Summit noted that there were no insuperable obstacles to Malta's adoption of the acquis. The Opinion published in 1993[19] focused on three main areas, Malta's political relations with the EU, in particular the neutrality issue, how its economy could be integrated with the EU's, and the institutional and administrative implications of admitting a small state.

Malta's neutrality was enshrined in the constitution in 1987. The amendment prohibits the installation of foreign military bases on Maltese territory and states that Malta is 'a neutral state actively pursuing peace ... by adhering to a policy of non-alignment and refusing to participate in any military alliance'. The Opinion argued that this might be incompatible with Title V of the Maastricht Treaty and might lead to problems over 'joint action'. In September 1992, following the Lisbon Summit, the Maltese Government had sought to reassure the EC by submitting a memorandum reaffirming its commitment to the Treaties (including the Maastricht TEU) and stating that:

> The Maltese Government believed it to be in Malta's interest to subscribe to the EU's foreign and security policy, including the eventual framing of a common defence policy which might, in time, lead to a common defence.[20]

As has been the case with other neutral states, Malta has sought to reconcile its official policy with Europe's new geopolitical realities. Given the uncertainties over the future of the CFSP, Malta's neutrality is unlikely to pose insuperable obstacles to accession. However, the constitution may have to be amended, requiring a two-thirds majority in the Parliament which, given the traditionally polarised politics in Malta, might be difficult to reach.

Although the Opinion argued that Malta would have few legal problems adopting the acquis, its economy was unprepared for the level of competition in the Internal Market. The Opinion identified a dualistic economy in which the majority of small companies employ fewer than five people, and have been protected by high tariffs, quotas and licences. The Opinion argued for an extensive programme of reform, including the introduction of VAT, the liberalisation of capital movements and the adoption of competitive policies as necessary preconditions of accession.[21] These factors were linked to concerns about the capacity of a small state to assume the obligations of membership, particularly in terms of its ability to provide enough trained personnel to staff the EU's institutions, to carry an EU Council Presidency, and to implement the growing burden of EU legislation.

The Commission argued that Malta should be sent a positive signal that accession should not be postponed indefinitely, and proposed a programme of technical assistance to speed up the necessary reforms. The Maltese Government subsequently tackled the reform process, liberalising the economy, and introducing VAT in January 1995. In March 1995, the Commission strongly endorsed the reform programme and linked Malta's application to Cyprus', offering to open accession negotiations six months after the conclusion of the 1996 IGC.[22] It is unlikely that the negotiations themselves would be difficult. However, membership is still an issue in Maltese domestic politics. Following the election of a Labour Government in October 1996, Malta's EU application was suspended, though not formally withdrawn.

CONCLUSION

The classical method would not present major obstacles for Malta and Cyprus. Both could take on the acquis without lengthy negotiations or transition periods. Their small size would reduce the need to make side payments to existing members. However, the biggest challenges to Malta's and Cyprus' applications are those posed by the reform of EU decision making. The EU has been concerned about its overall effectiveness if 'micro-states', such as Malta and Cyprus, have to assume the same level of EU responsibilities as large states. Further concerns focus on the power of blocking coalitions of small states to frustrate the ambitions of larger states. Should the veto powers of small states be limited, then the sovereignty debate within the applicants, in particular Malta, could become more contentious. However, the evolution of European integration makes the alternatives to full membership for small states such as Malta and Cyprus look even less attractive. The constraints of membership are likely to be accepted more willingly than the uncertainties of independence.

Turkey remains a special case, a reminder to the EU that states on the border of Europe raise uncomfortable questions, not only about the acquis and the classical enlargement method, but about European identity and the fundamental eligibility criteria of EU membership.

12 Conclusion
Can the classical method survive?

Through the four enlargement rounds to date, the EC has had to internalise a wide range of political and economic diversity, from
applicants with different capabilities and levels of commitment to the
integration process. Yet the continuing attraction of membership
suggests that the dynamics of the process do bring benefits to both
new and existing members, even if the experience is different from the
expectation. The classical enlargement method is central to this
process. Given the unpredictability of the political and economic
forces released by enlargement, a core set of mutual expectations
about the process and procedures of accession is a valuable reference
point. Though the classical method has been stretched almost to
breaking point on several occasions, it has endured and, arguably, has
been strengthened by its continuous trials.

Yet the preceding analysis of the four enlargement rounds, and of
the evolution of the EC's policies and institutions suggests that the
challenge of further enlargement requires more fundamental thinking
if the benefits of the Community method are to be preserved and
extended. The issue of differentiation, between existing members and
future applicants, and between policy areas and decision-making
processes, always implicit in the discourse of European integration, is
now more explicitly in the centre of the debate.

This concluding chapter, therefore, brings together the themes of
the book, first by reviewing the extent to which the classical method
has been affected by the four enlargement rounds, and the developments in the EC's policy domain and institutional processes. Second, it
examines options for the development of the EU to cope with further
enlargement pressures.

How has the classical method withstood the enlargement test? Each
of the core principles are examined in turn in order to assess its
durability.

Principle 1   Applicants must accept the acquis communautaire in full. No permanent opt-outs are available.

This bedrock principle is derived from the strongly held belief that new members are joining a club with a rule book rather than entering into a free collective bargain. The determination with which this principle has been enforced, initially by De Gaulle in 1963, always comes as a shock to applicants. Despite the clarity with which this principle has been reiterated, most applicants believe that their own circumstances are unique and deserve an equality of respect, even when this might challenge a principle of at least part of the acquis. The UK, for example, believed that its wider trading links merited special consideration. The realisation that such consideration would not be forthcoming was particularly humiliating, given that the UK had been invited to participate in forming the acquis in 1955–57. Since then, other applicants have approached the EC with the presumption that at least some of their special interests are virtually non-negotiable. Spain's fishing industry, the ownership of forests in Finland, second homes in Denmark, alpine transit in Austria, regional industrial incentive schemes in Ireland, and the Common Fisheries Policy for Norway are all such examples. Often the initial hard line position is for domestic political consumption in order to sustain a carefully constructed domestic coalition, and is softened once real negotiations commence. However, the case of Norway suggests that some national interests really are non-negotiable, and that accepting the principle of the acquis is not just an administrative and technocratic requirement of membership.

Yet the experience of four enlargement rounds demonstrates just how few of these special interests are acknowledged as such by the EC. Despite the enormous expansion in the acquis, this basic position has not softened. Indeed, successive enlargements have seen the principle stated more explicitly. The gradual acceptance that enlargement to Eastern Europe will take place has been accompanied by restatements of the orthodox position, for instance at the Copenhagen Council in June 1993. Successive policy statements, such as those accompanying the Internal Market White Paper have reminded applicants that any pre-accession strategy and framework is 'without prejudice' to actual accession negotiations.

This basic principle is very durable, even if parts of the acquis itself are less so. Indeed, the growing complexity of the acquis reinforces it. Accepting permanent opt-outs would put at risk a greater number of bargains carefully constructed by existing member states, which might otherwise start to unravel. The integration process is not perceived as so irreversible that member states are willing to try radical innovations during accession negotiations, even though objective circumstances might argue in their favour.

Principle 2   Accession negotiations focus exclusively on the practicalities of the applicants taking on the acquis.

The classical method relies heavily on the use of transition periods to facilitate the adaptation process. The basic instrument has been the five-year transition for the reciprocal removal of tariffs, quotas and other restrictions. This period has been considered long enough for new members to undertake the necessary political and economic restructuring, but short enough to force a realisation that the demands of membership cannot be postponed indefinitely. Safeguard clauses have been inserted where anxieties have persisted. This classic transition has been modified on a number of occasions, usually when existing member states have difficulties with sectoral interest groups. Thus Spain's 'sensitive' Mediterranean agricultural exports were subjected to a seven-year transition. The CFP has seen transition periods stretched to ten years. Transition periods have also been qualified by agreements as to what should happen at the end of the period. Where the new member has real difficulties with aspects of the acquis, an agreement to review the policy area, without prejudice, after transition is written into the accession Treaty. Some of these adaptations, for instance the maintenance of EFTA's environmental standards for four years following the 1994 enlargement, extend beyond the practicalities of implementation and raise issues of principle. Yet they are carefully worded so that the first classical enlargement principle is not publicly compromised.

The transition period, linked to agreed convergence objectives, is also likely to remain a feature of the enlargement process. It ensures the credibility of the first principle whilst permitting pragmatic flexibility to take account of the differences that each applicant brings, and the problems that this might pose for existing member states.

Principle 3   The problems arising from the increased diversity of an enlarged Community are addressed by creating new policy instruments overlaid on existing ones, rather than by fundamental reform of the latter's inadequacies.

Adherence to the first and second principles reinforces the third. Over four enlargements, the EC has added new policies and extended its domain, particularly in the 'cohesion' area in response to structural economic problems, some caused by other EC policies and more blatant special pleading. Though some of the design faults in the original policies, in particular the CAP, have been recognised, their reform has been too slow to prevent accretion of new policies, and the entrenchment of a complex pattern of special interests. This principle, though now well rooted in the realities of the Community bargaining process, is largely an unintended consequence of the weight given to the first two principles. Whilst acknowledged as necessary to constructing accession package deals, its limitations are also widely recognised. There is an emerging debate within the EU about whether and how the whole cohesion policy area can be recast.

Principle 4   New members are integrated into the EC's institutional structure on the basis of limited incremental adaptation, facilitated by the promise of a more fundamental review after enlargement.

This principle has again helped to overcome the difficulties of accepting the acquis, with the promise of a 'nameplate and a microphone'. It has supported the second principle in particular by keeping accession negotiations focused on specific and realisable objectives. Maintaining this principle has required some delicate finessing of negotiations. Applicants have to be persuaded that, even though the institutional decision-making system may create real difficulties for them, for instance in areas where they might be vulnerable to being outvoted in the Council, they nevertheless can have real influence after accession.

Principle 5   The Community prefers to negotiate with groups of states that already have close relations with each other.

With the exception of Greece, this principle has endured. For both practical reasons, in managing parallel accession conferences and for reasons of policy linkage, this principle has served the needs of the EC, though some applicants have found it frustrating. The Greek, single-member style of accession is unlikely to be repeated because the pressures of further enlargement require active and politically difficult choices by the EU on the scheduling of accession, and the EU has never before been faced with more than four applicants at any one time.

Principle 6   Existing member states use the enlargement process to pursue their own interests and collectively to externalise internal problems.

The development of the CFP is the clearest example of the EC developing a new policy in anticipation of enlargement. This proved very difficult for the UK and Spain, and impossible for Norway. Many other, smaller, side payments feature as part of enlargement packages. Here the EU faces major challenges over future enlargement, particularly over structural spending and cohesion policy. Were existing EU member states to externalise their difficulties over Structural Fund reform, for instance by changing eligibility criteria in order to limit their liability to future applicants, new problems would arise. The cases of Spain and the UK, though in some respects different, do not provide happy precedents.

The experience of the four enlargement rounds to date suggests that the core of the classical method of enlargement will continue. However, new contextual factors will force some modification. Two sets of factors are important. First, the diversity of the applicants, and their level of economic development, would stretch to the limit the use of classical transition periods. Baldwin calculated in 1994 that it would take between ten and fifteen years for most of the CEECs to attain budget neutrality. Using the experience of previous enlargements, he calculated that enlargement was improbable for twenty years.[1] Though Baldwin's calculations have been much debated, they nevertheless capture the scale of the challenge confronting the EU. Classical transitions will not be enough to carry the adjustment burden.

The second set of factors concerns the determination of the EU to move to full Economic and Monetary Union (EMU) around the year 2000. This commitment has already caused strains amongst the EU's present membership and is likely to become even more critical at the moment when enlargement pressures are also building up. Whilst there is no realistic expectation that the CEECs would be early participants in EMU, the preoccupation of the EU with simultaneous deepening and widening increases strains. The experience of previous enlargements suggests that deepening and widening are not necessarily incompatible. Iberian enlargement, in particular, demonstrated that widening can enhance deepening when applicants are enthusiastic about the integration process, and where suitable package deals with side payments can be put together.

The scale of the widening and deepening pressures has stimulated a debate as to how far models of differentiated integration may be appropriate to cope with these strains. Since the 1970s, a range of concepts has been discussed to encapsulate these pressures for differentiation. Their key concepts are described here, before their contribution to the enlargement debate is examined.[2]

'Multi speed Europe'   Originally attributed to Willy Brandt, the former West German Chancellor, the multi speed concept implies that some member states are more capable economically of moving quickly towards greater integration. The concept is implicit in the plans to move towards EMU, which accept differences in timing if not the agreement to the ultimate goal itself. However, it has pejorative overtones for those states which might be left behind as the speed of the integration process increases.

'Variable geometry'   Originally a French concept, this was intended to imply that different configurations of members could develop different and overlapping policy areas according to their capabilities and preferences. Thus, some combinations of member states may wish to move faster towards monetary integration, whilst others might pursue closer foreign policy and defence integration.

'Europe à la carte'   Originally used by Ralf Darendorf in 1979, to imply that some parts of the acquis might no longer be appropriate for new circumstances, this term has become synonymous with a 'pick and choose' approach to integration.

'Europe of "concentric circles"'   This model implies that the EU could be comprised of an inner group which accepted the full acquis, including EMU, the Single Market and the CAP, and thereafter, wider circles of countries accepting lesser commitments (for instance, some of the freedoms of the Single Market), with the outer circle just accepting free trade in industrial goods. The concentric circles model conceptualises the European framework which is centred on the EU and is supported by the EEA, as originally conceived, as well as by other forms of association, such as the Europe Agreements for the CEECs, EuroMediterranean partnerships, and Trade and Cooperation agreements with the countries of the former Soviet Union.

All of these models attempt to capture the diversity in the integration process and accept that some measure of differentiation is inevitable. Indeed, there has always been a greater degree of differentiation in the implementation of the acquis than a strict reading of the Treaties would suggest.[3] This has been reinforced by the adaptation methods used during the four rounds of accession negotiations.

Yet the classical method clearly imposes limits on the degree of diversity that is acceptable to present EU members. Also most applicants themselves wish to join a durable, coherent Union. Though partial integration, even if openly offered, might seem an attractive option for some applicants, the 'half-way houses' such as Association Agreements on the European Economic Area have not proved attractive to enough countries to regard them as permanent pillars of the European architecture. Underpinning all the models of differentiation is the assumption that the viability of the integration process depends on deepening for a core of policies and countries. Whilst there may not always be an exact fit between the policies and the countries promoting them at any one time, it suggests that the integration process still requires a 'motor' if it is to command the attention and respect of potential members. Therefore, the deepening agenda, as defined by the core countries of the EU, France and Germany, remain critical for the future of the enlarging Union.

Retaining the core of the classical method whilst responding to new levels of diversity, is likely to prove challenging. How might the principles of the classical method need to be modified to cope with these challenges?

The first principle concerning acceptance of the inviolability of the acquis is virtually immutable. There is no evidence that the EU would allow permanent derogations from the acquis for new members. All of the policy statements issued since the Copenhagen Council reinforce this orthodoxy. This is not to argue that the acquis itself is immutable. Institutional and policy reform is firmly on the EU's agenda until around the year 2000. The IGC, scheduled for conclusion in 1997, will be followed by negotiations over the EU budget in 1998 and the reform of the Structural Funds in 1999. All will be linked to enlargement, though not necessarily in ways helpful to EU applicants. Whatever the outcome of these internal reforms, however, applicants will still be expected to sign up for the full acquis and then seek further reforms as insiders, as others have done before them.

The second principle, concerning the practicalities of applicants taking on the acquis, offers more scope for flexibility. In theory, transition periods could be lengthened and temporary derogations could be extended almost infinitely. Ingenious ways could be found to reconcile special national interests with the letter of the acquis. In practice, this is unlikely to happen. Twenty-year transition periods would amount to partial membership and would be unacceptable to existing members and applicants alike. Though the classic five-year transition is unlikely to be long enough to manage the full burden of adaptation, other methods may be employed, including prioritising and sequencing the adoption of the acquis. The decision to make the Internal Market the centrepiece of the pre-accession strategy was an implicit decision that the Internal Market constitutes the core of the acquis. This was itself the outcome of complex negotiations within the Commission who eventually chose to delineate the Single Market acquis as measures ensuring the free movement of goods, services, capital and people. This opens the way to the phasing in of the acquis, with the initial stress on competition policy and the control of state aids, followed by product standards. More expensive social and environmental legislation could be left until later.[4] Such sequencing, which has, in effect, started already, does not materially affect the first principle of the classical method but is a more flexible interpretation of the second principle than has been the case in previous enlargements.

The third principle concerning policy overlay faces some fundamental challenges. Successive enlargements have increased structural spending, and the complexity of the cohesion policy area. Further incremental extension using existing criteria is unrealistic. Net payers, in particular Germany and the UK, would be unwilling to underwrite such an extension. The possibility of capping cohesion spending, using GDP per capita criteria has been suggested.[5] The preference of some applicants, such as the Czech Republic, for full market access, even without any access to cohesion spending, also suggests that the underlying arguments about the importance of cohesion spending as a measure of EU solidarity may be changing. However, the existing beneficiaries are unlikely to accept reforms which substantially reduce their own receipts from the Structural Funds unless some other forms of compensation can be developed. A reform packaged deal in 1999, more radical than the 1988 and 1992 deals, will need to be constructed.

The fourth principle, concerning the institutional integration on the basis of limited incremental adaptation is also very well entrenched. However, unlike in previous enlargement rounds, some modifications to decision-making processes is likely *before* further enlargement. The Reflection Group preparing for the IGC noted that the EU's institutional system, conceived for six members, had probably reached its limits with the fourth enlargement. The Report noted the gradual deterioration in popular representation in the weighting of qualified majority voting as a result of the under representation of the people of the more populous states, and the growing number of less populous states in the Union.[6] Given that further enlargement would, on the basis of existing weighting criteria, further exacerbate this imbalance, this is a key issue for the next enlargement round. Proposals involving reweighting to better reflect population size, and the use of 'double majorities' (of states and aggregated population) under QMV, have been put forward.[7] However, there is no consensus amongst member states concerning decision-making reform. EU applicants are not present at the IGC, although they are normally kept informed of progress, and will have to live with the outcome.

The fifth principle concerning the EU's preference to negotiate with states which already have close relations with each other is also likely to be severely tested. By mid-1996, twelve states had submitted formal applications to join the EU. The EU/EC has never before negotiated accession with a group larger than four. The conclusions of the December 1995 Madrid European Council, that accession negotiations may start six months after the conclusion of the IGC, possibly in January 1998, means that, in theory, twelve parallel accession conferences could be convened. Again, in practice this is unlikely, and a more limited group, similar in size to previous enlargement rounds is probable. However, this will still involve the EU in making some politically difficult decisions about which countries should be in the first wave. The importance given by Germany to stability in Central Europe suggests that the Visegrad Four would be given priority. However, other member states, such as the Scandinavians, are likely to press the case of the Baltic States. All applicants will lobby hard so as to not be left behind. Here, the classical method, by convening separate conferences for each applicant, and treating each applicant, at least nominally on its own merits, sets up competitive dynamics between applicants. Potential members have few incentives to co-operate with one another when they know that only the fastest and fittest amongst them will be in the first group of entrants.

The sixth principle, that existing member states use enlargement to pursue their own interests is also deeply rooted. Limiting access to the Structural Funds, whilst making side payments to existing members, is a real possibility in 1999. However, member states are also aware of the dangers of new members bringing new grievances into the EU, and this is likely to act as a balancing factor.

Overall, the classical method is likely to survive, so long as flexibility is shown over how it is deployed. As the four enlargement rounds to date have shown, there has always been a gap between EC rhetoric concerning the vision of a wider, more inclusive Community, and the reality of the hard bargaining necessary to achieve this. The next phase of enlargement involves bridging a wider gap. The classical method can help in this task by disciplining negotiations and focusing mutual expectations. Yet it also requires a willingness on both sides to see beyond short-term interests if the integration process in a wider Europe is to be sustained into the next millennium.

Appendices

Appendix 1: Voting Weights in the Council of Ministers

	1957	1973		1981	1986	1995
Germany	4	10				
France	4	10				
Italy	4	10				
Belgium	2	5	Voting			
Holland	2	5	weight			
Luxembourg	1	2	as			
Denmark		3	before			
Ireland		3				
UK		10				
Greece				5		
Spain					8	
Portugal					5	
Finland						3
Austria						4
Sweden						4
Total votes	17	58		63	76	87
Votes required for QMV decision	12	41		45	54	61

Appendix 2: Distribution of Seats in the European Parliament

	1957[1]	1973[2]	1979[3]	1981	1986	1995
Germany	36	seats	81			99
France	36	as	81			87
Italy	36	before	81			87
Belgium	14		24			25
Holland	14		25	seats		31
Luxembourg	6		6			6
Denmark		10	16			16
Ireland		10	15	before		
UK		36	81			15
Greece				24		87
Spain					60	25
Portugal					24	64
						25
Finland						16
Austria						21
Sweden						22
Total seats	142	198	410	434	518	626

Notes
1) European Assembly composed of nominated national parliamentarians
2) Seat allocation for direct elections to European Parliament
3) Sea redistribution following 4th enlargement and German unification

Notes

CHAPTER 1

1 Treaty of Rome, Article 2.
2 Treaty of Rome, Article 237.
3 See Harrison, R.J. (1974) *Europe in Question* London, George Allen & Unwin.
4 Avery, G. (1994) 'The European Union's Enlargement Negotiations' *Oxford International Review*, Summer, p. 28.
5 Treaty of Rome, Article 237.
6 Avery, G. *op. cit.,* p. 27.
7 Avery, G. *op. cit.*
8 Avery, G. *op. cit.*, p. 27.
9 Quoted in Avery, G. *op. cit.*, p. 29.
10 Avery, G. *op. cit.*, p. 29.

CHAPTER 2

1 Camps, M. (1964) *Britain and the European Community, 1955–64* Oxford, Oxford University Press, p. 7.
2 Camps, M. *op. cit.*, p. 25.
3 Camps, M. *op. cit.*, p. 46.
4 Camps, M. *op. cit*, pp. 58–61.
5 See: Pedersen, T.I. (1994) *European Union and the EFTA Countries: Enlargement and Integration* London, Pinter.
6 See Charlton, M. (1983) *The Price of Victory* London, BBC Publications, pp. 233–39.
7 Conclusions of European summit. Bonn Declaration on European Union, 18 July 1961.
8 Applications from Ireland, Denmark and Norway were also made on the same day.
9 Cmnd 1565, November 1961, 'The United Kingdom and the EEC'.
10 Cmnd 1565, *op. cit.*, para 11.
11 See Nicholson, F. and East, R. (1987) *From Six to Twelve. The Enlargement of the European Communities* Harlow, Longman.
12 The speech is quoted in full in Nicholson and East *op. cit.*, pp. 30–32.
13 See Nicholson, F. and East, R. *op. cit.*, p. 44.

14 See Nicholson, F. and East, R. *op. cit.*, p. 46.
15 Cmnd. 4289, 1970 'Membership of the European Communities'.
16 Nicholson, F. and East, R. *op. cit.*, p. 49.
17 European Commission: 'Opinion on the Application for Membership from the UK, Ireland, Denmark and Norway *Bulletin of the EC* Supplement 11/1967.
18 Nicholson, F. and East, R. *op. cit.*, p.54.
19 Nicholson, F. and East, R. *op. cit,*, p.56.
20 See Lord, C. (1993) *British Entry to the EC under the Heath Government of 1970–74* Aldershot, Dartmouth, p. 54.
21 See Lord, C. *op. cit.*, p. 55.
22 European Commission Opinion submitted to the Council concerning the applications for membership from the UK, Ireland, Denmark and Norway. *Bulletin of the EC* Supplement 9/10/1969.
23 See Wallace, H. (1989) 'Widening and deepening: the European Community and the New European agenda' London, Royal Institute of International Affairs, Discussion Paper 23.
24 See EC Commission Opinion 1969 *op. cit.*
25 Cmnd. 4289, 1970 'Britain and the European Communities, an economic assessment', para 101.
26 See Kitzinger, U. (1973) *Diplomacy and Persuasion: How Britain joined the Common Market* London, Thames and Hudson, p. 345.
27 Nicholson, F. and East, R. *op. cit.*, p. 65.
28 See *The Times* 1 July 1970.
29 See Lord, C. *op. cit.* pp. 68–69 for an account of these opening negotiating disputes.
30 Cmnd. 4715, July 1971, 'The United Kingdom and the European Communities'.
31 Cmnd. 4715, para. 77.
32 Cmnd. 4715, para 77.
33 Cmnd. 4715, para 96.
34 Lord, C. *op.cit.*, p. 73.
35 Nicholson, F. and East, R., *op. cit.*, p. 166.
36 Nicholson, F. and East, R., *op. cit.*
37 See Lord, C. *op. cit.* Chapter 6.
38 See Maher, D.J. (1986) *The Tortuous Path: The Course of Ireland's Entry into the EEC 1948–73* Dublin, Institute of Public Administration, p. 56.
39 Maher, *op. cit.*, p. 77.
40 Maher, *op. cit.*, p. 138–44.
41 Irish Government: 'Membership of the European Communities – Implications for Ireland' Prl 1110, April 1970, Dublin.
42 The White Paper drew particular attention to Article 5, which states that Ireland is a sovereign independent democratic state, and Article 6.2, which provides for the exclusive exercise of legislative, executive and judicial powers by organs of the state.
43 Maher, *op. cit.*, p. 306.
44 Strictly interpreted, the tax exemption given to Irish export earnings was incompatible with Article 98 of the Treaty. The Community agreed to treat all Ireland's industrial incentives as vital to its economic development, to be reviewed by the Commission after accession.

45 Irish Government: 'Accession of Ireland to the European Communities'
    Prl. 2064l and 2231, Dublin, January 1972.
46 Thomson, B.N. (1993) 'Denmark's road to Europe 1957–63' in Thomson,
    B.N. (ed.) *Denmark and European Integration 1948–1992* Odense, Odense
    University Press, pp. 25–27.
47 Christensen, J. 'Denmark, the Nordic Countries and the EC 1963–1972'
    in Thomson, B.N. (ed.) *op. cit.*, p. 35.
48 Christensen, J. *op. cit.*, pp. 39–42.
49 The negotiations are covered in Christensen, J. *op. cit.*, pp. 43–44.
50 Nicholson, F. and East, R., *op. cit.*, p. 120.
51 Nicholson, F. and East, R., *op. cit.*, p. 124.

CHAPTER 3

1   The provisions of the Association Agreement are covered in Tsalicoglou,
    I.S. (1995) *Negotiating for Entry: The Accession of Greece to the European
    Community* Aldershot, Dartmouth, pp. 10–15.
2   Tsoukalis, L. (1981) *The European Community and its Mediterranean
    Enlargement* London, George Allen & Unwin.
3   Tsoukalis, L. *op. cit.*, p. 21.
4   Tsoukalis, L. *op. cit.*, p. 34.
5   See Tsakaloyannis, P. (1980) 'The EC and the Greek–Turkish Dispute'
    Journal of Common Market Studies vol. 19.
6   Commission of the EC: 'Opinion on Greek Application for Membership'
    Bulletin of the European Communities 2/1976.
7   Commission Opinion *op. cit.*, p. 8.
8   Commission Opinion *op. cit.*, p. 8.
9   Tsalicoglou, I.S. *op. cit.*, p. 34.
10 See Tsalicoglou, I.S. *op. cit.*, p. 37.
11 Tsalicoglou, *op. cit.*, p. 39.
12 Tsalicoglou. *op. cit.*, p. 83.
13 Commission Opinion *op. cit.*, p. 18.
14 Commission Opinion *op. cit.*, p. 16.
15 Tsalicoglou, I.S. *op. cit.*, p. 43.
16 Commission Opinion *op. cit.*, p. 17.
17 Tsalicoglou, I.S. *op. cit.*, p. 43.

CHAPTER 4

1   Tsoukalis, L. (1981) *The European Community and its Mediterranean
    Enlargement* London, George Allen & Unwin. p. 80.
2   Tsoukalis, L. *op. cit.,* p. 81.
3   Nicholson, F. and East, R. (1987) *From Six to Twelve. The Enlargement
    of the European Communities* Harlow, Longman, p. 215.
4   Nicholson, F. and East, R., *op. cit.*, p. 244.
5   Dominguez, L. (1988) 'Agriculture and the third enlargement of the EC'
    PhD Thesis, University of Edinburgh.
6   Tsoukalis, L. *op. cit.,* p. 50.
7   Tsoukalis, L. *op. cit.*, p. 1.

8 European Commission: 'Opinion on Spain's Application for Membership *Bulletin of the European Communities* Supplement 9/78.
9 Commission's Opinion on Spain *op. cit.*, p. 9.
10 European Commission: 'Opinion on Portugal's Application for Membership *Bulletin of the European Communities* Supplement 5/78.
11 Commission's Opinion on Portugal *op. cit.*, p. 7.
12 Dominguez, L. *op. cit.*, p. 161.
13 European Commission: 'The Challenge of Enlargement' *Bulletin of the European Communities* Supplement 1/78.
14 European Commission: 'The Challenge of Enlargement' *op. cit.*, p. 11.
15 European Commission: 'The Challenge of Enlargement' *op. cit.*, p. 14.
16 European Commission: 'The Challenge of Enlargement' *op. cit.* p. 13.
17 European Commission: 'Report on the Progress of Enlargement Negotiations *Bulletin of the European Communities* Supplement 8/82.
18 European Commission: 'Report on Progress of Enlargement Negotiations *op. cit.*, p. 7.
19 Dominguez, L. *op. cit.*, p. 299.
20 Dominguez, L. *op. cit.*, p. 335.
21 Dominguez, L. *op. cit.*, p. 338.
22 Dominguez, L. *op. cit.*, p. 80.
23 Dominguez, L. *op. cit.*, p. 340.

CHAPTER 5

1 See House of Lords Select Committee on the European Communities, 14th Report Session 1989–96: 'Relations between the Community and EFTA' pp. 6–9.
2 See EFTA Trade 1988, Economic Affairs Department, EFTA, Geneva.
3 Delors, J. (1989) Debates of the European Parliament 1988–89 Session, Proceedings from 16 to 20 January 1989.
4 See Pedersen, T. (1994) *European Union and the EFTA countries* London, Pinter.
5 See Wallace, H. (1989) Widening and Deepening: the European Community and the New European Agenda London, Royal Institute of International Affairs.
6 Bruntlund, G.H. (1988) 'Norway, the EC and European Co-operation' Oslo, Office of the Prime Minister.
7 See Saeter, M. and Knudsen, O.F. 'Norway' in Wallace, H. (ed.) *The Wider Western Europe* London, Royal Institute of International Affairs.
8 Government of Sweden (1987) 'Sweden and European Integration: Proposition 1987/88: 66 Stockholm.
9 See Stalvant, L.E. and Hamilton, C. (1991) 'Sweden' in Wallace, H. (ed.) *op. cit.*, pp. 194–214.
10 See Antola, E. (1991) 'Finland' in Wallace, H. (ed.) *op. cit.*, pp. 146–49.
11 See Kristinsson, G.H. (1991) 'Iceland' in Wallace, H. (ed) *op. cit.*, pp. 159–79.
12 See Schneider, H. (1989) 'Austria and the EC' London, Royal Institute of International Affairs.
13 See Senti, R. (1991) 'Switzerland' in Wallace, H. (ed.) *op. cit.*, pp. 215–33.

14 See Church, C. (1993) 'Switzerland and Europe: problem or pattern?' European Policy Forum.

15 See House of Commons (1990) 'Trade with EFTA' Trade and Industry Committee Session 1989/90, 4th Report.

16 See Pedersen, T. *op. cit.*

17 See Miles, L. (1993) 'Scandinavia and European Community enlargement: aspects and problems for Sweden, Finland and Norway' European Community Research Unit, University of Hull.

18 European Court of Justice 'Opinion of the Court on the Draft Agreement Between the Community and EFTA Relating to the Creation of the EEA' Opinion 1/91, 14 December 1991.

19 See Miles, L. *op. cit.*, section 7.

20 European Commission 'Opinion on Austria's Application for Membership' *Bulletin of the European Communities* Supplement 4/92, p. 18.

21 European Commission: 'The Challenge of Enlargement' *Bulletin of the European Communities* Supplement 3/92.

22 European Commission: 'The Challenge of Enlargement' *op. cit.*, para. 6.

23 European Commission: 'The Challenge of Enlargement' *op. cit.*, para. 21.

24 European Commission: 'Opinion on Sweden's Application for Membership' *Bulletin of the European Communities* Supplement 5/92.

25 European Commission: 'Opinion on Finland's Application for Membership' *Bulletin of the European Communities* Supplement 6/92.

26 European Commission: 'Opinion on Norway's Application for Membership' *Bulletin of the European Communities* Supplement 2/93.

27 European Commission: 'Opinion on Finland's Application for Membership' *op. cit.*, pp. 10–12.

28 European Commission: 'Opinion on Sweden's Application for Membership' *op. cit.*, pp. 11–12.

29 'CFSP and Enlargement' text agreed in European Political Cooperation, 4 November 1992.

30 European Commission 'Opinion on Sweden's Application for Membership' *op. cit.*, p. 30.

31 See Granell, F. (1995) 'The European Union's enlargement negotiations with Austria, Finland, Norway and Sweden' *Journal of Common Market Studies* vol. 33, no. 1, March, p. 129.

32 See Granell, F. *op. cit.*, p. 129.

33 See Kaiser, W. (1995) 'Austria in the European Union' *Journal of Common Market Studies* vol. 33, no. 3, September, pp. 411–27.

34 See Sogner, I. and Archer, C. (1995) 'Norway and Europe: 1972 and now' *Journal of Common Market Studies* vol. 33, no. 3, September, pp. 389–411.

CHAPTER 6

1 Lintner, V. (1994) 'The Economics of EC Enlargement' London, Guildhall University.

2 Myrdal, G. (1957) *Economic Theory and Underdeveloped Regions* London, Duckworth.

3 el-agraa, A. (1983) *Britain within the European Community* London, Macmillan, 1983.

4 European Commision: 'Britain in the Community, 1973–83: Ten Years in Europe' 1983.

5 Lintner, V. and Mazey, S. *The European Community: Economic and Political Aspects* Maidenhead, McGraw Hill, 1991, p. 149.

6 See Demekas, D.G. *et al.* (1988) 'The effects of the Common Agricultural Policy of the EC: a survey of the literature' *Journal of Common Market Studies* vol. 27.

7 The development of the EC budget is examined in Chapter 7.

8 Lintner, V. and Mazey, S. *op. cit.*, p. 151.

9 Lintner, V. and Mazey, S. *op. cit.*, p. 151.

10 Winters, A.L. (1987) 'Britain in Europe: a survey of quantitative trade studies' *Journal of Common Market Studies* vol. 25, pp. 315–35.

11 See Gregory, F.E.C. (1983) *Dilemmas of Government: Britain and the EC* Oxford, Martin Robertson, pp. 55–73.

12 See Gregory, F.E.C. *op. cit.*, pp. 153–83.

13 See Richardson, J. and Mazey, S. (1993) *Lobbying in the European Community* Oxford, Oxford University Press.

14 See Bongers, P. (1992) *Local Government in the Single European Market* Harlow, Longman.

15 See Thomson, N. (1993) 'The EEC in Danish politics, 1972–79' in Thomson, B.N. (ed.) *The Odd Man Out? Denmark and European Integration* Odense, Odense University Press.

16 See Branner, H. (1992) 'Danish European policy since 1945: the question of sovereignty' in Kelstrup, M. *European Integration and Denmark's Participation* Copenhagen.

17 See Worre, T. (1993) 'Denmark and the European Union: public opinion and the Referendum of June 1992' in Thomson, B.N. (ed.) *op. cit.*, pp. 87–107.

18 See Worre, T. (1995) 'First No, then Yes: the Danish Referendums on the Maastricht Treaty 1992 and 1993' *Journal of Common Market Studies* vol. 33, no. 2, June, pp. 235–59.

19 Tsoukalis, L. (1993) *The New European Economy: The Politics and Economics of Integration* Oxford, p. 251.

20 Tsoukalis, L. *op. cit.*, p. 251.

21 See Laffan, B. (1991) 'Government and Administration' in Keatinge, P. (ed.) *Ireland and the EC Membership Evaluated* London, Pinter, pp. 187–90.

22 Tsalicoglou, I. *Negotiating for Entry* Aldershot, Dartmouth, 1995, p. 169.

23 Tsoukalis, L. *op. cit.*, p. 255.

24 Tsoukalis, L. *op. cit.*, pp. 258–59.

25 See Hine, R.C. (1989) 'Customs union and enlargement: Spain's accession to the European Community' *Journal of Common Market Studies*, September.

26 See Hine, R.C. *op. cit.*

27 EFTA Economic Affairs Department: 'Effects of "1992" on the manufacturing industries of the EFTA countries' *Occasional Paper* 38, Geneva, 1992.

28 See Lopes, J.D.S. (ed.) *Portugal and EC Membership Evaluated* London, Pinter, 1993, pp. 7–30.

CHAPTER 7

1 Lindberg, L. (1963) *The Political Dynamics of European Economic Integration* Stanford.
2 Haas, E.B. (1968) *The Unity of Europe* Stanford.
3 Harrison, R.J. (1974) *Europe in Question* London.
4 See Harrison, R.J. *op. cit.*, pp. 75–99.
5 Hooghe, L. and Keating, M. (1994) 'The politics of European Union regional policy' *Journal of European Public Policy* vol. 1, no. 3, pp. 367–95.
6 European Commission: 'Report on the Regional Problems in the Enlarged Community' (Thomson Report) COM (73) 550 final.
7 See Wallace, H. (1977) 'The establishment of the Regional Development Fund: common policy or pork barrel?' in Wallace, H., Wallace, W. and Webb. C. (eds) *Policy Making in the European Communities* Chichester, Wiley.
8 See Preston, C. (1984) 'The politics of implementation: the European Regional Development Fund and EC Regional Aid to the UK 1975–81' PhD Thesis, University of Essex.
9 European Commission: 'The Challenge of Enlargement' *Bulletin of the European Communities* Supplement 1/78, p. 11.
10 Mawson, J., Martins, M. and Gibney, J. (1985) 'The development of EC regional policy', in Keating, M. and Jones, B. (eds) *The European Union and the Regions* Oxford.
11 See European Commission: 'The European Union's Cohesion Fund', Luxembourg, 1994.
12 See Bongers, P. (1992) *Local Government in the Single European Market* London, Longman.
13 Hooghe, L. and Keating, M. *op. cit.*, p. 380.
14 See Tsoukalis, L. (1993) *The New European Economy* Oxford, Oxford University Press, Chapter 6.
15 See Lintner, L. and Mazey. S. (1991) *The European Community: Economic and Political Aspects* London, McGraw Hill, Chapter 8.
16 European Commission: 'The Challenge of Enlargement' *op. cit.*, p. 11.
17 See Lintner, L. and Mazey, S. *op. cit.*, Chapter 8.
18 See Wise, M. and Gibb, R. (1993) *Single Market to Social Europe* Longman, London, Chapter 6.
19 See House of Lords Select Committee on the European Communities: 'A Community Social Charter' Session 1989–90, 3rd Report.
20 See Tsoukalis, L. *op. cit.*, Chapter 3.
21 Balassa, B. (1961) *The Theory of Economic Integration* London.
22 European Commission: 'Completing the Internal Market' White Paper from the Commission to the European Council, June 1985.
23 See Moravscik, A. (1991) 'Negotiating the Single European Act' in Keohane, R. and Hoffman, S. (eds) *The New European Community: Decision Making and Institutional Change* Boulder Colorado, Westview Press.
24 See Swann, D. (ed.) (1992) *The Single European Market and Beyond* London, Routledge.
25 See Woolcock, S. (1994) *The Single European Market: Centralization or Competition Among National Rules?* London, Royal Institute of International Affairs.

26 European Commission: '1992: The Benefits of a Single Market' (the Cecchini Report) 1988.

27 'Report to the Council and the Commission on the Realisation by Stages of EMU in the Community' (Werner Report) *Bulletin of the EC* Supplement 3/70.

28 See Krugman, P. (1990) 'Policy problems in a monetary union.' in de Grauwe, P. and Papademos, L. (eds) *The European Monetary System in the 1990s* London, CEPS.

29 Committee for the Study of Economic and Monetary Union: 'Report on Economic and Monetary Union in the EC' (Delors Report) Luxembourg, 1989.

30 The UK and Denmark negotiated opt-outs from the timetable.

31 See Tsoukalis, *op. cit.*, p. 263.

32 European Commission: 'Report on the Progress of Enlargement Negotiations' *Bulletin of the European Communities* Supplement 8/82.

33 See Denton, G. (1984) 'Restructuring the EC Budget: implications of the Fontainbleau Agreement' *Journal of Common Market Studies* vol. 23, no. 2, December, pp. 117–40.

34 See Tsoukalis, L. *op. cit.*, p. 269.

CHAPTER 8

1 See House of Lords Select Committee on the European Communities: 'External Competences of the European Communities' 16 August Session 1984–85.

2 Pedersen, T. (1994) *European Union and the EFTA Countries' Enlargement and Integration* London, Pinter.

3 Hine, R. (1985) *The Political Economy of European Trade* Brighton, Wheatsheaf.

4 Hine, R. *op. cit.,* p. 50.

5 Hine, R. *op. cit.,* p. 62.

6 Hine, R. *op. cit.,* p. 83.

7 European Commission 'The Challenge of Enlargement' *Bulletin of the European Communities*, Supplement 1/78, p. 12.

8 Tsoukalis, L. (1992) *The New European Economy* Oxford, p. 320.

9 Hine. *op. cit.*, p. 132.

10 Pedersen, T. *op. cit,* p. 70.

11 Pedersen, T. *op. cit.*, p. 76.

12 Pedersen, T. *op. cit.,* p. 104.

13 Cable, V. and Henderson, D. (1994) *Trade Blocs? The Future of Regional Integration* London, Royal Institute of International Affairs.

14 GATT (1991) Report on Single European Market.

15 See Rollo, J.M. and Smith, M.A.M. (1993) 'The political economy of Central European trade with the EC: why so sensitive?' *Economic Policy* vol. 16.

16 Nuttal, S. (1992) *European Political Co-operation* Oxford, Clarendon, pp. 50–54.

17 Nuttal, S. *op. cit.*, pp. 127–36.

18 Nuttal, S. *op. cit.*, pp. 173–74.

19 Nuttal, S. *op. cit.*, p. 254.

CHAPTER 9

1 See Burrows, B., Denton, G. and Edwards, G. (eds) (1977) *Federal Solutions to European Issues* London, Macmillan for the Federal Trust.

2 See Wallace, H. (1982) 'Negotiation, conflict and compromise: the elusive pursuit of common policies', in Wallace, H., Wallace, W. and Webb, C. (eds) *Policy Making in the European Community* (2nd ed.) Chichester, John Wiley, pp. 43–81.

3 Harrap, J. (1979) *The Political Economy of European Integration* Aldershot, Edward Elgar, p. 24.

4 See Budden, P. and Monroe, B. (1993) *Decision-making in the EC Council of Ministers* Washington DC, European Community Studies Association, Washington DC.

5 Report on European Union by Leo Tindemans, *Bulletin of the European Communities* Supplement 1/76.

6 European Commission: 'The Challenge of Enlargement' *Bulletin of the European Communities* Supplement 1/78.

7 Tsalicoglou, I. (1995) *Negotiating for Entry: The Accession of Greece to the European Community* Aldershot, Dartmouth, p. 69.

8 See Budden, P. and Monroe, B. *op. cit.*, p. 14.

9 Ad Hoc Committee on Institutional Affairs (Dooge Committee), March 1985.

10 See Moravscik, A. (1991) 'Negotiating the Single European Act' in Keohane, R. and Hoffman, S. (eds) *The New European Community: Decision Making and Institutional Change* Boulder, Colorado, Westview Press.

11 See Keohane, R. and Hoffman, S. (1991) 'Institutional Change in Europe in the 1980s' in Keohane and Hoffman (eds.) *op. cit.*, pp. 1–41.

12 Moravscik, A. *op. cit.*, p. 61.

13 Keohane, R. and Hoffman, S. *op. cit*, p. 14.

14 Keohane, R. and Hoffman, S. *op. cit.*, p. 16.

15 Budden, P. and Monroe, R. *op. cit.*, pp. 3–4.

16 See Wessels, W. 'The EC Council: the Community's decision making centre' in Keohane, R. and Hoffman, S. *op. cit.*, p. 147.

17 Sloot, T. and Verschuren, P. (1990) 'Decision-making speed in the European Community' *Journal of Common Market Studies* vol. 29, no. 1, September.

18 European Commission: 'The Challenge of Enlargement' *Bulletin of the European Communities* Supplement 3/92.

19 See Widgren, M. (ed.) (1995) *National Interests, EU Enlargement and Coalition Formation* Helsinki, Research Institute of the Finnish Economy.

20 Budden P. and Monroe, R. *op. cit.*, p. 19.

CHAPTER 10

1 Pinder, J. (1991) *The European Community and Eastern Europe* London, Royal Institute of International Affairs.

2 Pinder, J. *op. cit.*, p. 61.

3 See Rollo, J. (1992) *Association Agreements between the EC and the CSFR, Hungary and Poland* London, Royal Institute of International Affairs.

4 Kramer, H. (1993) 'The EC's response to the New Eastern Europe' *Journal of Common Market Studies* vol. 31, no. 2, June, p. 225.

5 European Commission: Association agreements with the countries of Central and Eastern Europe: a general outline *Commission Communication to the Council* (COM/90/398) Brussels, 27 August 1990.

6 See Baldwin, R. (1994) *Towards an Integrated Europe* London, Centre for Economic Policy Research.

7 See Baldwin, *op. cit.*, pp. 130–39.

8 See Phinnemore, D. (1995) 'The European Economic Area, Europe Agreements and the future of Association' Paper presented to UACES Research Conference, Birmingham, September.

9 See Sedelmeier, U. (1994) 'The EU's association policy towards Central and Eastern Europe: political and economic rationales in conflict' *Sussex European Institute Working Report* no. 7.

10 European Commission: 'The Challenge of Enlargement' *Bulletin of the European Communities* Supplement 3/92. p. 18.

11 European Council: *Conclusions of the Presidency* Copenhagen, June 1993.

12 European Council: *Conclusions of the Presidency op. cit.*

13 Commission Communication to the Council: 'The Europe Agreements and Beyond: A Strategy to Prepare the Countries of Central and Eastern Europe for Accession' COM(94) 320 final, 13 July 1994.

14 Commission Communication to the Council: 'White Paper: Preparation of the Associated Countries of Central and Eastern Europe for Integration into the Internal Market of the Union' COM (95) 163 final, Brussels, 3 May 1995.

15 Commission White Paper *op. cit.*, p. 18.

16 Commission White Paper *op. cit.*, p. 16.

17 Johnson, D. and Miles, L. (1995) 'Small states and the Integration dilemma: The case of Hungary' UACES Research Conference, Birmingham, September.

18 Gyula Horn: Hungarian Prime Minister, Reuter's News Service 23 January 1995.

19 Johnson and Miles *op. cit.*, p. 9.

20 Hughes, G.A. and Hare, P.G. (1991) 'Competitiveness and industrial restructuring in Czechoslovakia, Hungary and Poland' *European Economy* Special edition no. 2.

21 *Financial Times* 2 August 1995.

22 *Financial Times* 10 July 1995.

23 Baldwin, R. *op. cit.*, p. 171.

24 Baldwin, R. *op. cit.*, p. 169.

25 Anderson, K. and Tyers, R. (1993) 'Implications of EC expansion for European agricultural policies' Centre for Economic Policy Research Discussion Paper no. 829.

26 Courchene, T. (1993) 'Stable money – sound finances' *European Economy* no. 53.

27 Baldwin, R. *op. cit.*, p. 170.

28 Baldwin, R. *op. cit,*, p. 170.

CHAPTER 11

1 Redmond, J. (1993) *The next Mediterranean Enlargement of the European Community* Aldershot, Dartmouth, p. 21.
2 Redmond, J. *op. cit.*, p. 31.
3 European Commission: 'Opinion on Turkey's Request for Accession to the Community', SEC (89) 2290 final, Brussels.
4 See European Commission: 'The Turkish Economy: Structure and Developments' Annex to 'Opinion on Turkey's Request for Accession' *op. cit.*, p. 57.
5 Redmond, J. *op. cit.*, p. 43.
6 European Commission: 'Europe and the Challenge of Enlargement' *Bulletin of the European Communities* Supplement 3/92, p. 17.
7 See *Financial Times* 7 March 1995.
8 See Schliam, A. and Yannopoulos, G.N. (eds) (1976) *The EEC and the Mediterranean Countries* Cambridge, Cambridge University Press.
9 European Commission: 'Opinion on Turkey's Request for Accession' *op. cit.*
10 European Commission: 'Europe and the Challenge of Enlargement' *op. cit.*, p. 17.
11 European Commission: 'Opinion on the Application by the Republic of Cyprus for Membership' *Bulletin of the European Communities* Supplement 5/93.
12 European Commission: 'Opinion on the Application by Cyprus' *op. cit.*, p. 17.
13 European Commission: 'Opinion on the Application by Cyprus' *op. cit.*, p. 17.
14 See Wilson, W. (1992) *Cyprus and the International Economy* London, Macmillan.
15 See Warrington, E. (1993) 'Political and institutional considerations of a European policy for a small state: the case of Malta' Centre for Euro-Mediterranean Studies, University of Reading.
16 European Parliament: 'Report on Malta and its Relationship with the European Community' (Prag. Report) PE 121.461/final, Brussels, 1988.
17 Department of Information, Malta 'Report by the EC Directorate to the Prime Minister and Minister of Foreign Affairs Regarding Malta's Membership of the EC', 1990.
18 Malta Labour Party: 'Malta and the EC: Economic and Social Aspects' Information Department, Valetta.
19 European Commission: 'Opinion on Malta's application for membership' *Bulletin of the European Communities* Supplement 4/93.
20 European Commission: 'Opinion on Malta's Application for Membership' *op. cit.*, para. 8.
21 European Commission: 'Opinion on Malta's Application for Membership' *op. cit.*, paras 25–36.
22 *Financial Times* 7 March 1993.

CHAPTER 12

1 Baldwin, R. (1994) *Towards an Integrated Europe* London, CEPR, p. 178.
2 See Wallace, H. and Wallace, W. (1995) 'Flying together in a larger and

more diverse European Union' Netherlands Scientific Council for Government Policy.

3 Ehlerman, C.D. (1984) 'How flexible is Community law?' *Michigan Law Review* 82, pp. 1274–93.

4 See Wallace, H. *et al.* (1996) 'The European Union and Central and Eastern Europe: preaccession strategies' Sussex European Institute Working Paper no. 15.

5 See *Financial Times* 24 October 1995.

6 See 'Interim Report of the Reflection Group on the Inter Governmental Conference' (Westendorp Report) Brussels, 17 November 1995.

7 See Westendorp Report *op. cit.*, pp. 31–34.

Index